Doing Research/Reading Research

Master Classes in Education Series

Series Editors: John Head, School of Education, Kings College, University of London and Ruth Merttens, School of Teaching Studies, University of North London

Working with Adolescents: Constructing Identity
John Head *Kings College, University of London*

Testing: Friend or Foe? The Theory and Practice of Assessment and Testing
Paul Black *Kings College, University of London*

Doing Research/Reading Research: A Mode of Interrogation for Education
Andrew Brown and Paul Dowling *both of the Institute of Education, University of London*

Educating the Other: Gender, Power and Schooling
Carrie Paechter *School of Education, The Open University*

Curriculum, Construction and Critique
Alistair Ross *University of North London*

Master Classes in Education Series

Doing Research/ Reading Research:
A Mode of Interrogation for Education

Andrew Brown and Paul Dowling

 The Falmer Press

(A member of the Taylor & Francis Group)
London • Washington, D.C.

UK   Falmer Press, 1 Gunpowder Square, London, EC4A 3DE
USA Falmer Press, Taylor & Francis Inc., 1900 Frost Road, Suite 101, Bristol, PA 19007

First published in 1998

A catalogue record for this book is available from the British Library

ISBN 0 7507 0728 3 cased
ISBN 0 7507 0719 4 paper

Library of Congress Cataloging-in-Publication Data are available on request

Jacket design by Caroline Archer

Typeset in 11/13 pt Garamond and printed by
Graphicraft Typesetters Ltd., Hong Kong.

Every effort has been made to contact copyright holders for their permission to reprint material in this book. The publishers would be grateful to hear from any copyright holder who is not here acknowledged and will undertake to rectify any errors or omissions in future editions of this book.

Contents

Contents

Tables and Figures

Acknowledgments

This book has arisen out of our research and research methods teaching over the period of the last ten years. In respect of the teaching, we have benefited enormously from the active participation and criticism of students on doctoral and masters courses at the Institute of Education, University of London, from masters students based in Hong Kong and Cyprus and, most recently, at the University of Ceara in Fortaleza, Brazil.

Of particular importance has been our participation in an Overseas Development Agency sponsored link between ourselves and the Universities of Cape Town and of the Western Cape in South Africa. The remit for the link concerns the development of research capacity in the Western Cape. We are grateful for the active participation of students and staff who have attended our sessions at these universities and, especially, to Paula Ensor, of UCT, and Cyril Julie, of UWC. The link agreement was Paula's initiative and she has been responsible for managing the South African end of it as well as for substantial intellectual input into our project. Parin Bahl has attended and contributed to most of our sessions in the Western Cape and has also provided continuous critical commentary on both our teaching and this book as they have developed. This has proved invaluable, as has the support provided by Diane Mayers and Michael Brown.

We would like to acknowledge participants on other research methods programmes that we have run individually. We are grateful to members of the Southern African Association for Research in Mathematics and Science Education for inviting Dr Dowling to be a plenary speaker at their 1994 conference and for organizing a brief lecture tour of South Africa during his visit. The active participation of staff and students at the University of Transkei, the University of the North, and the University of the Witswatersrand, during this tour, was highly productive. We are also grateful to the participants on the Institute of Education masters programmes directed by Andrew Brown as part of the IBRD Indonesian Primary School Teacher Development project.

We are particularly grateful to Professor Tim Dunne of the University of Cape Town for critical comments and statistical advice on an earlier draft of Chapter 7. Ultimate responsibility for the final version as it appears here is, of course, ours.

The list of due acknowledgments in relation to our research is potentially very extensive and is dissipated in our research publications. We should, however, recognize our indebtedness to Basil Bernstein, who was the adept in respect to both of our research apprenticeships.

In terms of the processes of production of the book, we are grateful for the support of the Institute of Education and, in particular, our colleagues in *Culture Communication and Societies* in allowing us leave of absence for the writing phase.

Finally, we are grateful for critical comments by John Head and Ruth Merrtens on an earlier draft of the book.

The photograph in Figure 6.1 is by John Gaps and is reproduced by permission of Associated Press.

Figure 6.2 is reproduced from Barthes, R. (1972) *Mythologies,* translated from the French by Annette Lavers, London: Jonathan Cape by permission of the publishers, Jonathan Cape (UK) and Hill and Wang (US) and the Barthes Estate. *Mythologies* was first published in French by Les Editions du Seuil in 1957.

Table 7.1 is reproduced from Luria, A.R. (1976) *Cognitive Development: Its Cultural and Social Foundations,* translated from the Russian by Martin Lopez-Morillas and Lynn Solotaroff and edited by Michael Cole, Cambridge, Mass.: Harvard University Press (© 1976 by the President and Fellows of Havard College) by permission of the publishers. Luria's book was first published as *Ob istoricheskom razvitii poznavatel'nykh protsessov* by Nauka (Moskow, 1974).

Series Editors' Preface

It has become a feature of our times that an initial qualification is no longer seen to be adequate for life-long work within a profession and programmes of professional development are needed. Nowhere is the need more clear than with respect to education, where changes in the national schooling and assessment system, combined with changes in the social and economic context, have transformed our professional lives.

The series, *Master Classes in Education*, is intended to address the needs of professional development, essentially at the level of taught masters degrees. Although aimed primarily at teachers and lecturers, it is envisaged that the books will appeal to a wider readership, including those involved in professional educational management, health promotion and youth work. For some, the texts will serve to update their knowledge. For others, they may facilitate career reorientation by introducing, in an accessible form, new areas of expertise or knowledge.

The books are overtly pedagogical, providing a clear track through the topic by means of which it is possible to gain a sound grasp of the whole field. Each book familiarizes the reader with the vocabulary and the terms of discussion, and provides a concise overview of recent research and current debates in the area. While it is obviously not possible to deal with every aspect in depth, a professional who has read the book should feel confident that they have covered the major areas of content, and discussed the different issues at stake. The books are also intended to convey a sense of the future direction of the subject and its points of growth or change.

In each subject area the reader is introduced to different perspectives and to a variety of readings of the subject under consideration. Some of the readings may conflict, others may be compatible but distant. Different perspectives may well give rise to different lexicons and different bibliographies, and the reader is always alerted to these differences. The variety of frameworks within which each topic can be construed is then a further source of reflective analysis.

The authors in this series have been carefully selected. Each person is an experienced professional, who has worked in that area of education as a practitioner and also addressed the subject as a researcher and theoretician. Drawing upon both pragmatic and theoretical aspects of their experience, they are able to take a reflective view while preserving a sense of what occurs, and what is possible, at the level of practice.

Doing Research/Reading Research

The practice of educational research is not deep-rooted as can be seen by the fact that such well-established journals as *Research in Education* and the *British Educational Research Journal* only go back respectively to 1969 and 1975. In more recent years there has been a vast expansion of activity, not least because of the funding arrangements which can reward research within universities.

Unfortunately, this increase in quantity has not been matched by a concomitant consistency in quality. Possibly part of the problem is that our very familiarity with education — we have all had considerable experience of it and several hundred thousand people are employed in the field — leads to a belief that it should be easily researched. In fact, it presents a challenging, complex, multidisciplinary task, and often involves methods which are relatively new and untested.

A further problem is that we too often look to research to provide simple answers to practical problems and, as the authors of this book remind us, research and practice are widely separated. To take one contemporary example, research can be interpreted as indicating that co-education might be recommended for boys but not for girls in secondary schools. The fact that this finding does not provide a simple solution to the debate about the value of co-education does not deny the validity of the research finding. What it does tell us is that either we have to develop new procedures within the schooling system which captures most of the advantages for both boys and girls, or we have to recognize that we are making a choice between options, each of which disadvantages one gender. The research findings clarify our thinking even if they do not point to simple resolution of practical problems.

The authors of this book have taken pains to spell out the difficulty of undertaking and using research properly. They warn us of the dangers of looking for a simple outcome which can be used to justify a policy or validate a practice. Rigour is required both in our thinking about the issues and in all stages of the actual carrying out of the empirical procedures. They provide a comprehensive review of the field. Although this enterprise may seem intellectually demanding, the mastery of this text will give the reader the tools to read critically the diverse literature and commence their own research from a position of understanding and integrity.

John Head
Ruth Merttens

Series Editors

1 Introduction: The Three Rs of Educational Research

This book has emerged very gradually out of work on which we have been engaged, individually and collaboratively over a period of ten years or so. Its central motivation has developed out of two fields of commitment and experiences. These have shaped and been shaped by the general approach to the reading and doing of research which constitutes the principal theme of the book. That is, that research is properly conceived, not, primarily, as a sequence of stages, nor as a collection of skills and techniques, nor as a set of rules, though it entails all of these. Rather, it should be understood, first and foremost, as the continuous application of a particularly coherent and systematic and reflexive way of questioning, a **mode of interrogation**.

Our first commitment is to **research** as a distinctive attitude. The products of educational research are currently being thrust more than ever before into the public domain of political positioning and manipulation. But all too much of this output is interrogated exclusively in terms of its summary conclusions and never in respect of its methodological integrity. Under these conditions, 'research' is very easy. Say we want to argue that homework is good for you. Well, all we have to do is select half a dozen schools that have received positive inspection reports and some others that were negatively evaluated. We then count the number of hours homework that each school sets. A fast piece of arithmetic on the back of an envelope and, lo and behold, we find that the good schools set more homework than the bad schools. Solution: advocate a national homework policy or, alternatively, leave it to the schools to decide, so long as they publish their individual policies (which headteacher is going to declare themself with the baddies?). Both sides of the political game get ammunition for their manifesto and happily sponsor the 'researcher' to keep up the good work. Or they just might employ another one who looks better on the TV — after all, just about anyone can do this!

In the heady atmosphere of serious political debate, no one notices that, since the criteria for positive inspection include setting homework, the 'research' can hardly be described as adding a great deal to the sum of human knowledge.

Our own experience of research is that it is difficult and frustrating and that it takes a lot of time and causes a lot of tears. But eventually, it can generate ways of looking at the world which you didn't have before and which can motivate real developments in your professional practice as well as spur you on to further research activity.

Our second commitment is to **teaching** as a distinctive attitude. And here, teaching is not to be understood as a relay of performance objectives to be measured by standardized tasks by a functionary whose relation to the content is challenged rather than fostered by bureaucratic authority. Nor is teaching itself to be conceived as a sequence of phases, a set of skills and techniques, or a set of rules, although, again, it entails all of these. We see teaching as the establishment of an apprenticing relationship between a relatively experienced and a relatively inexperienced practitioner. The aim is the transmission of the practice from the former to the latter; we make no apology for the use of the expression 'transmission'.

The teaching or transmission of one's practice relates to, but is different from, the doing of one's practice in its own right and for its own sake. We propose that the relationship between a practice and its transmission is to be understood as one of constructive dialogue. This is particularly apposite where the practice concerned is educational research: research and teaching, then, cast their respective interrogative gazes upon each other; each stands as a critic with respect to the other. The motive force of the dialogue is, of course, sustained only so long as the two do not tend to dissolve into each other. In our own research, we describe the distinctions between practices such as research and teaching in terms of the distinctive nature of the structures of social relations which constitute the fields in which they respectively operate. These relational structures include peer group evaluation, in the case of research, and a hierarchical, apprenticing relationship between transmitter and acquirer, in the case of teaching.

As we have announced, our commitments to research and to teaching have shaped and have been shaped by our **general methodology**, which is to say, our general theoretical framework which we apply in our own research and in our pedagogic practices. This general methodological position is referred to, by Dowling, as **constructive description** and is presented in detail in his own work (Dowling, 1998). In this work, Dowling also presents his more specific language of description,[1] **social activity theory**, which has informed our presentation of the research mode of interrogation.

These commitments to research and to teaching have also arisen from particular sets of experiences during the ten year period of gestation of this book. We have, for example, both benefited enormously from our own research apprenticeships. In both of our cases, this has included a substantial period of time working under the supervision of Basil Bernstein, at the Institute of Education, University of London. A dominant figure in educational research since the 1960s, Bernstein is also an inspirational teacher of research. We do not, of course, make any claims on his allegiance to our particular approach. The mark of a good teacher is the production of constructive practitioners rather than acolytes.

Our own teaching, during the past decade, has included a sub
amount of work on higher degrees programmes, including the super
of masters dissertations and doctoral theses. We have also been devel
a general course in doing and reading educational research which has directly resulted in this book. The course arose out of teaching that we were
initially doing in London, but which has since been taken around the world.
In particular, we have taught the course in South Africa, Hong Kong, Cyprus
and, most recently, Brazil. In presenting the course, we have employed
a diverse range of pedagogic techniques, including the use of computer
mediated communication modes for the supervision of coursework following the face-to-face components.[2] The interests of course members have
varied from a diverse range of curriculum subject and phase specialisms to
cross-curricular interests, such as health education, educational media and
information technology, the more general disciplines such as educational
management, educational philosophy, psychology, and sociology. In our
experience, it is very often the teacher who gains most in the pedagogic
encounter. In a very real sense, then, our production of this book owes a
great deal to the enthusiastic participation of and critical evaluation by the
members of these courses.

Our practice in presenting the course is to adapt it to the linguistic,
national and disciplinary interests of the members of the particular programme we are running and, naturally, to develop the general structure and
specific activities which comprise the course on the basis of experience and
feedback each time we run it. The book, however, represents a transition.
Clearly, we cannot target our readership in quite the same way. We do,
nevertheless, have an audience in mind.

We envisage that readers of our book will comprise intending producers and consumers of research in the academic and professional fields of
education. The kind of producer we have in mind might be someone who
wishes to conduct a small-scale piece of research. Commonly, this might
form part of an academic course of study, such as a masters or doctoral
programme. Alternatively, it might be a response to a problem or a question
that arises in the course of the professional educational activity of, for example, a teacher, an educational administrator, or a health education officer.
Whatever its origins, the research will involve the collection and analysis of
information, which is to say, it will be empirical research. The research will
also entail a systematic enquiry which attempts to be self-conscious about its
assumptions, method of approach, and its limitations.

The producer of research will need to draw on existing work which is
associated with their particular interest, that is to say, they will also be consumers of research. Within an academic context, the author is required to
situate their work within the field of research. This means that they must
make their consumption explicit. Professional research may or may not place
a high value on its bibliography. Nevertheless, the professional researcher as

well as the academic researcher can gain from a consideration of previous research, not least in respect of the ways in which other researchers have selected and deployed their methods of data collection and analysis and organized their arguments.

The category 'consumer' of research is, however, more extensive than that of producer. Whereas all producers are (or, at least, should be) consumers, not all consumers are producers. Much of the public output of both academic and professional educational research is aimed at a practitioner as well as a researcher audience. This book, then, is as much about reading research as it is about doing research.

Of course, the producer of research will generally want to address an audience of their own in relaying their work. So, in this book, we shall also address the writing of research. Reading, pRoducing and wRiting: the three Rs of Research.

Our readership, thus defined, will have diverse interests, backgrounds and needs in terms of research activity. We cannot hope and nor shall we attempt to meet them all. This book is not, for example, a summary of widely used data collection and analysis techniques. Nor do we spend very much time discussing the epistemological, ontological, and political debates that take research itself as an object of study. Nor have we compiled a collection of anecdotes on the practical experiences of researchers in the field. There are excellent publications available in each of these categories. We have referred to some of them in our annotated bibliography.

What we have attempted to do can be summarized as four aims. Firstly, and as we have suggested above, this book is not neutral. We approach educational research from a particular position. This position understands research as a particular coherent and systematic and reflexive mode of interrogation. Our first aim is to establish and present this mode of interrogation in a form which is accessible to the beginning researcher, as we have described them. In other words, to apprentice our reader to the research mode of interrogation. We should point out, however, that we have not made major concessions in the sense of diluting the principal ideas in the book. This is a serious position statement as well as a pedagogic resource. Readers will find some, though by no means all of the book hard work. Secondly, we aim to achieve this within the context of an introduction to and some development of the language and techniques of research methods. Thirdly, we aim to signal some of the difficulties entailed in research and to provide practical advice on their management. Fourthly, we aim to present our approach such that it can be applied in the reading and doing and, ultimately, the presentation of educational research.

The structure of the main body of this book is as follows. Following this introduction, we have included two chapters which focus on the clarification of the context of a research project. Chapter 2 considers the first stages of the development from a general area of interest to the sketching out of relevant theoretical and empirical fields within which the research is to take place. Chapter 3 takes this development further to the sharper delineation of the research problem and empirical setting, including the definition of variables, sampling procedures and so forth.

Chapters 4 and 5 focus on issues of data collection. Chapter 4 focuses on observational approaches and the generation of researcher accounts; Chapter 5 considers the eliciting of accounts from others, including the use of questionnaires and interviews. Chapters 6 and 7 move to issues and techniques of data analysis, Chapter 6 emphasizing qualitative analysis and Chapter 7 providing a limited introduction to quantitative approaches. Essentially, whilst we would like readers to read the book in the order in which it is presented, it is possible to read these four chapters in any order, making use of the cross-references where necessary.

In Chapter 8 we present the research mode of interrogation in a schematic way, drawing on the discussions of the previous chapters. Chapter 9 focuses on the points of entry to and exit from the research process. In the first half of Chapter 9 we shall revisit the initial phase of the research process that is introduced in Chapter 2. This time, we will be able to make use of some of the terminology that has been developed in the intervening chapters. In the second part of the chapter, we shall give some consideration to the process of writing-up one's research. Finally, in Chapter 10, we return to some of the issues raised in this introduction and present our 'manifesto' for educational research.

We contend that, in terms of reading on research methodology, it should be possible for a beginning researcher to produce a good quality piece of work in the form of, say, a masters dissertation without going beyond this book. We would not, however, advise it. We have, therefore, included an annotated bibliography that will enable the reader to broaden their methodological understanding both technically and in terms of general methodology.

We have also constructed a keyword index for fast reference and cross-referencing purposes. All of the words which are included in the keyword index are emboldened in the text. The keyword index has three forms of page reference. References in bold are the principal references which locate a definition or gloss of the term. Other relevant references are in plain text. Italicized references refer to annotated bibliography entries.

Finally, we must emphasize that this book cannot turn you into a researcher. Ultimately, you can make that transition only by involving yourself in the practices of research, preferably alongside a more experienced practitioner — possibly your tutor on a higher degree programme. This is why, whenever we teach this course ourselves, it is very much a practical activity. We cannot replicate this practical nature in a book, nor are we attempting to. The book stands in relation to your developing research practice in the same kind of relationship as that which we are claiming obtains between educational research and professional educational practices. That is, as a mode of interrogation. Its fundamental role is to challenge you to greater coherence and systematicity and reflexiveness in the research practice which you are now beginning.

This concludes our introduction, save to say that at the end of Chapter 10 we have included an invitation to send us your responses to the book (and your suggestions for future editions). We are giving advance warning of this here so that you can make notes as you go along.

Notes

1 The expression, 'language of description' was coined by Basil Bernstein and is discussed in Bernstein, 1996. See also Dowling (in press).
2 The Cyprus government actually denies foreigners the right to teach Higher Education courses on Cypriot soil. It was therefore necessary to fly the Cyprus cohort of students to London for the face-to-face element of their course.

References

BERNSTEIN, B.B. (1996) *Pedagogy, Symbolic Control and Identity: Theory, Research Critique*, London: Taylor & Francis.

DOWLING, P.C. (1998) *The Sociology of Mathematics Education: Mathematical Myths/ Pedagogic Texts*, London: Falmer Press.

2　Declaring an Interest: The Empirical and Theoretical Contexts of the Research

Empirical and Theoretical Domains and the Research Process

As we have announced in the introduction, this book is concerned with empirical research within the general field of education. By **research**, we mean an enquiry which seeks to make known something about a field of practice or activity which is currently unknown to the researcher. In referring to the research as **empirical**, we mean that the enquiry should, in part, justify any claims that it makes in terms of reference to experience of the field to which these claims relate. We shall refer to this field as the **empirical field**. By introducing this definition, we are trying to establish an attitude, rather than rule out certain kinds of enquiry. For example, suppose that you are interested in the relation between gender and secondary school academic performance. There is clearly a whole range of approaches which you might adopt in addressing this topic. Firstly, you might go to the library and find a book on the subject. This might qualify as 'research', subject to additional expectations that you may have concerning systematicity and extensiveness. However, it would be difficult to maintain that reading the book gave you any direct experience of secondary schooling. Rather, the author must impose principles of selection and organization, that is, principles of **recontextualization**, upon their own experience of secondary schooling in mediating it to you as reader.

Alternatively, you might consult the published statistical data relating to the GCSE performances of boys and girls in England and Wales in 1994. Clearly, this narrows the field to a national context and also to a particular year. However, it also imposes other principles of recontextualization that mediate direct experience of this field. For example, it provides a simple binary scale for the category 'gender'. This means that the data treat all girls as the same and all boys as the same. You may feel (and there is evidence to support this) that there are very considerable differences in the attitudes towards and experiences of secondary education of girls and boys that vary according to dimensions such as ethnicity and socioeconomic status. Additionally, of course, academic performances do not begin and end with GCSE examination results. However, your data source would make any such differences opaque to your enquiry.

A third approach might be to attempt to get closer to the intended field by conducting interviews with participants, such as students and/or teachers. This narrows the field somewhat further, so that we are now beginning to talk about an **empirical setting**. In conducting an interview one is generally engaging in one setting — that of the interview itself — in order to access information about another — performance in the examination room, for example. As with the library sources, this information is again mediated by principles of recontextualization which are imposed on their experiences by your subjects. These principles may be imposed self-consciously or otherwise. In either case, you have no clear line of access to them. You may try to overcome the effects of the unknown recontextualization principles by adopting the position of observer in the intended setting itself. But there are limits to what you can possibly observe. You will have only so much time available (and you can only be in one place at a time) and you can't observe, far less record, everything that goes on in a particular situation. You must be selective and encode your observations in some way if you are to record them. This is the case even with a video recording. The complexity of even the apparently most simple situation is such that you will be unable to make explicit all of the principles which you impose on your observation and recording activities even if it were possible to be conscious of all of them, which, of course, it isn't. Furthermore, you can rarely discount completely the effect of your presence in a situation as an observer.

Confronted with such apparently insurmountable difficulties, you may be forced to the conclusion that the only settings which you can validly research are those in which you naturally and routinely participate yourself. Unfortunately, this still does not eliminate the impact of recontextualization. The act of taking up the position of observer or commentator is, of necessity, a shift in perspective from that of participant. This point has been very powerfully argued by the French sociologist, Pierre Bourdieu.[1] Whether in prospect or in retrospect, the objectification of your activities is always a different experience from your experience of those activities themselves. You will be familiar with this outside of research; planning and evaluating a lesson are very different activities from actually teaching it. We shall refer to this as the **epistemological paradox**: the act of making your experience explicit of necessity entails its transformation.

There is, then, no position or method that you can adopt which will give you an indisputably clear view of the empirical field (or of any empirical setting within it) which you want to investigate and about which you want to make statements. There is no such thing as the correct method, or even the best method for addressing a particular research interest or question. This does not, however, mean that all methods and positions are as good as each other for the purposes of empirical research. If they were, we could hardly justify writing a book on research methods. A common response to the inevitable shortcomings of any particular approach is to employ two or more approaches to the same problem. This is called methodological triangulation. The term **triangulation** refers, metaphorically, to the police or military procedure of using geometry to locate an illicit or 'enemy' radio transmission from direction readings at two reception points. In the context of educational research, we might employ a combination of, for example, interviews and direct observation in attempting to gain access to teachers' classroom practices.

There is a fundamental difference, however, between the assumptions which are being made in the radio and the educational research contexts. Essentially, the radio triangulator is making the assumption that there is a unique location for the transmitter which will be revealed by the process. This assumption is empirically justified when the illegal transmitter is found and arrested (or shot). The assumption is justifiable because there is already a coordination between the method of finding out and the method of moving to the coordinates of the transmitter. The means of defining the locations of the transmission point and the reception points are coincident. Nothing is being measured that is not already encoded into the practice.

The situation in educational research is, generally, very different. As we have argued, the act of taking up the position of observer entails a necessary break with that which is being observed. The observational 'position' is to be defined in a way which is distinct from the way in which the empirical setting, or observed position, is being defined. If the result of applying methodological triangulation is the production of multiple observational positions, then your research will be incoherent. Reconciling these multiple positions into a single observational position will merely return you to the original problem. Methodological triangulation, then, may be of value in expanding the empirical setting. It cannot overcome the epistemological paradox.

To explain further, we must return to our definition of empirical research. We have already asserted that it must justify any claims that it makes in terms of reference to the empirical field. More specifically, it must justify claims in terms of reference to the empirical setting, which is the local space in which the researcher is working within the empirical field. We must focus on the word 'justify'. Claims must be justified, which entails that the reasoning must be made as explicit as possible. In addition, it will clearly help if the presentation of claims and their justification can be made as systematically as possible so that the lines of argument are visible. This will not only assist the reader, but will enable the researcher to detect faults in their reasoning.

So, you will need to be as explicit as possible about the empirical setting of your research and about the relation to it of any information that you gather. However, this is not enough. We have suggested above that you cannot approach a field or setting without some preconceptions about the nature of that setting. Most obviously, you cannot set out to research the school without having some idea of what you mean by 'school'. Your pre-conceptions will comprise commonsense knowledge about how schools work and who works in them and about how you can distinguish between good and bad schools and so on. You may also have access to more academic knowledge about the learning and teaching processes or about management practices etc. Furthermore, you may affiliate to moral and political views about how schools ought to work or what they should be aiming to do and so forth. Whilst these preconceptions will certainly impact upon your observation or interviewing or reading, they will not all be present in your consciousness at the time. You cannot be at all sure, in other words, of your own bias even though you must recognize that it is there. Thus, in justifying the claims that you will make about your empirical territory, you must also try to make as available as possible the conceptual structure that you bring to bear on that territory. This conceptual structure is the theoretical **problem** with which your research is concerned.

We have now introduced two arenas within which empirical research takes place. The first has thus far been described in terms of two levels, one local and the other general. The **empirical setting** refers to the local region of experience about which you want to make claims; the observed position. The setting is a specified region within a broader empirical field. Thus, secondary school teachers' classroom practices might constitute an **empirical field**; the practices of a small sample of teachers in a sample of their classrooms in a particular school in a particular location, etc, might constitute the empirical setting. We have also introduced two levels of the second arena. The **problem** refers to the conceptual structure which enables you to think about the empirical setting; the observational position. However, this also must relate to a broader field of discourse incorporating, perhaps, academic and professional knowledges and debates. This is the **theoretical field**. Later, we shall introduce third levels in each of these arenas. Research entails the **specializing** of a theoretical framework within a more general field and the **localizing** of an empirical setting within an empirical field. It is the bringing to bear of the theoretical framework on the empirical setting that enables you to make both theoretical and empirical claims.

As a beginning researcher, you will probably find it very difficult to give an adequately explicit and coherent description of your empirical setting. You are unlikely to have a clear idea of a problem. You may have initial ideas about an aspect of educational practice or process that interests you. You may also have a feeling for the kind of theoretical approach that you are drawn to; whether, for example, the problem is to be conceived of as a psychological or a sociological one, whether it relates to management or health promotion and so forth. But these ideas are unlikely to have been developed very far at this stage. In other words, you are likely to have some initial feeling for your general empirical and theoretical fields. Educational research does not necessarily begin with clearly defined and articulated problems and empirical settings. Rather, we are asserting that the research process itself is properly conceived of as the construction of the theoretical and empirical as increasingly coherent and systematically organized and related conceptual spaces. It is, in other words, a continuous and productive process. This poses the additional problem of knowing when to stop. We will leave this question for the moment. We will continue this chapter with a discussion on the initial moves in the formation of the theoretical and empirical contexts that constitute the research interest.

Declaring an Interest: First Steps Towards a Research Question

As we have announced in the introduction and, indeed, in the title, this book is as much about reading research as it is about doing research. In many ways (that we hope will become clear) each of these processes entails the other. We are not, therefore, offering separate sections on doing and reading. Rather, we will be looking at the various stages of the research process in terms of both doing and reading research. Clearly, we need to make reference to publicly available research in considering reading. We have decided to use a very famous and very influential piece of work carried out in the 1930s in the Soviet Union by Alexander Luria and published in English about twenty years ago. Luria was a student and colleague of Lev Vygotsky. Their work is now becoming increasingly influential in the general field of educational research. The particular item that we shall be referring to is Luria's (1976) *Cognitive Development: Its Cultural and Social Foundations.*

Apart from the influential status of this work, its principal appeal for our purposes is its clear definition of its theoretical and empirical contexts. It is, in this respect, a very good piece of research. A third reason for its selection is precisely its time and place of origin. Its distance from us in time and general cultural context gives it a degree of strangeness which makes it comparatively easy to bring into relief the contours of its argument. Vygotsky's and Luria's work also incorporates theoretical ideas which we shall be referring to at various points in this book. We intend to provide sufficient information about Luria's study to enable the reader who is not familiar with it to negotiate our text. However, we strongly recommend that you read Luria's text for yourself at some point.

In respect of the doing of research, we shall include references to several pieces of small-scale work. Most of these have been or, in some cases, are being carried out by students on diploma, masters and doctoral programmes with which one or both of us has been associated. In referring to this work, we are not seeking, here, to evaluate it. Rather, we are hoping that our discussion of the kinds of questions and approaches that these beginning researchers have adopted will concretize the more general statements that we shall be making. We shall also be referring to work that we have carried out ourselves, individually and jointly. Again, we are not presenting this as exemplary of good (or bad) practice. It is simply providing material for our methodological exposition. We shall begin our discussion of the initial stage of the research process with a brief introduction to the general theoretical and empirical field which was occupied by Luria's study.

An Initial Description of Luria's Theoretical and Empirical Spaces

The title of Luria's book gives us a good indication of the **theoretical field** in which he is working, cognitive development: its cultural and social foundations. The main title tells us that Luria is operating within the general field of psychology. The subtitle gives us a clue, should we need one, to the kind of theoretical explanation that he wants to offer. It indicates that he grounds cognitive development in the sociocultural; the level of development of an individual's consciousness is, in some sense, a function of the kind of society in which they live. In his introduction, Luria clarifies his interest:

> ...psychology has barely begun to study the specific sociohistorical structures of mental processes. We still do not know whether changes in sociohistorical structures or changes in the nature of social practice result only in broadened experience, acquisition of new habits and knowledge, literacy, and so forth, or whether they result in radical reorganization of mental processes, changes at the structural level of mental activity, and the formation of new mental systems. Proof of the latter would be of fundamental significance for psychology as a science of social history. (Luria, 1976; p. 12)

Here, Luria is indexing a debate within the field of psychology at the time. It was a debate that also held an interest for anthropologists, in particular, Franz Boas and Lucien Lévy-Bruhl. Boas adopted the former of the two positions referred to by Luria. That is, he maintained that the thinking of individuals from culturally different groups varied only in the categories used. Lévy-Bruhl, on the other hand, argued that there were structurally different forms of thought which related to each other in developmental terms. That is, people from 'primitive' societies are characterized by a 'primitive' mode of thought. In the above extract, Luria also hints at his own preference.

There are other dimensions to Luria's interests. Whilst his work and that of Vygotsky often stood in opposition to the Marxist psychology of the Soviet Union of the day, his general approach must be described as itself Marxist. Specifically, his understanding of social development related to the organization of the relations of production. Luria also adopted Vygotsky's interest in and understanding of language as providing the basis for the structuring of thought. Literacy, in particular, constitutes language as a comparatively context-independent system and thus potentially facilitates a radical transformation in the mode of thinking. Thus, his disciplinary interests were very broad, ranging across psychology, sociology, anthropology and linguistics. So, we can begin to get an idea of the theoretical space within which Luria was working. It is a space which identifies particular discourses and debates within an even broader, multidisciplinary field. It will become more sharply defined in the subsequent chapters of this book. How about his **empirical field**?

As we have indicated, Luria's interest is in the relationship between social and cultural organization and cognition. Empirically, Luria wants to look at differentiation in people's productive relations, in their literacy, and in their thinking. The Soviet Union of the 1930s was a society in transition (some might say turmoil). Luria therefore had the opportunity to work in settings which spanned developmental levels. Some of his subjects would be engaged in individualized subsistence production, others might work on a collective farm; some of his subjects would be illiterate, others would have received access to schooling and literacy. He chose to work in 'remote villages of Uzbekistan and also a few in the mountainous regions of Kirghizia', where such variations could be found (Luria, 1976; p. 14).

Luria's choice of **empirical setting** was motivated by his theoretical field and, more particularly, by his specific problem. This problem constituted his position within the academic field. The choice also involved taking advantage of an opportunity to study cognition during what Luria conceived to be a particular kind of social transformation. In this respect, the choice was motivated by Luria's contingent location in the Soviet Union in the early 1930s. By definition, beginning researchers have yet to clarify their position within a field of research and the achievement of this clarification will be an important aspect of their research. Very often, however, they will occupy professional positions and will be familiar with and interested in some of the discourses and debates relating to these positions. They will also be immersed in a professional practice within which problems and issues of interest may arise. The initial steps towards a **research question** may well involve the articulating of localized observations and problems with more general professional discourses and debates. We will now consider the inaugural stage of such a study.

Opening Your Theoretical Space: Using the Library

One primary school teacher remarked on a child's reference to 'a vampire in his or her coffin'. It was this observation, she claimed, that led to her

interest in the more general issue of children's use of gender-specific pronouns. The observation indexes the teacher's local professional context as
the emerging empirical setting. It also leads to an area of professional literature relating to the issues of gender and language acquisition and use in the
primary school. Further, it leads to a more academic literature base in a
number of possible fields, including sociology, linguistics and psychology.
At this stage, the empirical setting seems fairly well defined, whilst the theoretical space looks dangerously expansive and uncoordinated. It is, therefore, in this space that some initial clarification must be made.

The initial approach might be to try to specify more precisely what
aspect of the inspirational observation particularly interests you. This will
direct you to relevant areas of the literature. There are a number of possibilities relating to the above example. For example, your main interest
may lie in gender as a structural feature of the primary school and of
wider society. In this case, children's gendering of their language would
be regarded as instances of a gendered culture. Alternatively, you might be
interested in children's language development, either in linguistic or cognitive terms or in relation to children's reading materials. There again, you
may be interested in exploring policy in relation to language and gender
in primary schooling. Making a decision in these terms is probably about as
far as you can go without doing some work in the **library**.

An academic educational library can be a daunting place for the beginning researcher. It will contain at least seven kinds of resources.

    (i)   The collection of books about education and educational research
and associated topics and disciplines: some of these will be targeted primarily at an academic audience. This category will include 'classical' research in fields such as psychology and sociology
as well as work by academic authors focusing specifically on
education. Other books will be more deliberately aimed at professionals and, possibly, other groups. This category will include,
for example, governmental reports and enquiries as well as books
written by professionals for professionals.

    (ii)   The collection of journals: again, both academic and professional
journals are likely to be included.

    (iii)   The archive of dissertations and theses of former masters and
doctoral students.

    (iv)   Reference materials of various kinds including, for example,
statistical data relating to education.

    (v)   A collection of educational materials, such as school textbooks.

    (vi)   Various resources which enable the interrogation of the library
collection and of educational literature more generally. There
will be a library catalogue which, nowadays, will usually include
a computer search facility enabling users to find specific items,

the works of particular authors, or to search using topics or keywords. Most academic libraries will also contain indices of educational research, including the **British Education Index** and the **Education Resources Information Center** (**ERIC**). Commonly, these indices will be available in the form of regularly up-dated CD-ROMs, so that they can be interrogated using computer searches.

(vii) The library staff who will be able to give expert advice on all of the above resources and who are generally rather more tolerant than a computer.

Suppose that you have decided that what caught your attention in the observation about the politically correct vampire was the contrast between this young child's apparent sensitivity to gender as a variable in comparison with what you perceive to be a general tendency amongst adults to the use of the masculine as generic. Could it be that there is a difference in the gendering of language by primary-age children and adults? Might any such difference relate to the expressions used or to the intended or perceived meaning of the expressions or both? What might be responsible for any such differences? These questions suggest a sociological interest. That is, they suggest an interest in the structuring of social practices by gender and by age. What is needed, at this stage, is some literature which is directly concerned with sociology, language and gender.

You do not need to carry out a full literature search at the moment. You are not trying to claim that you have read everything that has ever been written on these subjects. Rather, you are trying to make an entrance into this literature in order to define your research question more clearly. A number of strategies are available apart from, of course, asking someone for assistance. The simplest approach might be to look through the contents pages of the available sociology journals covering the past five years or so. Alternatively, you might try a simple computer search, using either the library catalogue — if you want a book — or one of the educational research indices if you are looking for journal articles. The latter is particularly useful if you are not entirely clear which journals might cover your particular interests.

Using our computerized library catalogue at the Institute of Education, University of London we carried out a **key word search**. Initially we entered the terms language and gender. In this kind of search the computer looks for the terms given in the titles, the short descriptions of each book and the key words appended to each record on the system. It displays those records that contain both terms. Not surprisingly, given that we used just two very broad terms, this search gave us 674 matches. Scanning quickly through some of those identified as close matches gave some indication of the breadth of the field and the types of material available. Some of the work was clearly aimed at the development of classroom practice, for example Goddard, A. (1989) *The Language Awareness Project Years 4 and 5 (Key Stage 2): Language and Gender Pack One*, Lancaster: Framework Press. Whilst this was of interest with respect to the forms of action teachers might take to address language and gender issues with primary age children, it is of limited interest at this early stage of refining our question and establishing an approach. The existence of this kind of material should reassure us that our general area of interest has attracted the attention of other practitioners.

Some of the references looked more promising. A 1985 collection of papers edited by Walkerdine, V., Unwin, K. and Steedman, A. *Language, Gender and Childhood*, London: RKP provided us with an indication of the range of approaches taken to our general area of interest and began to provide possible theoretical resources for the development of our study. A 1983 collection edited by Thorne, B., Kramarae, C. and Henley, N. *Language, Gender and Society*, Rowley, Mass: Newbury House fulfils a similar function and specifically indexes the articulation of gendered language use and wider social practices. Collections like these help us to develop a better feel for the field in which we are working. Both collections are, however, rather dated and very broad in their concerns. One of the references provided is more recent and more clearly focused: Coates, J. (1993) *Women, Men and Language: A Sociolinguistic Account of Gender Differences in Language*, 2nd edition, London: Longman. This is clearly relevant to our study, although no direct reference is made to the school or classroom in the title or summary.

Rather than plough through all 674 references we narrowed down our search by including the term sociology. This gave us seventy-one hits. Amongst these we found an Australian study by Evans, T. *A Gender Agenda: A Sociological Study of Teachers, Parents and Pupils in their Primary Schools*, Sydney: Allen and Unwin which was of some interest. The collection by Walkerdine *et al.* did not appear in the results of this search. This illustrates the importance of carrying out both broad and narrow searches.

The library catalogue is obviously not good for locating recent research. For this we need to turn to journals. Searching the **ERIC database** using the key words language and gender gave seventy hits. An attempt to narrow this search by adding the term sociology reduced this to zero hits. As would be expected, many of the seventy references turned up by the initial search were well outside our area of interest. The *Southern Illinois Working Papers in Linguistics and Language Teaching, Volume 1*, for instance, consisted of five research papers in applied linguistics by members of one university linguistics department. One of these papers concerned gender differences in second language acquisition, hence the appearance of the collection in our search. The ERIC database includes abstracts for all entries, so identification of relevant items is straightforward. Often the abstracts alone give sufficient detail for you to be able to identify which items are central to your area of interest and which are peripheral. The search facilities are powerful and easy to use. The results of a search can be inspected on screen, printed out or downloaded onto disc. The latter enables the results of a search to be transferred into a bibliographic database, such as Endnote, on your own PC.

Of the seventy references provided by the ERIC search, eight are in the North American journal *Language Arts*. These papers focus on either children's books or on children's own writing. Whilst the issues discussed are clearly relevant to our general area of research, the journal is aimed at a professional audience and few of the papers draw on original empirical research. Nonetheless, the eight papers, all published in 1993, demonstrate that there is significant professional interest in the issue of children's gendered language and how this relates to what they read and how they write. One of the papers identified in the search provides a critical review of literature relating to language, gender and education (Corson, D.J. (1992) 'Language, gender and education: A critical review linking social justice and power', *Gender and Education*, **4**, pp. 229–54.) which is clearly relevant. It also indexes a relevant journal, *Gender and Education*, available in our library and a possible source of additional material.

None of the references provided by the ERIC search directly address our interest in differences in the gendering of language by young children and adults. A number of papers look at the language experience and language use of pre-school children. One questionnaire-based piece of research indicates that the use of gender specific language is not considered to be an issue in the selection of books to read to pre-school children for the majority of teachers surveyed (Patt, M.B. and McBride, B.A. (1993) 'Gender equity in picture books in preschool classrooms: An exploratory study', paper presented at the Annual Meeting of the American Educational Research Association, Atlanta, GA, April 12–16). Another strand in the literature addresses shifts that have taken place in the general use of gender inclusive and gender exclusive language (for example, Zuber, S. and Reed, A.M. (1993) 'The politics of grammar handbooks: generic "he" and singular "they"', *College English*, **55**, 5, pp. 515–30). Searches carried out using the **British Education Index**, the **Australian Education Index** and the **Canadian Education Index** turned up a similar range of references. These indexes do not provide abstracts, which makes it more difficult to evaluate the relevance of the items selected.

Some of the items might be in journals that are not available in your library. It is often possible to order copies of these papers either through ERIC or through the inter-library loan system. Thesis and dissertations are not universally available in this way. Getting hold of, or access to, any of these items will always involve a time delay and can sometimes incur a financial expense. You need to weigh up these possible costs against any benefits you might hope to gain from reading the work.

The outcome of this brief literature search indicates that the area which we have identified is worth investigating. A good range of relevant work has been identified and professional and academic interest in key issues has been established. By following up the most relevant references we can begin to develop the theoretical framework and state the problem more clearly. At this stage in the development of the research, the review of literature should act as both an inspiration and affirmation.

The Theoretical and Empirical Spheres

In this chapter we have made a distinction between the theoretical and the empirical contexts of educational research. The theoretical field is the broad area of academic and/or professional knowledge, research and debates which contains your general area of interest. Theoretically, your research will involve the selection and development of a region of this field as a specialized problem. This framework will comprise your theoretical propositions or hypotheses or your research questions and, ultimately, your conclusions. The empirical field is the general area of practice or activity or experience about which you intend to make claims. Empirically, your research must involve the selection and elaboration of a region of this field as a localized empirical setting. This setting will contain the specific site of your empirical work.

We are approaching the reading of research in books and articles in precisely the same way as we are treating the doing of research. It is the responsibility of the critical reader of research to determine the specific problem and local empirical setting of the work. These may be stated, in the book or article, in greater or lesser clarity and detail. They may be described separately or they may be intertwined. They may be given in different forms at different points of the book or article. In particular, the specific problems addressed by educational research are often very hard to pin down in theoretically well-defined terms. Your initial foray into the piece will provide you with a general feel for the theoretical and empirical fields of the research. As you re-read and study the piece, you should begin to formulate a clearer picture of the problem and empirical setting.

The distinction between the theoretical and empirical spheres is crucial in establishing clarity in doing one's own research and in the interrogating of the research of others. However, these spaces are not to be hermetically sealed with respect to each other. As the details of the problem and empirical setting become sharper, they must also be related explicitly to each other. It is to the processes involved in the articulation of the theoretical and the empirical spheres that we shall turn in Chapter 3.

Note

1   See, for example, Bourdieu, 1977, 1990.

References

BOURDIEU, P. (1977) *Outline of a Theory of Practice*, Cambridge: Cambridge University Press.
BOURDIEU, P. (1990) *The Logic of Practice*, Cambridge: Polity.
LURIA, A.R. (1976) *Cognitive Development: Its Cultural and Social Foundations*, Cambridge MA: Harvard University Press.

3 Articulating the Theoretical and Empirical Fields

In Chapter 2 we described two spaces which, we maintain, are the concerns of any piece of empirical research. We have indicated that Luria's theoretical problem emerged within a context of disciplined academic writing and debates. Beginning educational researchers may be interested in similarly academically located debates in respect of their theoretical position. Alternatively, they may see themselves as entering a field of professional debate concerning, for example, curriculum policy or management practice. These are different, but equally valid starting points. It is not, in our opinion, the particular referential field that defines the theoretical quality of the research. Rather, it is the extent to which the research attempts a systematic and explicit organizing of its theoretical space as a theoretical framework.

Luria's empirical setting was an opportunistic one. It is likely that the beginning educational researcher's empirical setting will also be selected on the basis of opportunity. Again, this is unimportant in terms of the empirical quality of the research. What matters is the extent to which the research attempts to make explicit its empirical conditions and the extent to which it justifies the links between its empirical observations and its theoretical categories. Where it is possible, of course, a part of such justification may derive from a more deliberately selected or constructed empirical setting.

In this chapter, we shall make the move to the formulation of specific research questions or theoretical propositions — the problem — on the one hand, to questions about the empirical setting, on the other. We are, then, dealing with the articulation of the theoretical and empirical spaces. However, in this chapter, we are moving from the theoretical to the empirical. Moves in the opposite direction will become important in Chapters 4–7. We do not have the space to introduce alternative theoretical positions. Because of this, we shall refer most of our discussion in this chapter to the work by Luria that we have already introduced.

The Problem

The first phase of development of the theoretical field involves making explicit a nebula of debates and theories and, indeed, empirical findings about the area of your concern. These are theoretical because they entail general statements in relation to the local context of your particular empirical setting.

This process may be thought of as a crystallizing out of what you will consider to be key pieces of work (in relation to your own) from a more general context. We refer to this key region of the theoretical field as the **problematic** within which you will be working.

The next phase involves the formulation of more precise statements or propositions or questions in terms of specific concepts. This is where you begin to specify your **problem**. It is important, at this point, to stress that by the expression 'next phase', we are referring to the phase which logically follows the initial marking out of the problematic within the more general theoretical field. In chronological terms, it is sometimes the case that the problem does not emerge in its explicit stage of completeness until the very end of the research. Under such circumstances, the work of data collection and analysis that are the concern of the middle section of this book (Chapters 4–7) may be said to come in between the work of the previous chapter and this one. The point, however, is that data collection and analysis are empty activities unless theoretical development is a constant part of your active engagement with the research. For this reason, then, we must explain and exemplify what is meant by this phase at this early stage of the book.

Theoretical development, then, may occur, chronologically, at various stages of the research process. So, the presentation, in a book or article, of the problem as **propositions** or **hypotheses** to be tested, or as **questions** to be answered, or as observations or **conclusions** relates more to the form in which the argument is to be made than to the research process as actually experienced by the researcher. The report of the research must be understood as itself a **recontextualizing** of this process for the purposes of establishing a case. In his introductory chapter (entitled, 'The problem'), Luria presents his **problem** as both a **research question** and a **hypothesis**. In his conclusion, he re-presents it as a **finding**. We will quote from the conclusion, here:

> Our investigations, which were conducted under unique and non-replicable conditions involving a transition to collectivized forms of labor and cultural revolution, showed that, as the basic forms of activity change, as literacy is mastered, and a new stage of social and historical practice is reached, major shifts occur in human mental activity. These are not limited simply to an expanding of man's [sic] horizons, but involve the creation of new motives for action and radically affect the structure of cognitive processes.
>
> A basic feature of the shifts we observed is that the role of direct graphic-functional experience was radically altered in the transition to collectivized labor and new forms of social relations and with the mastery of rudiments of theoretical knowledge. (Luria, 1976; pp. 161–2)

As is commonly the case in social science and educational writing, the familiarity of many of the terms in this extract tends to conceal the specific and technical way in which they are being used. 'Activity', 'motive' and

Table 3.1:   Luria's theoretical proposition

Variable	Primitive society	Advanced society
social relations	individualized labour	collectivized labour
cultural practices	non-literate	literate
cognitive development	graphic-functional	theoretical

'action', for example, are the English equivalents of terms within a particularly Vygotskian theoretical framework. This framework was developed by another of his colleagues, Aleksei Leont'ev, and is now referred to as 'activity theory'. We shall try to make available the general nature of Luria's question/proposition/conclusion without recourse to an extensive theoretical elaboration of this theory.

Other expressions, such as 'graphic-functional experience', possibly, are more obviously technical. Graphic-functional experience is experience structured by the physical nature of the context within which it takes place. It is here being opposed to 'theoretical knowledge', which has the property of generalizability across contexts defined in physical terms.

Essentially, Luria is making the following proposition. Firstly, that societies move between different patterns of *social relationships*. Secondly, that these movements are associated with developments in *cultural practices*. Thirdly, that these social and cultural developments cause developments to take place in terms of individual cognition. In passing, we should also mention that Luria very much saw these developments as evolutionary in nature.

The basic form of the proposition, then, is that the terminal (i.e. adult) level of cognitive development is a function of the state of social and cultural development. Hypothetically, then, Luria can postulate two societies — respectively, primitive and advanced — for which his proposition enables him to map out their respective social and cultural properties and the levels of cognitive development of individuals within these societies. This has been done in *Table 3.1*, which presents the **proposition** in a rather more formal way than Luria does himself.

Levels of Measurement

You will note that the first column of *Table 3.1* is headed **variable**. A variable is a quality which can take a number of different values or states. The range of states that the variable can take constitutes its **scale**. Thus 'gender' is a variable which is generally scaled as masculine and feminine. In the case of gender, masculine and feminine are not usually thought of as being organized in any particular order. This kind of scale is called a **nominal scale**.

Luria's scales are rather different. This is because, as we have indicated, he saw social and cultural and cognitive development as evolutionary. Thus, there is a logical ordering of the scales of the three variables in *Table 3.1* which places the categories in the second column before those in the third, in

---

developmental terms. Scales which can be ordered in this way are called **ordinal scales**.

Sometimes, a variable is scaled in numerical terms. Thus a time variable may be scaled in terms of the years of the twentieth century: 1900, 1901, 1902, 1903, and so on. On this kind of scale, the interval between adjacent points is the same everywhere on the scale. In other words, the interval between 1900 and 1901 has the same meaning as that between 1935 and 1936 and that between 1990 and 1991. This kind of scale is called an **interval scale**. Arithmetical operations are permissible with this kind of scale, but not with nominal or ordinal scales. You can calculate the middle year in a scale, but the notion of an average gender or an average in terms of social relations is somewhat bewildering.

Interval scales, such as the calendar years may have a **conventional zero**, for example, 1 AD. However, if time were to be scaled in terms of, say, the number of minutes which had elapsed since the start of an experiment (or lesson), there would be an *absolute zero*. That is, the variable is defined in terms of its starting point — the start of the experiment. A scale which has an absolute zero is called a **ratio scale**. It is only on ratio scales that the most sophisticated mathematical operations may be performed.

Nominal, ordinal, interval and ratio are called **levels of measurement**. For most of our purposes in this book, we shall be dealing only with nominal and ordinal levels of measurement in terms of the scaling of **variables**.

Frequency

In addition to the scaling of variables, we will also refer to the measurement of the **frequency** of a category. This means the number of times that the category occurs. Here, we are clearly referring to a ratio level of measurement, since logically (although not necessarily empirically) the minimum frequency is zero.

In determining the level of measurement, it is important to distinguish between the scaling of a variable in terms of its possible values or states and the frequency with which these values or states occur. Thus, supposing you record that your sample consists of fifty-two females and forty-six males. You are recording the **frequency distribution** of the **variable**, gender, within your sample. That is, the frequency of each state or value of the variable. Gender remains nominally scaled, whilst it is the frequency which is ratio scaled.

So, Luria has defined his theoretical proposition as a statement of the relationships between a number of variables, each of which is ordinally scaled with two values. These are theoretical **concepts** or **concept variables**. Where the theoretical proposition is being presented as a hypothesis to be tested in a more experimental mode of design, you may want to refer to these as **hypothetical variables**. Luria's theoretical propositions could easily have been formulated as a question:

What is the nature of the terminal level of cognitive development, in terms of graphic-functional and theoretical thinking, in (a) a society exhibiting individualized social relations of production and a non-literate culture and (b) a society exhibiting collectivized social relations of production and a literate culture?

Whether or not an author presents a theoretical proposition or hypothesis, on the one hand, or a **research question**, on the other, depends upon the degree of openness which they wish to attribute to their initial predictions. Similarly, in doing research, whether one starts with a hypothesis or a question depends upon how much one knows about the theoretical and empirical contexts in terms of prior work and/or personal experience.

Note that the movement from theoretical proposition or hypothesis to research question does not entail any loss of precision. Just because it's a question does not mean that you should feel entitled to be vague. Theoretical development is precisely the generation of explicitness and systematicity in the definition of one's variables and the statement of the relationships between them. Naturally, this precision develops with the research process, but at the point of writing-up, it should have been achieved and can be demanded in your interrogation of other people's research reports.

Having tightened up the theoretical space somewhat, it is now time to move towards the empirical setting.

Operationalization: The Empirical Measurement of Theoretical Propositions

Luria's theoretical propositions clearly make certain demands of his empirical setting. However, they do not, as they are formulated, immediately specify exactly how the empirical work is to be carried out. It is clear that Luria needed to be able to access individuals in a way that allows him to measure their cognitive level and the nature of the society in which they live. He also needed to draw samples from each of the two kinds of society. But what counts as evidence that an individual's cognitive processes can validly be described as 'graphic-functional'; what are the principles whereby the samples should be drawn? The move from the statement of a theoretical proposition to its empirical measurement is called **operationalization**. We will now consider how Luria facilitated the movement between his theoretical framework and his **empirical setting**. We shall begin with the empirical measurement of the theoretical propositions.

There are three **concept variables** that must be measured: social relations; cultural practices; and cognitive level. The first is scaled as individualized as opposed to collectivized production; the second as non-literate as opposed to literate. Luria worked with five groups of subjects, which he describes as follows:

1   Ichkari women living in remote villages who were illiterate and not involved in any modern social activities. [. . .]
2   Peasants in remote villages, who continued to maintain an individualistic economy, to remain illiterate, and to involve themselves in no way with socialized labor.
3   Women who attended short-term courses in the teaching of kindergarteners. As a rule, they still had no formal education and almost no literacy training.
4   Active *kolkhoz* (collective farm) workers and young people who had taken short courses. They actively involved themselves in running the farms — as chairmen, holders of kolkhoz offices, or brigade leaders. They had considerable experience in planning production, in distributing labor, and in taking stock of work output. They dealt with other kolkhoz members and had acquired a much broader outlook than had the isolated peasants. But they had attended school only briefly, and many were still barely literate.
5   Women students admitted to a teachers' school after two or three years of study. Their educational qualifications, however, were still fairly low. (Luria, 1976; p. 24)

Luria classifies these groups as follows:

> Only the final three groups had experienced the conditions necessary for any radical psychological change. There now existed new motives for action, and also new forms of access to a technological culture and mastery of mechanisms such as literacy and other new forms of knowledge. The transition to a socialist economy brought along new forms of social relations and, with them, new life principles. The first two groups were much less exposed to the conditions for any such fundamental shifts. (*ibid*)

The principles whereby this classification is made are, essentially, encoded into the descriptions of the groups in the first extract. Subjects in the first two groups are simply asserted to be illiterate and not to be involved in collectivized relations of production. No further information is given, presumably because Luria considered these features to be self-evident properties of the subjects. The subjects in the third and fifth groups are described as having been exposed to schooling and, therefore (presumably), to literate culture. The fourth group had additional and active exposure to collectivized relations of production on a collective farm. Luria is careful to point out, however, that none of these subjects could be described as having had more than rudimentary schooling. The difference between the two groups is described in terms of zero as opposed to some exposure to modern society. Luria is hypothesizing (at this stage) that only a small amount of exposure is needed in order to trigger the expected psychological advances.

Now, you may feel that the description of the activities of the fourth group of subjects is sufficiently detailed to provide a plausible case that they are involved in collectivized relations of production. It is less clear, perhaps, that the description of the first two groups is sufficient to justify their social categorization, although you may be content to accept Luria's assertion that they were illiterate. The women in the third and fifth groups had participated in schooling, but not necessarily in collectivized relations of production. Is this important? These issues concern the **validity** of Luria's operationalization of the two variables, 'social relations' and 'cultural practices'.

Validity and Reliability

Validity concerns the relationship between theoretical, **concept variables** (or **concepts**) and empirical, **indicator variables** (or **indicators**). For example, supposing that your **problem** includes the variable 'gender', scaled 'feminine' and 'masculine'. Suppose, further, that your **empirical setting** includes a written list of the names of school students in alphabetical order of family name. You may decide that their first name provides a valid indicator of their gender, because you are confident that you can recognize girls' and boys' names. You, therefore, expect to be able to **code** each student correctly as either feminine or masculine. This would be an assertion of **face validity**; the first name is a plausibly valid indicator of gender.

There may, however, be ambiguities, such as names which may be written in abbreviated form (Chris, Pat, and so on), names with which you are unfamiliar by virtue of their and your ethnic origin etc, and names which are commonly associated with one gender but which may, contingently, be associated with the other (the actor, John Wayne's original first name was Marian, for example). In coding the list, you will have to make a decision, in the first two cases; you may not notice the third. These ambiguities weaken the validity of the variable 'first name' as an indicator of the concept variable, 'gender'. Validity, then, is a measure of the extent to which you are measuring what you think you are measuring.

In addition to relying on face validity, the results of coding according to one indicator may be compared with the results of coding according to another indicator which has previously been demonstrated to be valid. A statistical measure of the agreement, or **correlation**, between the two coding results provides a measure of the **criterion validity** or **convergent validity** of the new indicator.

Alternatively, you may be able to demonstrate that coding according to your chosen indicator bears out an already known relationship between two theoretical variables. This comparison provides a measure of the **construct validity** of your indicator.

Reliability is a measure of the consistency of a coding process when carried out on different occasions and/or by different researchers. As a test of reliability, a researcher may produce instructions for coding a set of information. The rules and the information (or some of it) are then given to two coders and their results compared. A measure of the correlation between the two coding results provides a numerical measure of reliability.

Luria is far more elaborate in describing his principles of recognition of the variable 'cognitive level'. For example, in his introduction to his findings on generalization and abstraction, he describes the previous findings of Goldstein in order to illustrate in concrete terms the distinction between responses in the two levels of cognition:

> In abstract or categorical classification, the normal subject forms a distinct category by selecting objects corresponding to an abstract concept. This kind of classification yields instances of abstract categories such as *vessels, tools, animals,* or *plants* in an appropriate group, no matter whether the particular objects are ever encountered together. An ax, saw, shovel, quill, and a knitting needle are all assigned to the category *tools* [. . .] Subjects who gravitate towards [concrete or situational thinking] do not sort objects into logical categories but incorporate them into graphic-functional situations drawn from life and reproduced from memory. These subjects group together objects such as a table, a tablecloth, a plate, a knife, a fork, bread, meat, and an apple, thereby reconstructing a 'meal' situation in which these objects have some use. (Luria, 1976; pp. 48–9)

Luria then provides his readers with examples of his experimental **protocols**, which is to say, transcripts and notes from his interview work.

> Subject: Rakmat., age thirty-nine, illiterate peasant from an outlying district; has seldom been in Fergana, never in any other city. He was shown drawings of the following: *hammer — saw — log — hatchet.*
>
> > 'They're all alike. I think all of them have to be here. See, if you're going to saw, you need a saw, and if you have to split something you need a hatchet. So they're *all* needed here.'
> >
> > *Employs the principle of 'necessity' to group objects in a practical situation.*
> >
> > [. . .]
> >
> > **Which of these things could you call by one word?**
> >
> > 'How's that? If you call all three of them a "hammer," that won't be right either.'
> >
> > *Rejects the use of general term.*
> >
> > **But one fellow picked three things — the hammer, saw, and hatchet — and said they were alike.**
> >
> > 'A saw, a hammer, and a hatchet all have to work together. But the log has to be here too!'
> >
> > *Reverts to situational thinking.*
> >
> > **Why do you think he picked these three things and not the log?**

'Probably he's got a lot of firewood, but if we'll be left without firewood, we won't be able to do anything.'

True, but a hammer, a saw, and a hatchet are all tools.

'Yes, but even if we have tools, we still need wood — otherwise, we can't build anything.'

Persists in situational thinking despite disclosure of categorical term.
(*ibid*; pp. 55–6)

By presenting this lengthy extract, together with his commentary (in italics), Luria is attempting to mark out resonances between this subject's responses and the description of situational thinking in the illustration involving the reconstruction of the meal situation. In this way, Luria is presenting an argument for the validity of his **coding** of the subject as employing situational or graphic-functional thinking. You will notice that no clear distinction is made between the **concept** and the **indicator** variables. This is because Luria has elaborated his theoretical propositions through the use of concrete illustrations and he has described his empirical data directly in terms of the concepts. In this way he brings the theoretical and empirical spheres closer together and this constitutes his argument in respect of the validity of his coding. We shall refer to this approach as **elaborated description**.

Elaborated description constitutes the apprenticing of the reader into Luria's coding principles. This apprenticing, together with the very substantial number of protocols that Luria provides may be taken to stand in the place of a formal test of the reliability of the coding principles. Had Luria given only one or two examples, you might feel entitled to ask him to demonstrate that one or more of his colleagues also coded the subjects in the same way as he himself did. Failure to employ one of these approaches might encourage the suspicion that he had selected only those cases for which the coding was clear and that these may not be representative of the sample as a whole.

One alternative to elaborated description is to provide explicit rules for the recognition of indicators. An example of this approach is discussed in Chapter 7 where we consider Dowling's use of textual 'icon' as an indicator for his concept 'localizing strategy'. Where the statement of the rules is sufficiently explicit to persuade the reader of the reliability of their application, there is clearly less need to provide large numbers of examples. Rather, the data can be summarized in quantitative terms. The quantitative representation and analysis of data is discussed in Chapter 7.

A second alternative to elaborated description is to **precode** the data. This would be appropriate in the use of a questionnaire which is designed so that the respondent makes their response by selecting from a range of possible responses. Precoding clearly addresses the issue of reliability.

However, there remains the question of the validity of the precoding. The scaling of questionnaire items must be justified in terms of the theoretical variables which they are intended to measure. We shall include some discussion of the use of questionnaires in Chapter 5.

In this section, we have looked at the empirical measurement of theoretical propositions. Our particular concern has been with the issue of the validity of the relationship between theoretical concept variables and their empirical realization. In the case of Luria's work, the distance between theoretical and empirical variables has been reduced through his use of elaborated description. In the next section we shall look at the issue of sampling, which is concerned with another aspect of validity.

Operationalization: Sampling Procedures

We have described the **empirical setting** as a **localized** region of the **empirical field**. Luria's empirical setting in Uzbekistan and Kirghizia was a localized region of the empirical field of social relations, cultural practices and cognitive processes in which people were engaged in the Soviet Union and globally. The setting also localizes the empirical field in terms of time, that is, during the period of Luria's fieldwork in the nineteen thirties. Luria's report of his fieldwork incorporates claims about this particular setting. However, Luria also wants to make claims about the empirical field more generally in bringing together his theoretical and empirical spheres. This being the case, the nature of the relationship between the local setting and the general empirical field is crucial.

Luria had also to act selectively on his empirical setting. There was clearly a limit to the amount and nature of information that he could gather in terms of both subjects and situations. Again, the principles of his selection procedures become important to the extent to which he wants to generalize beyond the information actually gathered.

The relationship between setting and field and between information actually gathered and information potentially available is concerned with **sampling procedures**. All empirical research involves drawing a sample. Attention to the sampling procedures is a necessary prerequisite to establishing or questioning the validity of claims which **generalize** beyond the sample itself. We shall describe three main categories of sampling procedure: opportunity sampling, theoretical sampling, and random sampling.

Opportunity Sampling

The selection of empirical setting is very often a matter of seizing an **opportunity**. A secondary school teacher, for example, wanted to observe the processes of marking and moderation whereby examination coursework was graded. As head of department, he had access both to teachers' written evaluations and to their discussions at a moderation meeting. A primary school teacher was interested in the possible impact that media images of politics and politicians might have on children. Fortunately, she was conducting her research across the period of a general election and so was able to compare students' political knowledge before and after the event. Robert Lawler (1985) wanted, for his doctoral research, to observe the cognitive development of young children across as wide as possible a range of contexts over an extended period of time. Luckily, he had a six-year-old daughter. He took her with him just about everywhere he went (or went with her wherever she went) during a period of six months. Conducting such a programme with someone else's child would clearly have been awkward.

An interesting example of an opportunity sample was provided by Howard Becker (1953) in his study of Marijuana users in Chicago in the early nineteen-fifties. The practice which Becker was studying was (and still is) an illicit one. This clearly presented him with difficulties in respect of drawing his sample of subjects. As it happened, however, Becker was himself involved in a practice which brought him into routine contact with marijuana smokers — in addition to being a social psychologist, he was a jazz musician. He therefore decided to interview his friends and colleagues whom he knew to be marijuana smokers. He also asked them to refer other smokers that they knew to him, acting as guarantors of confidentiality, as it were. These new contacts were similarly asked to refer additional subjects and so forth. For obvious reasons, this kind of sample is called a **snowball sample**.

Commonly, educational researchers attempt to put a gloss of deliberation onto their opportunity samples by referring to them as **case studies**. We have difficulties with this expression when either it is reified as a specific technique or method or when it is used to fudge the issue of **validity** in respect of **generalization**. Essentially, all research is case study research insofar as it makes claims about one or more specific cases of or in relation to a broader field of instances or phenomena. All research seeks to relate its own local findings to this more general field. Where the empirical setting is defined by an opportunity sample, the validity of generalization relies on the researcher marking out the continuities and discontinuities between the setting and the empirical field in an ad hoc manner. The resulting presentation will bear some similarity to the **elaborated description** employed by Luria in validating his empirical measurement of his theoretical proposition. We shall return, briefly, to the issue of case study research in Chapter 10.

Theoretical Sampling

The proposition that no **sampling** procedure can be independent of **theoretical** considerations follows from our discussion of the theoretical and empirical fields in Chapter 2. However, the extent to which theoretical considerations explicitly operate in the construction of the sample does vary. For example, although Luria's research involved the grasping of an opportunity, it was only recognizable as an opportunity in terms of Luria's well-developed theoretical framework. The societies in Uzbekistan and Kirghizia were recognized as transitional in terms of social and cultural development. Luria was thus able to recognize them as **critical cases**.

The study of a critical case must be opposed to an approach which attempts to draw a **representative sample**. In making this distinction in relation to Luria's research, we need to introduce another expression, the **unit of analysis**. This refers to the object which is to be described in terms of the research **variables**. Thus, Luria describes societies in terms of the variables, social relations and cultural practices. Focusing on the society as the level of analysis, we can describe the Uzbeki society as a **critical case**. However, the variable 'cognitive level' describes individual human subjects. When we focus on the human subject as the unit of analysis, it is less clear that Luria is looking for critical cases. He wants subjects that he can locate within one of his two categories of society. One group must be clearly located within 'primitive' society. His selection of subjects must result in representatives that can unproblematically be described in this way. The other group must be describable as having some measure of participation in 'advanced' society. The subjects chosen are thereby taken to be representative of this group as a whole.

The second group of subjects, but not the first, are closely associated with the critical nature of the societal case — they have only limited participation in 'advanced society'. They are, then, representatives of a critical class of subjects. Thus critical and representative cases are not necessarily mutually exclusive categories.

A third method of sampling theoretically is referred to as a **quota sample**. This approach is commonly used in market research, however, we will illustrate it using a hypothetical educational context. Suppose that a researcher wishes to investigate teachers' experiences of appraisal. Suppose, further, that they have decided to conduct interviews at a teachers' conference. It might legitimately be hypothesized that these experiences will depend on, amongst other variables, the subject's professional position defined in terms of, say, years of experience and position in the career structure. If the researcher wanted to make claims about the teaching profession as a whole, then it might be important that they select subjects who are representative in respect of each of these variables. The two variables might be scaled and **cross-tabulated** to produce a matrix similar to that in *Table 3.2.*

The next stage would be to determine how the teaching profession as a whole was composed in terms of the matrix. That is, the table would be completed in terms of the number of teachers in each cell of *Table 3.2.* Suppose that the researcher has the resources to interview a sample of 100

Table 3.2:   *Quota sampling matrix*

Years teaching	MPG	Career position Middle management	Senior management
0–4			
5–9			
10–19			
20+			

MPG = Main Professional Grade

teachers. A representative sample (in numerical terms) would be obtained by dividing the 100 subjects between the cells of the table in the proportions of the teaching profession as a whole. This would give a quota for the number of subjects to be interviewed in each cell. The sampling would then proceed as follows. The researcher would approach a teacher at the conference and ask their number of years in teaching and their career position[1]. This would locate them in the matrix. The interview would proceed only if the quota had not yet been filled.

Critical, representative and quota sampling procedures are not mutually exclusive. In particular, quota sampling is clearly one method of attempting to produce a representative sample. They have in common that they all depend upon a degree of theoretical development being done in advance of the definition of the empirical setting; hence the term, theoretical sampling. The level of theoretical development may be very advanced, as with Luria's work. Alternatively, it may hardly seem to merit the term 'theory', as in the illustration of quota sampling. Nevertheless, theoretical it is, because it consists of general hypotheses about the empirical field. It is to be hoped, of course, that theoretical development does not end at such a preliminary stage.

Random Sampling

The final category of sampling that we shall refer to is **random sampling**. Like quota sampling, this set of procedures is a strategy for achieving a **representative sample**. There has been a considerable amount of mathematical and statistical development in the theory of probability in relation to random sampling. This means that the use of random procedures can potentially allow the use of very sophisticated statistical tools in the analysis of the data. We have included in the book a chapter on **quantitative analysis** (Chapter 7). However, we shall not be able to get very far at all into probability theory. You are strongly encouraged to follow up our references to statistical manuals if your interest lies in that direction. Here, we shall simply describe some of the simpler techniques in drawing a random sample. At the outset, we must emphasize that 'random' certainly does not mean 'unprincipled'. Random sampling is a highly technical and theoretically informed and deliberate procedure.

The production of a random sample involves attempting to ensure that each member of the **population** that you are sampling has an equal chance or **probability** of being selected as a subject. The population is the notional class of possible subjects. It may be defined at any level of analysis. For example, your population might comprise all secondary school teachers in the UK, all secondary schools in the UK, or all local education authorities in the UK. In practice, the researcher will often not have immediate access to a complete list of the whole population. They will therefore have to draw up such a list as best they can. The list may be an approximation to the notional population as, for example, the electoral register may be taken as an approximation to the list of the adult population of a political constituency. When the list is drawn up and arranged in alphabetical order, it is referred to as the **sampling frame**. In practice, then, a random sample is one which ensures that each member of the sampling frame has an equal probability of being selected.

Suppose that you wish to draw a 10 per cent random sample of the students of a particular university. Suppose, further, that you have an alphabetical list of registered students which you are going to use as a sampling frame. Your procedure is as follows. You first find a list of random numbers in a book of statistical tables. You then take a pencil, close your eyes, and stab the random number list. If the digit nearest the pencil point is, say, seven, you take the seventh student in your sampling frame as your first subject. Thereafter, you select every tenth name on the list, that is, the 7th, 17th, 27th, 37th, . . . names. This gives you a sample of one out of every ten students, that is, a 10 per cent sample.

The procedure just described is used to draw what is called a **simple random sample**. Now it may be that you want to combine the statistical potential of randomization with the representative features of **quota sampling**. For example, suppose that you want your sample to consist of students of different genders and different courses of study in proportion to the representation of these groups within the sampling frame. You can achieve this by reorganizing or **stratifying** your sampling frame. You would first organize the frame in terms of the various courses — anthropology, biology, chemistry, and so on. Within the frame, each course list should be arranged as consecutive, alphabetical lists of female and male students. You would then proceed as before, using a randomly selected digit as the starting point. The stratification of your sampling frame would ensure the kind of quota representation that you want, provided, of course, that the number of students in each category was sufficiently large. If any of the groups are small in number, then your procedure might result in a sample of greater than or less than 10 per cent of these groups; a very small group (less than ten in number) might be omitted altogether.

The **stratified random sample**, as this procedure is called, deviates somewhat from the principle of randomization. This is because two elements of the sampling frame that occur sufficiently near to each other cannot both be selected. In the case of a 10 per cent sample, two elements must be separated by a multiple of ten if they are both to be selected. Applying a principled organization to the sampling frame clearly alters the nature of the sample by putting together elements sharing particular properties; it imposes a **bias** upon the sample. You might argue even that simple alphabetical organization may not be entirely free of this kind of bias because of the ways in which different ethnic groups distribute family names differently within the alphabet. This is certainly a valid point. All you can do, however, is try to be aware of possible sources of **unintentional bias** and, if you can't eliminate them, at least try to take account of them in qualifying any inferences you may make on the basis of your analysis.

In some cases, the sampling frame may be so extensive that you cannot, in practice, compile it. Under such circumstances, it may be possible to **cluster** it. For example, suppose that you want to draw a random sample of all students currently registered in universities in the UK. The compilation of the sampling frame is clearly a major task in itself and may be beyond your resources. An alternative would be to compile a preliminary sampling frame which consists of the universities rather than the students. You could then draw a simple or stratified random sample of universities from this sampling frame. This would leave you with the task of compiling sampling frames of registered students only for each of the universities in your sample.

This approach is also useful if you actually intend to visit the subjects in your sample personally. Drawing an unclustered sample from the UK electoral register, for example, would be very likely to result in an enormous amount of travelling between your subjects. Alternatively you could cluster the sample by constructing a sampling frame comprising all of the electoral constituencies in the UK and draw a random sample from this. You could then compile sampling frames comprising all of the postcodes for each constituency in your sample and draw a random sample of postcodes from each. Finally, you could compile sampling frames of electors for each postcode in your sample and draw random samples from these. This would generate clusters of subjects with the same postcodes and clusters of these clusters each within the same constituency.

You would certainly save petrol by using such a cluster sample. Again, however, your reorganization of your ideal sampling frame will have resulted in deviations from the principle of randomization. As is commonly the case in educational research, your decisions are likely to be compromises between ideals and practicalities. What is important is that they are considered compromises and that you take into account any deviation from the ideal in your conclusions.

Moving into the Field

In this chapter we have discussed, firstly, the development of the problem in the formulation of research questions or theoretical propositions in terms of theoretical concept variables. We then considered the development of the empirical setting and its articulation with the problem. We were concerned, initially, with the measurement of concept variables in terms of empirical indicator variables. Key issues here were validity and reliability. Finally, we looked at the issue of sampling.

We have not finished with any of these topics. They will feature throughout the rest of the book. However, the discussion so far has been strongly led from the theoretical side of things. In the next four chapters we shall move to an emphasis on the empirical setting and on the collection and analysis of data. Chapters 4 and 5 are concerned with data collection. Chapters 6 and 7 deal with analysis. We have designed these chapters so that they can reasonably be read in any order, although cross-references are indicated where appropriate and via the emboldened terms which are entries in the keyword index.

Note

1   The researcher would need to develop a way of precoding responses to these questions. This would involve making advance decisions on, for example, how to count part-time teaching experience and how to distinguish between middle and senior management.

References

Becker, H.S. (1953) 'Becoming a marihuana user', *American Journal of Sociology,* **59**, pp. 235–42.

Lawler, R.W. (1985) *Computer Experience and Cognitive Development: A Child's Learning in a Computer Culture,* Chichester: Ellis Horwood.

Luria, A.R. (1976) *Cognitive Development: Its Cultural and Social Foundations,* Cambridge: Harvard University Press.

4   Experience and Observation: The Collection of First Hand Data

In previous chapters we have stressed that empirical educational research must be involved with both empirical and theoretical development. We have also suggested that, at different stages of the research, one or other of these spheres may move into the foreground of attention and the other may be temporarily backgrounded. This is also the case in our consideration of the research process. In this chapter and in Chapter 5 we are moving into the (empirical) field, as it were. Therefore, whilst we will try not to lose sight of the theoretical problem, we shall be foregrounding issues relating to the empirical setting and its management. In particular, we shall be focusing mainly (but not exclusively) on operational issues relating to the measurement of indicator variables rather than on their theoretical conceptual development. This is a pragmatic choice. In order to survey a range of approaches to research we shall need to draw on a wide empirical field. Unfortunately, we do not have the space to develop these empirical resources in to a theoretically adequate level.

In this chapter we are going to look at a number of ways of collecting first hand data, that is data obtained through the researcher's direct experience of the setting being explored. This covers a wide range of techniques, from the systematic observation of behaviour in the context of a highly structured, experimental study through to making incidental fieldnotes as a participant in an everyday setting. Our intention is to outline the major forms of observational data collection, to consider why a researcher might select a particular way of collecting data and to develop the means to evaluate both other researchers' and one's own practice. In describing different forms of observational data we will focus on, firstly, the degree of manipulation by the researcher of the context within which the observations are being made and, secondly, the extent to which structure is imposed on the observations and the point at which this happens. As we discuss different forms of data collection, we will also consider the question of research design.

Manipulation of Context: From Experiments to Participant Observation

Experimental Research Design

Researchers adopting an experimental approach attempt to establish a relationship between **variables** by exercising very tight control over key aspects of the setting with which they are concerned. The simplest form of **experimental design** would enable the researcher to manipulate one variable (known as the **independent variable**) and to observe the effects that this has on another variable (the **dependent variable**). For example, a researcher wishing to explore whether the adoption of a particular teaching strategy has a positive effect on children's scientific reasoning could conduct a simple experiment. The teaching strategy would be the independent variable and the children's scientific reasoning the dependent variable.

As they stand, neither variable is sufficiently well defined. In order to construct an experiment, the teaching strategy in which you are interested has to be translated into an explicit procedure which can be repeated with a high degree of consistency. This constitutes the **experimental treatment** you are to carry out. You also need to be clear about how you will gauge any changes that occur in the children's scientific reasoning, the dependent variable. You thus require an **indicator**, or cluster of related indicators, of the quality of children's reasoning in order to render this visible and measurable. Having clarified what you mean by 'scientific reasoning', and how you might recognize different levels of this, you could measure each child's level of scientific reasoning using a test of some sort. Alternatively you could devise some tasks for children to carry out, and make an assessment of their level of scientific reasoning on the basis of your observations of their performance on the tasks. Whatever form of measurement of 'scientific reasoning' you choose, it is essential that you can establish both the validity and reliability of the judgments you make.

In order to investigate the relationship between the dependent and independent variable you have to decide on the form that your experiment will take. There are a number of alternative designs from which to choose. You could select a group of children, administer the treatment (i.e. teach them using the teaching strategy in which you are interested) and see what effect this has had on their scientific reasoning. To do this you would need to test the children before and after the treatment. This design is known as the one group **pre-test–post-test design**. A design such as this would be adopted in an attempt to establish causality. In this case, to establish that the use of a particular teaching strategy causes the observed changes in the scientific reasoning of the children.

There are, however, a number of possible influences on the performance of the children that you would be unable to control. This is particularly acute if your treatment takes place over an extended period of time, say over a series of science lessons covering a school term or semester. In this case you would not know whether the observed changes were due to the treatment or to activities that were taking place outside the experimental session. Even the general maturation of the children over the period of time may be important. Whilst these factors cannot be directly manipulated, an attempt can be made to **control** for their effects through the design of the experiment. The introduction of a second group of children, who do not receive the treatment, into the design is one way of doing this.

In a **pre-test–post-test control group design**, an **experimental group** and a **control group** are selected. The members of the experimental group, but not those of the control group, receive the treatment. In all other respects, the two groups have, as far as possible, the same characteristics and experiences. Both groups are tested before and after the treatment is given to the experimental group. These pre- and post-tests enable us to compare changes in the performance of the subjects who receive the treatment with those who do not.

If the two groups are actually **matched** in terms of their characteristics and experiences, then, once any differences in performance on the pre-test have been allowed for, differences in post-test performance can be attributed to the treatment received by the experimental group. The matching of the groups is vital as the design is based on the assumption that the effects of all the non-manipulated factors can be accounted for by making a comparison between two groups with as near identical characteristics as possible.

The **random** selection and **allocation** of individuals to groups is one way of achieving this. In randomly selecting subjects from a population there should be nothing motivating the selection and allocation of a particular person to any particular group. With a numerically large sample, the profile of each group should be similar to that of the population from which the sample is drawn. An alternative strategy is to **pair** subjects with similar characteristics and to assign one person to the control group and the other to the experimental group. In this way it is possible to construct two groups that are similar in particular ways. To do this one has to be clear about which characteristics of the individual matter with respect to the study being carried out. If we are examining teaching strategies in science it is unlikely that we will feel that it is important to match individuals in terms of hair colour, but we might feel it is important to match them in terms of attainment in science. Producing matched groups in this way requires reference to prior research and/or theoretical development relating to the object of our study. Confidence that matched groups can be produced by random allocation, on the other hand, is based on probability theory.

The strict demands made by experimental designs create a number of problems for educational research. Randomly assigning pupils to groups is disruptive and likely, in most circumstances, to be impractical. The conditions necessary to construct groups in this way, and to be able to manipulate the treatment received by these groups with sufficient precision, leads us away from the classroom and towards tightly controlled experimental settings. This raises questions regarding both the typicality of behaviour within experimental contexts and the transferability of treatments from an experimental setting to the classroom. These questions relate to concerns about the **ecological validity** of experimental research in which phenomena are explored in contexts other than those in which they naturally occur.

There are also potential **ethical** problems in the manipulation, for the purpose of research, of the circumstances in which school students are taught. It is obviously important not to embark on a course of action which, it is thought, could be harmful to the educational progress of a group of school students. Similarly, one has to take care that the research design does not lead to beneficial forms of action being withheld from particular groups for extended periods of time. If teachers and/or children are participating in an experiment, it is important that they are aware of this. On the other hand, this awareness might itself compound the research by what is known as the Hawthorne effect.

The Hawthorne Effect

Influenced by the 'scientific management' techniques of F.W. Taylor, the management of the Western Electric Company plant at Hawthorne, USA set out to determine which working conditions were most conducive to high productivity. In a series of studies conducted in the 1920s and 1930s (reported at length by Roethlisberger and Dickson, 1939) researchers attempted to investigate the effects on the productivity of workers of changes in variables such as the length of the working day and the level of heating and lighting in the plant. The results were highly ambiguous.

In the 'Illumination Study' they attempted to find out if increasing the level of lighting would cause workers assembling electrical relays to produce more. As the lights grew brighter, productivity increased, suggesting a relationship between level of illumination and productivity. However, when the lighting intensity was subsequently reduced, productivity remained high. In response to this, the researchers attempted to take into account both physical and economic factors and to conduct the investigation in more tightly controlled circumstances. In the 'Relay Assembly Room Study' they selected six workers to work in a special observation room. They varied wage incentives, heating, lighting and other working conditions. Irrespective of the conditions, the output of the workers increased steadily over the two year period of the study. On the basis of their observations the researchers hypothesized that the changes in productivity were the result of the special attention being paid to the workers as the subjects of a research study. In this case the effects of 'being researched' far outweighed the influence of any of the physical and economic factors the researchers were exploring. This phenomena clearly has implications for all forms of observational research. The possible effect on behaviour of being studied has subsequently come to be known as the **Hawthorne effect**.

These kinds of effects can be controlled for in a **laboratory setting**. Outside the laboratory this is more difficult. In the testing of new drugs, an experimental group can be given the drug being studied and the control group given a **placebo**. This is a treatment that appears to be similar to the test drug, but which has no physiological effects. The research subjects do not know whether they are in the experimental group or the control group. In this way allowance is made for the effects of participation in a study. It is of course possible that the person administering the treatment will behave differently according to whether they are administering the test drug or the placebo. For this reason a **double-blind design** is generally used. In this design, neither the person administering the treatment nor the subject know whether the test drug or placebo is being used.

In an attempt to overcome the problems associated with experimental designs when applied to the study of complex social contexts such as schooling, some researchers adopt compromise, **quasi-experimental designs**. Rather than make a comparison between two groups constructed for the purpose of research, comparison can be made, say, between two classes within the same school, one receiving a particular treatment, the other acting as a control group. There is no pretence here that precise **matching** of subjects can be achieved in this way and thus the researcher cannot make inferences about the effects of the treatment with the same degree of confidence that would be possible if the groups were matched in the ways described above. It becomes increasingly difficult to establish a clear relationship between the independent variable and the dependent variable as it is no longer possible to say that the effects of the multitude of non-manipulated variables are the same for the two groups. In other words, the quasi-experimental design makes the control of these non-manipulated variables more difficult.

In the discussion of experimental studies thus far we have made the assumption that the treatment that takes place is a purposive, pre-designed **intervention** of some form. This need not be the case. We could, for example, use a simple experimental design to examine the effects of a 'natural' event which is beyond our direct control. The event would be the independent variable and the researcher would need to gather data relating to the dependent variable before and after the event.

An example of such a 'natural experiment' is the study referred to in the section on *Opportunity Sampling* (p. 29). This study was carried out by a primary school teacher. She had a particular interest in the political knowledge of young children and how this relates to representations in the mass media. She took advantage of an imminent general election to explore the effect on children's knowledge of high levels of media coverage of national politics. In order to do this she had to test the political knowledge of a group of children (in this case the children in her own class — an opportunity sample) before the lead up to the election and again after the election had taken place. She used a questionnaire of her own design for data collection.

Here, a kind of single group pre-test–post-test design is being used, but the form of intervention (increased media coverage of politics) is beyond the control of the researcher. Being a single group study makes it difficult to establish that any differences found in the children's political knowledge has been caused by the 'intervention'; no control for other variables is being exercised. The use of the pre-test (essential if the logic of the design of the research is to be followed) might indeed have a profound effect. It could sensitize the children to political issues and make them more likely to pay close attention to political coverage in the media. The sensitizing effects of pre-tests are recognized by experimental researchers. In order to account for these effects, additional experimental and control groups are added. These groups match the original groups closely but are not given the pre-test. By administering the post-test to all groups, the effects of the pre-test can be estimated. In the case of the study of the children's political knowledge this would mean the administration of the post-test questionnaire to another class of children whose characteristics matched those of the teacher's own class.

It is also possible to explore the effects of a treatment that has already taken place. This is known as **ex post facto research**. Here the researcher explores the possible causes, or influences upon, a currently observable state of affairs by looking back at antecedent conditions. You might, for example, wish to examine the proposal that the earlier introduction of a staff appraisal scheme in a school has produced a high level of teacher involvement in continuing professional development (CPD) activities. A study exploring the relationship between a past event (the independent variable in this case) and a current situation could also take the form of a comparative study. You could, for instance, compare levels of CPD involvement in a group of schools in which formal staff appraisal had not been implemented with a group of schools where formal staff appraisal has been established.

In ex post facto research, the adoption of a quasi-experimental design in a **natural** setting allows the possibility of making comparisons between similar groups which, for some reason, are already receiving different forms of treatment. An interest in the effects of whole class teaching on primary school children's attainment in mathematics might lead you to look at two samples of primary school classes. You might take one set of classrooms in which whole class teaching is used in the teaching of mathematics and another in which there is no formal whole class teaching. Teaching method is the independent variable (the treatment) and is scaled according to the presence or absence of whole class teaching. Attainment in mathematics is the dependent variable. In lieu of a specifically designed pre-test you could use already available data on the children's mathematical performances at a particular point in time and measure changes in this performance over a given period.

Here we have moved away from the artificiality of direct manipulation of contexts and planned interventions, and towards the investigation of more 'natural' phenomena. Whilst an approximation to an experimental design has been retained, the compromises regarding sampling and procedure that have been made have, to an extent, undermined the logic of the design. This weakens its potential to provide support for a causal relationship between the variables. It also weakens the potential for the generalization of the results.

This is often forgotten. Seductive accounts of, say, the apparent success of whole class teaching in countries in the Pacific rim may be compared with apparent failure of individualized methods used in the UK. These comparisons may be based on descriptions of teaching methods observed in classrooms and on the attainment of school students based on international tests. However, there are clear difficulties in matching samples. There are also difficulties in control. An adequate comparison would seek to take into account variables relating to differences in the social and cultural relationships between, for example, the state, the family, schooling and employment. The incommensurability of societies at such macro-levels makes it impossible to establish that the teaching methods observed cause, or are even a major influence on, the observed differences in attainment. Unable to support a causal relationship, we are left with a **correlation** between the use of a particular teaching method and high attainment. Our data will not enable us to rule in or out a possible third variable, or cluster of variables, which lies behind the observed association between whole class teaching and high attainment. In passing, we should also point to the difficulty of constructing a valid and reliable cross-cultural measure of attainment, especially given the lack of theoretical development that generally characterizes international surveys.

In this section we have illustrated how the basic experimental design may be adapted in addressing concerns regarding ecological validity and the ethics of manipulation. In these kinds of study an attempt is made prior to the conduct of the research to isolate key variables and to organize these in the form of a possible causal relationship. For the design to be tenable we must be able to measure the variables with a degree of precision. In many cases it may not be desirable or possible to preconceptualize and/or organize the phenomena in which one is interested in this way. The difficulties involved in the application to complex social settings of an experimental logic, inspired by research design in the physical sciences, has led some researchers to reject this model. One result of this is the growth of ethnographic studies of education.

Ethnographic Research

Ethnographic approaches draw inspiration from anthropological research in which the researcher sets out to understand and describe a setting with which they are, in most cases, initially unfamiliar. The development of this understanding involves the immersion of the researcher in the practices in the empirical setting and sustained interaction with participants. The predominant means of collecting data is through highly detailed observation. In the classic social anthropology of the early twentieth century, the researcher would have been a Western academic and their object of study would have been a distant 'exotic' culture (see, for instance, Malinowski, 1922). Through direct experience, the researcher would collect detailed information about the society, or a particular segment of the society, and generate a description of this 'novel' setting. Minimally, this enterprise would involve learning the language of the people being studied, observing what they do in a variety of situations and, from this, constructing an account of how the society works.

The legitimate site for anthropological work was originally the distant, 'exotic' culture. Over time the number of little known distant cultures about which to 'bring back news' has reduced. The association of this kind of work with the self-assumed colonial authority to produce accounts of 'other' cultures has also made it less acceptable. As a consequence ethnographers have brought their investigations closer to home, for instance the study of AIDS support groups, weight watchers, wholefood co-operatives, parent–teacher associations and even groups of ethnography students (see Burawoy et al., 1991). Ultimately we can look to our own lives and the contexts within which we operate as settings for ethnographic research. Rather than entering an unfamiliar setting as an outsider and attempting to make sense of this, we are in the position of already being a participant in a familiar setting. The challenge is to be able to strip away our assumptions and everyday understandings to render the world around us 'anthropologically strange'. For the educational researcher the adoption of an ethnographic approach makes possible the exploration of the processes of teaching and learning in the classroom, the 'lore' of the playground, power relations amongst school staff, the relationship between the home culture of children and the culture of the school and so on.

The immediate appeal of this kind of approach is that the actions of participants are studied in the context in which they naturally occur. Furthermore, the researcher is making no attempt to manipulate what happens, but merely to observe and record. The fluidity of the research process also allows the researcher to analyse data as they collect it and thus to refocus their study as they go along and specifically seek out particular information or look for counter examples. There are, however, a number of issues about this method of collecting data and conducting research that need to be addressed.

Firstly, as we pointed out in Chapter 2, data collection and description inevitably involves a process of **recontextualization**. This process includes the imposition of principles of selection or recognition. For the ethnographer the process of selection of what counts as relevant information starts very early in the research process and the principles of this selection are often not made clear. Why have they chosen a particular empirical setting for their research? Why have they chosen certain people as guides and informants? How do they establish the genuineness and typicality of what they see and what they are told? When the researcher observes, why do they notice some features of what is around them and not others? How do they decide what to record from their observations?

The researcher must also impose principles of interpretation or realization. Ironically, perhaps, the more familiar a setting may seem, the greater the danger of bringing your own unexamined interpretive frameworks in making sense of what you see. Educational practitioners researching educational practices are clearly vulnerable in this respect. The following extracts are taken from a study which included classroom observation in three schools in Brazil; they refer to pedagogic practices in two of the schools:

> The process of creation, re-creation and discovery of concepts and principles was emphasized to the detriment of the mere storing of facts and information. Correspondingly, experimenting and investigating, observing and drawing conclusions, and organizing results and reporting, were used more often than filling in textbooks or worksheets of factual and fragmented questions. The purposes and procedures of every activity were fully presented to the children, and they also had opportunity to discuss them. (da Silva, 1988; p. 61)

> The extensive use of solitary drills and exercises excluded the use of other modes of teaching and types of activities. There was an impressing sameness to the type of work in these classrooms. Besides children working individually at their desks, short presentations of new topics by teachers and occasional dialogues between the teachers and the pupils, little else, as far as schoolwork is concerned could be seen there. (*ibid*; p. 62)

The descriptions of these two modes of pedagogic practice are quite clearly coloured by the researcher's preconceptions of what constitutes appropriate pedagogy. However, whilst an educationalist might recognize constructivist and behaviourist pedagogies in the respective descriptions, the researcher does not explicitly theorize pedagogic practice. To do so would require some theoretical articulation between, shall we say, transmission and acquisition. In the absence of such clarification in the area of the problem, nothing is learned by the observation. This kind of reporting of observational data is little more than the rehearsal of one's prejudices.

This is not to suggest that there should be a circular relationship between theory and data. If our theory predicts precisely what it is that we will find when we enter the field then, again, there would be little point in conducting the research. What theory provides here is a way of making visible how, why and with what consequences we make particular decisions in the various phases of the design and conduct of the research. In this way the integrity of the process of collecting and analysing data is open to scrutiny by others. Similarly, as readers of ethnographic work, we need to be able to see how selections and interpretations are made and how conclusions are drawn in order to be able to evaluate the research.

The second issue concerns the scope for a tension between extremes of '**objectivism**' and '**subjectivism**'. Some ethnographers may regard the above description of the approach as unduly 'objectivist'. The ethnographic researcher may legitimately be concerned with the meanings that events and phenomena within a particular setting may have for participants in that setting. The object of study becomes the means by which the symbolic world of the participants is produced and maintained. From this perspective, the observer cannot simply record what they see and present this record as a set of facts.

However, this concern carries the attendant danger of abdication from one's responsibility as an analyst, of ignoring the principle of recontextualization. Having collected detailed notes from numerous observations and discussions, there is a temptation to present participants' own accounts of what they are doing as explanations of social and cultural phenomena. This is inappropriate. Neither the rules for producing acceptable performances nor the wider significance of particular practices are necessarily explicitly available to the participants. The ultimate responsibility for analysis lies with the researcher. In this sense, research is simply not a democratic activity.

This apparently obvious point is worth remembering. Commonly, the accounts of participants are indeed inappropriately presented as analysis rather than as data. Collecting together and summarizing the views of teachers on, say, the appraisal process and presenting these as research findings, whilst possibly making interesting reading, contributes little to our understanding of teachers and schools.

A third cluster of related problems concerns the extent to which the ethnographic observer is also a participant and the consequences of different levels of participation. The options for an observer are conventionally marked out on a continuum from complete **participant** to complete, non-participant, **observer** (see, for instance, Robson, 1993). Both ends of this continuum are problematic. Limits are placed on the possibility and desirability, of being a complete participant by the necessary differences between taking part in an activity, on the one hand, and the production of an analytic account of that activity, on the other. To become a participant an outsider has to learn how to recognize and produce legitimate performances within the setting they are investigating. As every setting has associated with it a number of legitimate identities that can be ascribed to and achieved by human subjects, the researcher has to learn to 'be' one of these. This entails coming to be recognized as a legitimate participant by the other participants.

This is more than taking on a 'role'; one cannot be who or what one wants independently of who one is seen to be by others. Let's say that we wish to conduct an ethnographic study of homeless people who live on the streets in London. There are a number of possible identities to which a researcher could aspire. There are the police officers who attempt to regulate the activity of homeless people, there are the 'passers-by' who might act as a source of income, there are the homeless people themselves and so on. Each group can be distinguished and can distinguish themselves from the others. There is also variation within each group. Each group member has some common expectations of others in their own group and of members of other groups. Clearly for the researcher, achieving membership of the 'homeless' group is likely to be more fruitful than becoming a 'police officer' or a 'passer-by' (they are probably already a member of the latter group). Thus it is vital to be aware of both the work involved in 'becoming' a participant and that the account produced will be dependent on where one places oneself with respect to the range of possible identities. If you wish to study the culture of disaffected youths at school, whether you participate as a disaffected youth (few educational researchers have this option) or as a teacher will clearly affect the data you collect and the account you produce.

Being seen as 'a researcher' will also affect what you are able to achieve and may affect the manner in which people behave. This raises the issue of whether one operates as an overt or covert researcher. There are clear weaknesses in adopting the former position, not least that you are immediately seen as not being a 'real' participant. These are counterbalanced by the obvious ethical problems associated with covert observation. These issues demand careful consideration before embarking on a piece of research. Such concerns clearly limit what it is possible to research and the ways in which research on certain topics can be approached.

The **practitioner researcher**, who might be studying an aspect of their own workplace, will not have to address the question of coming to be seen as a legitimate participant and producing contextually acceptable performances. They will, however, have to consider carefully the question of what they tell their colleagues, pupils and others about what they are doing. It is generally preferable to be open and honest. Nevertheless, care must be taken not to transform the behaviour of others by the manner or detail of your representation of your study.

Careful consideration also has to be given the relative status of the observed and the observer. What children do in front of parents, teachers and peers will differ. The way teachers act might, similarly, be different when observed by an inspector, their headteacher, a colleague, a trainee teacher and so on. Whatever form of observation one adopts, there are a range of possible observer effects that will have a bearing on what happens (see also discussion of the Hawthorne effect, page 39). It is important to take these into account in both your own work and your reading of other people's work.

As we pointed out in Chapter 2, the act of taking up the position of observer necessarily transforms the practice being observed. We referred to this as the **epistemological paradox**. This impacts on the ethnographic researcher whether they are an outsider negotiating a 'participant identity' or a practitioner researcher studying a familiar, everyday setting. In particular, in producing an analytic account as a researcher, both the descriptive resources that you will draw upon and the criteria by which your account is evaluated will, at least in part, originate outside of the activity that is the object of your study. In our view, this is a positive feature of research as a distinctive activity in itself. It encourages us to stand outside of our everyday practices and to scrutinize them in terms of what we have described as the research **mode of interrogation**. We shall return to this issue in Chapter 10. It will be clear already, however, that we view the proposition that an observer can be a full participant as highly questionable.

The notion that one can be a complete (non-participant) observer also presents difficulties. Researchers who aspire to being non-participant observers usually do so in an attempt to minimize the impact that the presence of an observer has on the setting. This involves keeping some distance from the activity in question and minimizing interaction with the participants. An observer in a classroom might, for instance, sit in the corner of the room, away from the pupils and the teacher, and make notes on what they see. They might have particular strategies for avoiding any discussion with participants and have previously prepared answers to anticipated awkward questions. Whilst it is obviously reasonable in some forms of work to attempt to minimize observer effects, it is not possible to eliminate them altogether. Some form of identity will be ascribed to the researcher by the participants, no matter how unobtrusive they attempt to be. What is important is to be as aware as possible of the effects that one's presence has on participants and how these affect the integrity of the data. This directs us away from trying to be 'invisible' and towards thinking carefully about the image that we project in a given situation. The performance of a teacher will be affected in particular ways by the presence of someone they think of as a school inspector or if they feel that information gathered by the observer will find its way to someone who is in a position of authority with respect to the teacher.

You will need to design your observation fieldwork so as to minimize effects that may compromise your study. You will also need to be able to judge the extent of the influence of those factors which you cannot control. One technique used by observers is to **habituate** participants to the presence of an observer. This involves entering the setting (in whatever position one has decided to adopt) a number of times before the collection of data begins. In this way participants become accustomed to the researcher being around. Although behaviour will initially be affected by the presence of an outsider, it is hoped that this will settle down into customary forms once the observer becomes familiar.

A similar technique can be used if an **audio** or **video recorder** is used. Some teachers or pupils might find being recorded in this way inhibiting. Habituation would involve introducing the recording device into the setting before actual data collection begins. If, for instance, you wish to study the discussions that take place when children collaborate on science investigations, you could record their conversations over a period of weeks but not use, say, the first three recorded sessions for your analysis. In a study similar to this, a teacher used an audio-tape recorder as the means by which children routinely made a record of what they had done. In this way they became used to the presence of an audio-tape recorder which could then be used as a means for the collection of data for analysis.

Not all researchers employing participant observation as a method for collecting data wish to minimize their impact on the setting. Ethnomethodologists, for example, have sometimes employed techniques that are specifically designed to disrupt the smooth running of everyday interactions and activities (see Garfinkel, 1967). **Ethnomethodology** is concerned with gaining an understanding of the manner in which everyday life is accomplished. The empirical work carried out often attempts to identify the taken-for-granted assumptions that operate in a particular social situation by asking the researcher to behave in an unusual manner. The intention here is to break some of the shared, but usually unstated, conventions that operate in everyday interactions and to examine the ways in which people respond. Through the disruption of social order, at the level of the everyday and the commonplace, the ethnomethodologist hopes to gain access to the manner in which the social reality of participants is achieved and maintained.

The disruptive techniques used are usually simple. For example, consistently using very formal modes of address when talking to friends or family, or constantly asking people 'what do you mean?' when engaging in everyday conversation. Here the researcher is a participant in everyday settings but is engaging in a form of social experiment. By 'being strange' they are manipulating the context in particular ways and producing uncharacteristic behaviours and forms of interaction between themselves and others. Their own experiences and observations constitute their data.

In this section we have discussed variation in the extent to which the context in which first hand data is collected is manipulated by the researcher. To do this, we have counterposed experimental designs and ethnographic work. We hope to have illustrated that, whilst these forms of research design are quite distinct, a clear contrast between high levels of manipulation and control in experimental studies and the apparent 'naturalism' of ethnographic studies is difficult to sustain. Relatively non-intrusive comparisons can be made between settings using a quasi-experimental design and such comparisons are common in ex-post facto research. Conversely, the aspirations of some ethnographic studies to describe 'natural' settings 'as they are' have been shown to be problematic. Like experimental work, participant observation can be used to achieve a variety of ends, including the testing of hypotheses.

Structure: From Schedules to Fieldnotes

It is helpful to make a distinction between **information** and **data**. Essentially, we are taking the term 'data' to refer to information that has been read in terms of an explicitly available theoretical framework and/or collected via an explicit methodological process. We shall return to this distinction in Chapter 6, where we shall be concerned with the application of theoretical interpretive frameworks. In this and the next chapter, we are interested in principles deriving from methodological considerations. The constitution of data from information entails the application of explicit **recontextualizing** principles of recognition (selection) and realization (interpretation). In doing this researchers are making important decisions. They need not only to have some basis on which to justify choices but also to be able to communicate to others precisely what it is that we are doing and why.

Observation Schedules

In the conduct of research based on **observation**, the extent to which and the point at which observations are structured may vary dramatically between studies. Take, for example, an observational study exploring possible differences in the way in which teachers interact with girls and boys in the classroom. We could, on the basis of previous research on classroom interaction, adopt a highly systematic approach to the collection of data by using an existing observation schedule. An **observation schedule** provides, firstly, a number of categories that the researcher uses to record their observations. Secondly, it includes a set of instructions describing the manner in which the schedule should be used. The categories relate directly to the phenomenon being investigated. The schedule should enable all forms of the phenomenon, in this case different forms of interaction, to be categorized. Clearly, a decision must be taken as to whether this should be limited to verbal interaction or should include non-verbal interaction as well. The descriptive power of the categories is a key element in establishing the validity of the schedule as an instrument for collecting data.

An observation schedule can be relatively straightforward, with just a handful of categories. One widely used schedule, the **Flanders' Inter-action Analysis Categories** for example, has just ten categories for the classification of forms of verbal interaction in the classroom. Flanders identifies seven categories of teacher talk.

1   *Accepts feeling.* Accepts and clarifies an attitude or the feeling tone of a pupil in a non-threatening manner. Feelings may be positive or negative. Predicting and recalling feelings are included.
2   *Praises or encourages.* Praises or encourages pupil action or behavior. Jokes that release tension, but not at the expense of another individual; nodding head, or saying 'Um hm?' or 'go on' are included.
3   *Accepts or uses ideas of pupils.* Clarifying, building, or developing ideas suggested by a pupil. Teacher extensions of pupil ideas are included but as the teacher brings more of his own ideas into play, shift to category five.
4   *Asks questions.* Asking a question about content or procedure, based on teacher ideas, with the intent that a pupil will answer.
5   *Lecturing.* Giving facts or opinions about content or procedures; expressing his own ideas, giving his own explanation, or citing an authority other than a pupil.
6   *Giving directions.* Directions, commands. Or orders to which a pupil is expected to comply.
7   *Criticizing or justifying authority.* Statements intended to change pupil behavior from nonacceptable to acceptable pattern; bawling some-one out; stating why the teacher is doing what he is doing; extreme self-reference. (Flanders, 1970; p. 34)

For pupil talk there are just two categories.

8   *Pupil-talk-response.* Talk by pupils in response to teacher. Teacher initiates the contact or solicits pupil statement or structures the situation. Freedom to express own ideas limited.
9   *Pupil-talk-initiation.* Talk by pupils which they initiate. Expressing own ideas; initiating a new topic; freedom to develop opinions and a line of thought, like asking thoughtful questions; going beyond the existing structure. (*ibid*, p. 34)

To ensure that the schedule is able to cover all possibilities, one final category is necessary.

10   *Silence or confusion.* Pauses, short periods of silence and periods of confusion in which communication cannot be understood by the observer. (*ibid*, p. 34)

In order to achieve such brevity, the schedule must either be narrow in its focus or have categories that are very broad. The former will provide us with detailed but specialized data, the latter will provide a wider ranging picture of the events observed but expressed in less precise terms. Having a small number of categories makes the schedule easier to use in practice. It is, for example, easier for the observer to learn the category descriptions which makes recording quicker and more reliable. For the **ORACLE study** of primary school classrooms (see Galton, Simon and Croll, 1980), more complex observation schedules were designed in order to construct a finer grained picture of teacher and student behaviour (and to examine the relationship between these). Two schedules were developed for the observation of teacher and students respectively. The categories used make fine distinctions between, for example, the kinds of questions asked (five forms of teacher questioning are listed), the types of statements made (nine forms of teacher statement are given) and the kinds of non-verbal interaction observed.

The attractions of a complex observation schedule are clear. The researcher has just one opportunity to record events and commonly wishes to bring back from the field as detailed an account as they can. However, making a distinction between, say, 'open' and 'closed' teacher questions is not always easy, particularly when under the strict time pressures of filling in an observation schedule. Recording using the ORACLE schedules, for example, takes place at twenty-five second intervals; using the Flanders schedule, they take place every three seconds. The more detailed the schedule, the more difficult it is to be consistent in making distinctions between one category and another. This in turn has an effect on the reliability of the schedule as an instrument for collection of data.

The sample for the ORACLE study was large and a team of observers were used to collect data. To ensure that similar interpretations of events were being made by all the observers, careful attention had to be paid to training people to use the schedule and to align their judgments. As an observer uses a schedule over a period of time, the interpretations made may change slightly, that is, there may be **category drift**. With multiple observers it is clearly important to ensure that everyone continues to be consistent in their use of the schedule. It is also important for the lone researcher to guard against this. The consistency of the use of a schedule can be checked using video extracts. By coding the same material at different points in the data collection process, the researcher can check to see if there have been any changes in interpretation over time.

To make it possible for an observation schedule to be used consistently across a number of contexts and, possibly, by a number of different people, it is obviously important that the categories are clearly and unambiguously defined. In addition to a set of categories, an observation schedule must have a set of explicit instructions for its use. The instructions will include details of the frequency with which one records events. This is a question of **sampling**. How often does one need to sample events in the classroom to be able to record them in a way that retains the distinctiveness of the distribution of events within different settings? Attention also needs to be given to the format in which recording takes place. The use of a grid, with the categories along one axis and a scale marked out in the time intervals being used along the other, enables a record of the sequence of coded events to be made. It then becomes possible to examine the characteristics of different phases of a lesson, or to look at the points at which particular behaviours or forms of interaction occur most frequently. It is also possible to explore the occurrence of particular pairs, or longer sequences, of coded events.

If the sequence of events is of central importance to the researcher, **interval sampling**, as used by both the coding systems discussed so far, may not be appropriate. By coding at regular intervals one gets an impression of the distribution of events across periods of time. However, because there may be other, non-recorded events between one recorded event and the next, some patterns or sequences may be missed. The alternative is to record specific events as they happen, rather than wait for a fixed period between the coding of events. This is known, not surprisingly, as **event coding**. In this way we could investigate, for instance, what kinds of interactions take place when a teacher asks an open question. Event coding can be very effective for gathering data on the relative frequency of particular events. Closer attention has to be paid to the definition of the **unit** that is being recorded and to recognition of the beginning and end of a codable event. These are less important issues for interval coding, where the observer need only consider, at the moment at which the coding is to be done, 'what kind of event is occurring now?'

In designing an observational study it is unlikely that an off-the-shelf schedule will do precisely what you want it to do. The two schedules mentioned above were both developed for specific purposes and are thus limited in their scope. The Flanders schedule, for example, was designed at a time when teacher centred, whole class teaching was the predominant mode of organization. Consequently, it does not work well in classrooms where alternative modes of classroom organization predominate. The schedule would be difficult to operate, for example, in a classroom in which the teacher moves between groups of students and interacts sometimes with individuals, sometimes with groups and sometimes with the whole class.

Further, as each schedule is developed from a particular theoretical perspective, its form and content will be based on a set of assumptions that might not be shared by other researchers. An alternative is to develop your own observation schedule. This is most appropriate if you are exploring an area in which some previous research has been carried out, or if you are working from a well developed theoretical position. Working with a clearly articulated problem will enable you to show how the categories of your schedule — your indicator variables — are derived from your concept variables.

Of course, the schedule must also be designed with direct reference to the empirical setting. It should provide a range of categories that enable all forms of the phenomenon in which you are interested to be easily classified, that is, the categories should be *exhaustive*. In addition, each coded event should fall into just one category, that is, the categories should be *mutually exclusive*. The schedule should be easy to use. It should have full descriptions of the categories and clear instructions for use. To maximize consistency in the use of the schedule, the coding of events should require a minimal amount of inference on the part of the observer. The more contextual information needed to make judgments and the more the observer has to make inferences from what they see in order to code an event, the greater the necessity for training in the use of the schedule to ensure that it produces data with a high degree of reliability.

A new observation schedule has to be **piloted** and any necessary changes have to be made before it is used for the collection of data for analysis. The reliability of the schedule can be tested by employing two independent observers to code the same sequence of events, either from live action or video tape. You will then need to consider the level of agreement between the two observers. This provides a good indication of the extent to which the categories are adequately defined. This procedure for checking the **inter-coder reliability** can be used wherever schedules or coding frames are used to categorize events. Not only does it test the explicitness, coherence and clarity of the framework, it also helps to identify any unintentional bias that might creep into the researcher's own coding.

As a way of collecting data, structured observation has both strengths and weaknesses. A major strength is that a well designed schedule allows data to be collected from a variety of settings and for comparisons to be made with a high degree of reliability. In describing a complex social setting in terms of a pre-formed set of categories much information is, however, lost. This can be either a positive or a negative feature, depending on the priorities of the researcher. On the one hand, making meaningful selections is what category systems are designed to achieve. They serve as effective focusing devices at the stage of data collection. On the other hand, your observations are available only in terms of these categories. No other information from the event can be reliably reclaimed. For this reason, systematic observation has been criticized for producing static representations of phenomena (see Hamilton and Delamont, 1974). Clearly, using this technique for the collection of data in a classroom misses much of what goes on. There may be important, but subtle features of classroom life that cannot be recorded using a schedule, no matter how detailed. Furthermore, the observer has only limited knowledge of the particular setting and can work only on the basis of what can be seen. The significance to participants of certain events, for instance the use of in-jokes, may not be immediately accessible to the observer. Misinterpretations, with respect to the meanings ascribed by participants, can thus occur.

Fieldnotes

An alternative to the highly structured approach is to engage directly in the setting being explored and to make *in situ* **fieldnotes** on what is experienced. This resembles an anthropological or ethnographic approach to educational contexts. Here the researcher enters the setting with a range of questions, interests and orientations. A description of the setting is developed through the successive compilation and analysis of fieldnotes. As with the use of observation schedules, the result is a **biased** account in that it constitutes an imposition of **recontextualizing** principles of recognition and realization. Consequently, as with the use of observation schedules, it is essential to make explicit the basis on which these selections and interpretations are made. There is, however, an important difference between the use of schedules and the use of fieldnotes. The schedule constitutes a pre-conceptualization of the empirical setting (particularly in the sense that only that which can be categorized can be recorded). With the use of fieldnotes, on the other hand, the structuring of the empirical setting can occur progressively across the period of the fieldwork as successive sets of notes are analysed and the researcher returns to the setting with more finely developed foci for their observation.

In other words, the distinction between structured and unstructured approaches refers to the point at which selection and structuring information from the empirical setting takes place. Bringing back fieldnotes, photographs, or even video or audio recordings of what has happened in the classroom defers the production of a structured account. This deferral can allow a more open exploration of a setting. Ultimately, however, a structured account of the empirical setting and associated phenomena has to be constructed. Without this we have nothing to say; we have no research findings.

There are important methodological and technical issues to be addressed when working with fieldnotes, just as there are with the use of schedules. The researcher will carry with them a number of presuppositions about what is being investigated. The fact that the observation process is not being pre-structured in a rigid way, does not mean that preconceptions can be ignored. On the contrary, there is a sense in which the interrogation of the researcher's preconceptions forms as important a part of the research process as does the direct observation of the empirical setting. Unfortunately, in many cases researchers do not examine their assumptions carefully and consequently they themselves are unaware of the presuppositions that are guiding their work. It is not that fieldnotes are unstructured but that, often, their structuring is not made explicit.

Working with fieldnotes, and other information and documents gathered when conducting fieldwork, requires a high level of administrative discipline. For instance, in making fieldnotes it is helpful to distinguish between the different kinds of information that one wishes to bring back from observation episodes. In our own study of three secondary schools in South Africa (Dowling and Brown, 1996) we followed classes of school students for entire days and took fieldnotes in all the lessons we attended. Our aim was to examine how pedagogic texts, very broadly defined, were used by teachers and pupils across a range of school subjects and in different kinds of schools. To guide the production of fieldnotes and to facilitate comparisons between the notes made by the three fieldworkers, we drew up a set of fieldwork guidelines. These included guidance on the format of the fieldnotes. For each lesson we recorded, at the head of the first page, contextual details, such as the number of children, the arrangement of the furniture, the manner in which the pupils were organized, the resources available and so on.

Underneath this opening section, the fieldnotes were divided into two columns. On the left hand side a chronicle of events was written. Each fieldworker kept a running record of what they observed including accounts of the teacher's actions, interactions between the teacher and the pupils, verbatim speech extracts, a record of what was written on the chalk board and so on. To speed up the process of recording, the use of abbreviations was useful. In the right hand column the fieldworkers made a note of their own ideas, links with other data and thoughts about preliminary analysis. At the foot of the fieldnotes for each lesson, a note was made of any additional information collected, including information gathered from conversations with the teacher and school students at the end of the lesson. Following each day's observations, we each read through our fieldnotes and added any additional information that we had not been able to note at the time. This included the addition of references to other material collected, such as copies of worksheets used. We also began to develop our analysis.

In making fieldnotes it is important to have a system that enables a clear distinction to be made between the notes that constitute the raw data (albeit already highly selected) and the emerging analysis. It is also vital to have a cross-referencing system that allows information to be easily recalled and for links to be made with other material collected. The adoption of the form of fieldnote organization described above enabled us to keep different forms of information separate. The event chronicle acted as a reference back to what we had observed in the classroom. This is a record of what, from our perspective, had happened and effectively acted as the empirical basis for our subsequent analysis. As all three fieldworkers observed the same lessons and were using a common fieldnote format, we were able to compare notes and reach a common account of the lessons we observed. Often one observer had been able to note down some details of a lesson that the others had not included in their notes. It is neither possible nor desirable to 'get it all down' and produce a completely unbiased account. Being able to compare notes does, however, help to guard against the dangers of inadvertent selective attention, recording and memory lapses. Contextual information was also shared and checked with the other fieldworkers. Our preliminary analytic notes, often just hastily scribbled ideas, where made in the righthand column and acted as a reminder of lines of enquiry that might prove to be fruitful. In this way analysis proceeds alongside the collection of data.

The form of recording we have described provides greater flexibility than the use of a schedule, and was more appropriate for the type of study we wished to carry out. The notes taken can provide an image of the classroom and the activity within it, remind us of key events and provide us with information for use in the development of our analysis and in writing this up. They do not provide us with quantitative data, nor can they be used as the basis for generating data of this sort. Our subsequent analysis does, however, impose structure on what we have observed. In developing and writing up our analysis we have to be every bit as clear, and explicit, about how we move from our observations to our results as the researcher using systematic observation has to be about the design and use of their schedule and the interpretation of the information gathered.

It is not always possible to make fieldnotes as the activity being investigated is taking place. Sometimes, especially in covert observation in sensitive settings, writing may not be an appropriate activity. Furthermore, when the observer is personally involved in the activity, for instance, a teacher observing interaction between children in their own class, taking notes may not be physically possible. In these cases notes have to be made as soon after the event as feasible. Under these circumstances, having some means of remembering information, such as the use of mnemonics, is particularly useful. Whatever the form of record that is made of an event, and whatever the circumstances, it is necessary to be clear about the status of the record — what precisely can the notes, or the completed schedules, tell us about the object of our investigation. This concerns the relationship between the theoretical and empirical contexts of the research, in particular the validity of the findings in relation to the problem.

Experience and Observation: Conclusion

The focus of this chapter has been on the details of the empirical setting. We have turned our attention to the specifics of the collection of first hand data in order to raise what we feel to be important methodological and practical issues. We have not attempted to provide a comprehensive survey of methods, nor have we dealt with any of the approaches in great detail. There are numerous general research methods texts and more specialized work to which the beginning researcher can turn for further advice. We have included those we feel to be the most useful in our annotated bibliography.

We initially distinguished between approaches in which manipulation of the research setting is paramount and those in which the researcher attempts to minimize their effect on the research setting. Both positions present problems. In social and educational research it is rarely possible to establish the high degree of control that is required in experimental designs. As a result, compromises are made and the experimental design logic on which many forms of educational research are predicated is weakened. On the other hand, it is also impossible for a researcher to have no effect on the settings in which they are working. The very presence of a researcher, indeed the knowledge that a setting is subject to study, will affect activity within that setting. This provides a challenge to the notion that it is possible to conduct a fully **naturalistic** enquiry. Once it is constituted as the object of research, a setting is transformed and can never be precisely what it was before. Furthermore, the production of an account requires choices to be made with respect to both what is described and how it is described. The claim that one is presenting a situation 'as it is' or 'as it is construed by participants' obscures the principles by which such selections are made and accounts constructed.

Our second distinction focused on the point at which structure is placed on the information in the production of data. We have argued that all forms of data collection and analysis involve the imposition of structure — this is fundamental to the conduct of research. The use of a structured observation schedule imposes structure at a very early stage in the research process. Once the schedule has been designed, data can only be collected in terms of the categories of the schedule. The structuring of data is less obvious in the use of fieldnotes, particularly in the early stages of research. This more open form of data collection allows the possibility of developing a focus as the research progresses. In the analysis of the data the researcher must identify patterns and relationships in the data. If the data remains unstructured, it has not been analysed.

We have chosen not to present the choice of a particular way of collecting data as indicating a strong affiliation to a specific **epistemological** position. In our view these associations are commonly post-hoc and are of limited help in either the design or interrogation of research. It is of greater importance in deciding how to collect your data, that you ensure that the methods you choose are consistent with the theoretical framework within which you are working. It is also important that you are clear about the status of your data with respect to your study. As we have argued, there is a great difference between the manner in which observations made in an experimental setting and narrative description brought back from the field can be used within a study. You have to take care to treat different forms of data in an appropriate manner and to be clear what your data represents. These issues will be taken up again in Chapter 5 in which we turn our attention to the collection of data from the accounts of others.

References

BURAWOY, M. *et al.* (1991) *Ethnography Unbound: Power and Resistance in the Modern Metropolis*, Berkeley: University of California Press.

DOWLING, P.C. and BROWN, A.J. (1996) *Pedagogy and Community in Three South African Schools: A Classroom Study*, at http://www.ioe.ac.uk/ccs/ccsroot/ccs/dowling_brown/1996.html.

FLANDERS, N. (1970) *Analysing Teacher Behaviour*, New York: Wiley.

GALTON, M., SIMON, B. and CROLL, P. (1980) *Inside the Primary School*, London: Routledge and Kegan Paul.

GARFINKEL, H. (1967) *Studies in Ethnomethodology*, Englewood Cliffs: Prentice-Hall.

HAMILTON, D. and DELAMONT, S. (1974) 'Classroom research: A cautionary tale', *Research in Education*, **11**, pp. 1–15.

MALINOWSKI, B. (1922) *Argonauts of the Western Pacific*, London: Routledge and Kegan Paul.

ROBSON, C. (1993) *Real World Research: A Resource for Social Scientists and Practitioner-Researchers*, Oxford: Blackwell.

ROETHLISBERGER, F.I. and DICKSON, W.T. (1939) *Management and the Worker*, Cambridge, Mass: Harvard University Press.

SILVA, T.T. DA (1988) 'Distribution of school knowledge and social reproduction in a Brazilian setting', *British Journal of Sociology of Education*, **9**, 1, pp. 55–79.

5 Gathering Information and Asking Questions: Interviews, Questionnaires and Accounts

In Chapter 4 we discussed ways of generating data by recording first hand experience, either by directly manipulating a setting and observing what happens, or by motivated observation of social interaction in a 'natural' setting. In this chapter we turn our attention to the ways in which other people's accounts, rather than the direct observations of the researcher, can be used as the main source of information. We have made a distinction between these two modes of data collection for pedagogic reasons. Researchers often employ complexes of methods so, in practice, it is often difficult to maintain the distinction. As we have already seen, an ethnographic approach to research can involve the use of informants from whom details of local practices are obtained. Discussion with participants can inform the development of an understanding of how they make sense of the world. Questionnaires and interviews can also be incorporated into experimental designs, for example to gauge changes in attitude associated with a particular intervention. It is thus possible that, in both reading and doing research, you will encounter data produced from a combination of both observational sources and personal accounts, questionnaires and interviews.

Many of the issues discussed in the previous chapter are relevant here. The contexts within which accounts are produced, for instance, can vary from settings created specifically for the purpose of direct questioning through to documents, such as diaries, that may be an incidental outcome of everyday activity. As with observational methods, the stage at which structure is imposed upon the accounts of others can also vary. Self-completion questionnaires distributed by post are usually highly structured, with respondents being asked to select answers from a predetermined list of possibilities. In contrast, some exploratory face-to-face interviews may resemble a conversation with little apparent pre-structuring of either form or content by the researcher. In considering the different approaches, we will look firstly at variations in the extent to which the researcher manipulates the context before moving on to discuss variations in the structuring of data collection.

Researchers clearly enter the field with different objectives, and select their data collection techniques accordingly. In considering observational techniques we had to take care to establish, for instance, the extent to which the researcher may be attempting to retain and describe the 'natural qualities' of the settings being observed and the activity taking place within them. We must address similar questions when considering the status of accounts. In general terms, we might distinguish between five broad categories of interests in terms of gathering accounts. That is, the researcher may be interested in: what people know; what people do or have done; what people think or feel; how people think; and/or how people construct meanings. In practice, however, these categories are rather more problematic than they may at first appear.

Manipulation of Context: From Clinical Interviews to Diaries

Clinical Interviews and Elicitation Techniques

The purpose of a **clinical interview** is to probe beneath the surface of events (such as the behaviour, including utterances, of an individual) in order to explore the underlying processes from which these events arise. It is concerned with *how people think* or *how they construct meaning.* In a clinical setting, the therapist organizes a context specifically for the examination of a client's condition. The ultimate aim is not only to explore possible causal relationships and develop a better understanding of the condition, but also to bring about a transformation, to alleviate the condition.

The manner in which the therapist makes sense of what the client says or does and the way in which they manage the interview procedure depend on the theoretical perspective from which they are working. The therapist has a particular way of 'reading' what the client says and does (a theory) and way of proceeding in terms of eliciting forms of behaviour that can be read in this way (a method). In some forms of therapeutic encounter the therapist is in clear control, asking specific questions, reacting to the client's responses in particular ways and guiding the course of the interview. In others, such as Rogerian approaches, the therapist responds in as neutral a manner as possible and attempts to put the client in control of the encounter. In both these types of approach, the clinical interview constitutes a specialized context, a setting that has been created, and is being manipulated, for a particular analytic purpose.

The aims of therapy and of research are clearly different. A form of clinical interview has, however, been fruitfully adopted by some social researchers. Luria, for instance, does more than just ask his interviewees a series of questions to which they are expected simply to give answers. Working from an initial stimulus, such as a syllogism or a classification problem, Luria confronts his subjects, probing and asking supplementary questions in order to explore the form of reasoning they employ. His theorizing of the relationship between forms of social organization and modes of human cognition leads him to explore whether or not his subjects are capable of particular ways of reasoning.

How a person reasons is not open to direct inspection. Luria thus needs to be able to recognize, from what his subjects say and do in particular situations, when they are engaging in certain types of reasoning. The probing that takes place in these interviews is thus designed to examine the way in which each subject approaches the problem given and to offer them every opportunity to look at the problem in an alternative way. The extract from the interview with Rakmat, discussed in Chapter 3 (see page 27), illustrates Luria's technique. Having explained the task and given a detailed example, Luria uses a set of cards with drawings of familiar objects on them to initiate a classification activity. On being shown the collection *hammer-saw-log-hatchet* and asked which ones are similar, Rakmat gives the following response:

> They're all alike. I think all of them have to be here. See, if you're going to saw, you need a saw, and if you have to split something you need a hatchet. So they're *all* needed here. (Luria, 1976; p. 55)

Rakmat has clearly failed to produce the 'correct' answer. Luria interprets Rakmat's response as indicating that he 'employs the principle of "necessity" to group objects in a practical situation' (*ibid*). Rather than simply record Rakmat as having produced a particular type of response when set a certain kind of problem, Luria pursues the matter further. As it is possible that Rakmat simply does not understand what is being asked of him, Luria attempts to explain the task by using a 'simpler example'.

Look, here you have three adults and one child. Now clearly the child does not belong in this group.

> 'Oh, but the boy must stay with the others! All three of them are working, you see, and if they have to keep running out to fetch things, they'll never get the job done, but the boy can do the running for them . . . The boy will learn; that'll be better, then they'll be able to work well together.' (*ibid*)

As the subject once again applies the same principle of grouping, Luria explores this further by providing more examples and additional prompts before returning to the original problem. He approaches this by continuing to probe with additional questions and statements. The transcript extract which is reproduced on page 27 illustrates the method.

This form of interview does not consist of a set of standard questions that are given to all interviewees in a fixed order, nor does it consist of a task at which the subject is judged to have succeeded or failed on the basis of a single response. Instead Luria has a range of tasks specifically designed to explore particular forms of reasoning. In administering these tasks he has a general strategy to guide the manner in which the interview is conducted. Through the exploration of the responses of the subjects, Luria tests and develops his own theory.

Probes and Prompts

A **probe** is a question used in an interview to gain further information, clarification, or which seeks to access underlying causes or reasons for a particular response. A **prompt** involves suggesting possible responses. The use of both probes and prompts interrupts the spontaneity of the response. This does not mean that they should be avoided; the use of probes, in particular, is a crucial strategy in many kinds of interview. You should, however, give careful advance consideration to the kinds of probes and prompts that you are prepared to use.

Luria made extensive use of both probes and prompts because his method involved trying to nudge his subjects into what he classified as a higher mode of cognition. Luria reasoned that if a subject failed to do so, despite his probing and prompting, then this indicated that the subject was unable to operate at the higher level.

Jean Piaget (for example, Piaget, 1953) used a similar form of clinical interview to examine children's reasoning, that is, to examine *how children think*. Piaget and his colleagues designed a range of tasks and problems to be given to individual children by a researcher. How the children made their judgments or solved the problem was explored through extended questioning. For Piaget, it was not enough to ascertain whether or not a child produces the 'correct' solution to a problem, but to look at the form of reasoning that took place in producing a solution or making a judgement. Each task provides a research context. The responses to the task and to the subsequent probing enable the researcher to make and support theoretically informed judgments.

Piaget's tasks, usually in modified form, have subsequently been used by other researchers as the basis for their own experimental research designs (see, for example, Donaldson, 1978). Here samples of children are set tasks under tightly controlled conditions. Rather than acting as the initial stimulus in a detailed exploration of forms of reasoning, the tasks are used as tests. It is certainly legitimate for researchers to draw inspiration from the work of others. Nevertheless, this recontextualization of Piaget's work is open to question. In particular, the probes used by Piaget and his colleagues are entirely or substantially eliminated in much of this subsequent work. Arguably, the researcher is thus more concerned with *what children think* than with *how children think*.

The starting point for the form of clinical interview conducted by Luria and Piaget is a task of some kind. The nature of each task relates to the substantive focus of the research (e.g. the exploration of generalization and abstraction in the work by Luria discussed above) and the theoretical standpoint adopted by the researcher. These also guide the form that the interview will take. Whilst there are clearly criteria for evaluation of the suitability of the task and the ultimate form of realization of each individual interview, there are no fixed techniques or procedures that are common to all interviews. George Kelly (1969), developed both a theory of personality and specific techniques for the elicitation (and analysis) of theoretically relevant information from interviewees. As a school psychologist, he worked initially from a clinical perspective. Kelly's prime interest was in the way in which individuals made sense of the world around them, that is, in *how people construct meanings*.

Kelly proposed that individuals come to a personal understanding of the world through attempts to predict and control events. Each individual, he argued, comes to conceptualize the world in terms of a limited number of **personal constructs.** These are conceptual dimensions marked out in terms of bi-polar oppositions, such as 'strong'/'weak' or 'good for me'/'bad for me'. These constructs are used to make sense of and evaluate phenomena with which the individual comes into contact (e.g. people, events, objects). These phenomena are referred to as **elements**.

Kelly's method is designed to identify the personal constructs by which individuals make sense of their world. This can be done by, firstly, eliciting key elements from the interviewee. The person might be asked, for instance, to note down, in a list or on cards, the people who are significant to them. Having produced a set of elements, the interviewee is asked to form groups of three in which two of the elements are the same in some way but differ from the third element. The way in which these elements are similar or different should be expressed as a bi-polar opposition, such as friendly/hostile, honest/dishonest, competent/inept. These are the constructs. The way in which two elements resemble each other is the **similarity pole** of the construct, the way in which these two elements differ from the third is the **contrast pole**. By working through the elements in this way a number of personal constructs can be elicited. Once this has been done a grid is drawn up. Each row of the grid represents a construct and each column an element. The interviewee is asked to take each construct in turn and indicate whether each element lies at the similarity pole or the contrast pole. The completed grid, known as a **repertory grid**, can be used to explore both how each construct is used and how the interviewee construes each element.

There is substantial debate amongst researchers drawing on Kelly's work regarding the process of constructing the repertory grid and its subsequent analysis. Engagement with these debates is beyond the scope of this book. For our purposes, Kelly's work offers an example of an empirical technique which is derived from theory. Personal construct theory provides principles for the construction of a particular kind of encounter and techniques for the analysis of information collected. It is potentially applicable either in a therapeutic/diagnostic setting or a research setting.

Diaries and Documents

The approaches discussed above involve a high degree of manipulation of the context within which an enquiry takes place. The interview is separated from the everyday activity of the subject and involves engagement with tasks designed specifically for the purpose of research. Accounts relating directly to everyday activity can be collected with less direct manipulation. In some forms of activity, accounts of various kinds are produced routinely by participants. Teachers, for instance, produce policy **documents**, teaching plans, student evaluations and so on. A researcher wishing to study, for instance, the relationship between school policies and the form of planning carried out by teachers could do so on the basis of the analysis of policy documents and examples of teachers' long term and short term planning drawn from a sample of schools.

As with all the forms of study we have discussed, there is a need for clarity about what constitutes relevant information and explicitness concerning the manner in which the information is organized and analysed as data. It is also important to be clear about the conditions under which the information has been produced and the status which is being accorded to it. In designing your study you will have to attend to questions of sampling and comparability. Whether or not you are manipulating the context in which the source information is generated, you still need to attend to fundamental issues in the design and conduct of research.

Brown (1993, 1994, forthcoming; Brown and Dowling, 1993) analysed documents produced incidentally by primary school teachers in the everyday activity of attempting to involve parents in the mathematical education of their children (these were schools taking part in the IMPACT project, see Merttens and Vass, 1990, 1993). These included examples of school mathematics activities sent home by teachers, booklets produced by teachers for parents and comments about mathematics tasks made by parents in IMPACT diaries (see Chapter 6 for some further details of this work). **Sampling** is clearly an issue here. Writing to schools and asking for, say, any booklets they have produced for parents is a viable approach to information gathering. However, when the booklets are analysed it is important to be quite sure what the sample that has been drawn represents. You cannot, for instance, claim that a sample collected in such a non-systematic manner is **representative** of booklets produced by schools. In fact, Brown chose to analyse all of the booklets in use in one Local Education Authority in one particular year. This avoided the possibility of being inadvertently selective.

It still left unanswered the question of the extent to which the booklets analysed could be taken as representative of a wider population.

Although the manipulation of settings is minimal in the collection of incidental or 'found' information, there are **ethical** considerations that you must address. This is because the information may originally have been generated for purposes which were quite different from those of your research. The producers of the information may be in no position to give consent to its recycling as research data. Consideration, then, must be given to anonymity. In most cases this is easily achieved by the use of fictional names and the exclusion of collateral information that would enable institutions and/or individuals to be identified. Particular care has to be taken over the use of **confidential** information. Schools, for example, keep much information that has a limited circulation and some that is highly confidential. Researchers have to consider carefully whether such information should be used at all and, if it is, how it should be treated and represented. Although you are not directly manipulating a setting, you are intervening. Here our discussion converges with the consideration of observation in the previous chapter.

In order to follow the activities of participants in their everyday lives you may ask them to keep a **diary** of events. This would enable you to look, for instance, at the proportion of time spent on various kinds of tasks. For example, you might be interested in the manner in which headteachers allocate time to different aspects of their work. To do this you could provide a number of categories of the types of activities which you feel typify the work of headteachers. A sample of headteachers could then be asked to keep a diary showing at what times during the day they took part in these activities (**event sampling**). Alternatively they could be asked to record what they are doing, in terms of the categories you have provided, at particular times of the day (**interval sampling**).

This kind of diary is a form of self-administered, structured **observation schedule**. It thus has both the strengths and weaknesses discussed in the previous chapter with respect to observation schedules. The categories have to be clearly defined and relatively unambiguous in order to be consistently applied by the members of the sample. With each person mapping out their own daily activity, you face all the difficulties of having multiple observers, with no automatic guarantee that everyone is interpreting the category descriptions in the same way. As with the construction of observation schedules you also have to have a fair understanding of the activity being investigated in order to construct a set of categories that have the potential to describe the activities adequately.

Diaries can be used in a more exploratory manner. Headteachers could be asked to keep unstructured, freeform notes on their activities as they take place or to look back on and describe the work they have done at the end of each day. This would not give the neatly categorized information of the structured diary but could give the researcher insight into the manner in which headteachers construe their work. In effect the subjects of the research are being asked to make fieldnotes on their own day-to-day activities. Although no observer is present, this kind of research is not free from observer effects. The awareness that one's behaviour is under scrutiny, even if the details of this are self-reported, can affect what one does (see the discussion of the Hawthorne Effect in Chapter 4). With self-reporting techniques we also have to be aware that subjects might present idealized accounts of what they do.

Structure: From Questionnaires to Conversations

Questionnaires

Self-completed **questionnaires** hold a number of attractions for the researcher who wishes to collect information from a large number of people but has limited time and resources. On the surface the process of construction, distribution and analysis of questionnaires appears to be straightforward. The appeal of the questionnaire is that, once the information required by the researcher has been identified, it appears to be relatively easy to construct a list of questions that get straight to the heart of the matter, to be delivered directly to chosen respondents to complete and return in their own time. There are, however, severe limitations on what can be achieved using a questionnaire. Even once these limitations are taken into account, the design of effective questionnaires is fraught with technical difficulties. Excellent advice on the construction of questionnaires is readily available (see Oppenheim, 1992, for instance). Even so, in our experience, beginning researchers frequently run into serious problems in the use of questionnaires and many invest a lot of time collecting information that is ultimately of little or no use to them.

As is the case with the use of structured observation schedules (discussed in Chapter 4), the strengths and limitations of the questionnaire are closely related. For instance, if information is to be of use to the researcher, it is necessary to standardize the questionnaire to ensure that the responses received are comparable. This entails more than simply giving the same questions to all respondents. The researcher has to be confident that each question will be interpreted by each respondent in a similar manner. The questions thus have to be as free as possible from ambiguity. The researcher must take care to keep the questions short and ensure that there are no **double-barrelled questions** (i.e. single questions that ask for two items of information). Questions must be checked carefully to ensure that they are free from bias and that they do not lead the respondent towards a particular answer. Technical language that may not be understood by all respondents should be avoided. Care has to be taken even with common, everyday terms. In cases where it is not clear that an important term will be understood in a similar manner by all respondents, a definition can be provided. This also carries problems.

To illustrate this difficulty we can consider the use of a questionnaire, distributed to school students, to investigate the incidence of bullying in a school. Although the terms relating to bullying are used in everyday speech, it is not clear that they are used in the same way by everyone. The question 'how many times have you been bullied this month?' becomes problematic if, across the sample, there is wide variation in what respondents consider bullying to be. Some students might see a single incidence of name calling as bullying whilst others view bullying as occurring across extended time periods and involving physical threat.

In response to this, the researcher might choose to include a definition of bullying in the questionnaire. This imposes a particular understanding of what it means to be bullied. The danger here is that by presenting bullying as an objectively defined phenomenon, the researcher is no longer gathering data on the extent to which people subjectively feel that they are being bullied. The provision of a definition might lead some respondents who feel they are, by their own definition, being bullied to indicate that, by the definition provided, they have not been bullied. Similarly, students who previously have not seen themselves as the victims of bullying might, in the light of the definition provided, indicate that they have been bullied.

The alternative is to accept the definition of each respondent and focus the research on the subjective feeling of being bullied, whatever this might mean to each individual. If relevant, the researcher could include items in the questionnaire that are specifically designed to draw out what each respondent understands by the term bullying. The decision to either include a definition of a key term or not, in this case, fundamentally affects the nature of the study. This decision is clearly not a technical issue. It relates back to the theoretical framework from which the problem being addressed is derived.

Whichever approach is adopted it is vital to carry out a **pilot study** with a sample which matches the profile of the sample for the main study. The questionnaire items can be trialled with the specific intention of gaining feedback from the respondents concerning their interpretation of the questions. This can be achieved through the addition of some open, free response questions asking respondents to reflect on how they interpreted the questions. Alternatively, a brief interview focusing on the questionnaire might be conducted. Attention also has to be paid to the ordering of questions, the division of the questionnaire into sections and the format of the questionnaire. All these aspects can be modified on the basis of the feedback obtained from a pilot study.

Difficulties with regard to interpretation can be exacerbated by the mode of delivery of the questionnaire. If questionnaire forms are sent out by **post**, the researcher has no opportunity to correct any obvious misunderstandings, probe or offer help, as they would in an interview. Consequently, forms might be returned with some sections not completed or incorrectly completed. Questionnaire forms might be passed on to other people to complete, or they might be consigned to the wastepaper basket. Low **response rates** and idiosyncratic responses do more damage than just reducing the sample size. They can also be a source of **unintentional bias** to the extent that there is a connection between the reasons for non-response and the topic of the research. There are no straightforward ways for correcting for sample bias caused by non-response. You simply have to do everything you can to foster a good response rate.

Improved response rates to postally distributed questionnaires can be obtained by taking such measures as inviting respondents to participate in the survey (either by phone or by letter) or by providing advance warning of the arrival of the questionnaire form. Explaining why the respondent has been selected and describing the nature (and importance) of the research also helps to allay fears and engender personal commitment. This is easier if the topic is likely to be of interest to the respondent. It also helps to let the respondent know who you are and what you intend to do with the results. The promise of **confidentiality** and the anonymity of each respondent (if you are able to make such assurances) can also have an effect. The appearance of the questionnaire form is also important. It must not look as if completion will be an onerous task nor that it will take a long time. The inclusion of a stamped addressed envelope can also encourage people to return the completed questionnaire. If responses are slow in coming in, a reminder can be sent. If anonymity has been promised, the reminder will have to go to the whole sample. Attention to detail in both the design and the use of the questionnaire will all enhance the quality of the study.

The researcher can enhance response rates by more closely supervising the administration of the questionnaire or by becoming more personally involved in its **distribution** and completion. The questionnaire may be given to a group of people (such as a class of children or a group of teachers attending a training course) who are asked to complete the questionnaire at a specific time. The completed questionnaires can be collected from them immediately. This, of course, increases the researcher time required and thus reduces one of the attractions of the questionnaire.

If we follow this path, the researcher could, ultimately, **administer** the questionnaire to each individual in the sample, either in person or by telephone. This overcomes some of the disadvantages of postal distribution, but negates a prime advantage. We effectively have a form of very structured interview. Both forms of administration mentioned have sampling implications. They both allow the inclusion of people who are unable to read or write. The telephone interview obviously excludes those people who are not accessible by telephone. Of course, even personal administration of the questionnaire does not guarantee a 100 per cent response rate; people can always refuse to take part.

It may be that, despite your efforts, the response rate is low. You may also be aware of a bias in the distribution of your responses. For example, you may have received very few responses to a questionnaire on school-based teacher training from headteachers of inner-city schools. Under such circumstances, it is important to state this bias and consider any implications it might have for your findings.

In using postal questionnaires the researcher operates at some distance from the respondents. This impersonality can lead to researchers making unwise decisions. No matter how interesting it might appear to investigate the views of people who have recently suffered a bereavement in their close families, they are unlikely to appreciate receiving a postal questionnaire probing at their feelings when they may still be experiencing great distress.

Questionnaires are particularly useful for gathering simple information on *what people do or have done* (although care must be taken to allow for the limitations of memory in the questions asked) and *what people know*. Details of a person's educational qualifications or of their reading habits can be gathered by using either closed questions with carefully selected alternatives to choose from (**pre-coded** responses) or simple open questions. In the latter case, the responses to which will have to be coded by the researcher after data collection. On the other hand, questionnaires are not always good for exploring *how people think* or *how people construct meanings*. It is possible to use a questionnaire to explore *what people think or feel*, although this requires great skill in the design of items. With this in mind, we shall now look at techniques designed specifically for the purpose of exploring people's opinions, attitudes and beliefs.

Exploring Opinions, Attitudes and Beliefs

The major difficulty in the use of a conventional questionnaire to collect information on the thoughts and feelings or **attitudes** of individuals stems from the complexity of the enterprise. If a researcher wishes to find out, for instance, how satisfied parents are with their child's school, they are immediately faced with a number of problems. They could ask 'how satisfied are you with your child's school?' They could provide a one-to-five scale on which parents are required to mark the degree of their satisfaction, from very unsatisfied to very satisfied. This would be difficult to respond to in a consistent manner as a parent is likely to be satisfied with some aspects of the school and not others. To address the question they have to decide what weighting they will place on each of these aspects in assessing their own overall satisfaction. With such a complex judgment, a slight rephrasing of the question might lead to a different response.

This makes it difficult to test the **reliability** of the item by asking the same thing in a different way and comparing the answers to the two questions. In addition, the notion of overall satisfaction might itself have little meaning for the respondent. A parent might, for instance, be very satisfied with respect to one of their children, but not at all satisfied with respect to another child. The complexity of the issue thus makes the use of just one question highly unreliable. The same question asked at another time may well get a different answer from the same person. In this case there are also doubts about the **validity** of the item. It is not clear precisely what a particular response to the item might indicate to the researcher.

The use of a set of questions, rather than a single item, would increase reliability. In assembling a number of items that relate to the same phenomenon, the effects of, say, an unintentional bias in one of the items or of an idiosyncratic response to one of the questions is reduced. Having a number of questions relating to the same topic also allows questions to be asked about different aspects of the topic. Satisfaction with schooling could thus be broken down into components and more focused questions constructed. The problem here is that, in order to reap the increased reliability benefits of having a set of questions rather than a single question, all the questions have to be considered together. Treating each of the questions individually reintroduces the difficulties that we are trying to overcome through the use of multiple questions. So, it is necessary to have a way of combining the responses to the individual questions in a set so that the set as a whole can be considered as one item. Our questions relating to parental satisfaction with schooling would together enable us to distinguish between those parents who are satisfied with schooling and those who are not with a comparatively high degree of reliability. It is thus important for the set of questions as a whole to have **discriminative power**.

Various techniques for the construction of scales for the measurement of attitudes have been developed to overcome these problems. The most straightforward, and most widely used, form of scale is the **Likert scale** (see Likert, 1932). A Likert scale consists of a number of statements, some positive and some negative, relating to the attitude being measured. The respondent is asked to indicate the degree to which they agree or disagree with each statement. This is commonly done using a five point scale from 'strongly disagree' at one end through 'disagree', 'neutral' and 'agree' to 'strongly agree' at the other end of the scale. Often these options are represented as a 1 to 5 numerical scale. In order to arrive at a score for each respondent, a numerical value is given to the response made to each statement, the values being reversed for positively and negatively worded statements. If the respondent 'strongly agrees' with a positive statement, a value of five is given, if they 'strongly agree' with a negative item a value of one is given, if they 'disagree' with a negative statement a value of four is given, and so on. These values are added together to give an overall score. Comparisons between respondents, or between groups of respondents, can now be made on the basis of these scores.

Great care has to be taken in the construction and use of a Likert scale. It is vitally important to understand the logic of this form of instrument, even if you are using a scale constructed by another person. For this reason we will outline briefly the process of constructing a Likert scale (see Robson, 1993; and Oppenheim, 1992, for more detailed accounts).

Suppose you wish to draw up a Likert scale to explore parental satisfaction with schooling. You need, firstly, to create a pool of statements, both positively and negatively worded, that relate to this issue. You can do this by referring to relevant literature, by taking statements from existing instruments, or by setting up a panel of people with particular knowledge of the field and asking them to suggest statements. The statements must have **face validity**, that is they must be seen to relate clearly to the topic being investigated. Your list might include statements like 'The work my children do at school is worthwhile' (positively worded) and 'Teachers do not give us enough information about our children's progress' (negatively worded).

Having compiled a preliminary list you need to reject extreme statements to which you suspect all or most respondents will react in the same way. This is because, if you are to distinguish between those parents who are satisfied with schooling and those who are not you must have statements which discriminate. To select the final statements for your scale you will need to compile a draft from the statements that you have collected, making sure to have approximately the same number of positive and negative statements. They should be arranged randomly. In order to test the discriminative power of each item, and to reject those which are the weakest in this respect, the draft should be given to a large **pilot** sample of respondents. The profile of the pilot sample should match that of the population you wish to investigate in the main study. On the basis of the scores obtained, the respondents should be placed in rank order and the power of each item to discriminate between the top 25 per cent and the bottom 25 per cent tested (see Robson, 1993, p. 258 for the procedure for this). The final scale should have around twenty-five statements (again with approximately equal numbers of positive and negative statements selected from those with the greatest discriminative power and again arranged randomly.

The aim of this procedure is to produce an instrument for the measurement of opinions, attitudes, beliefs or orientations which has face validity, is internally consistent, has discriminative power and is reliable. We have presented this to illustrate the difficulty in gathering information and making comparisons which go beyond collection of reports of personal experience and accounts of ready at hand knowledge. In our experience beginning researchers do not take sufficient care in the construction of these kinds of instruments. In particular there is a temptation to treat the responses to individual statements in Likert, and similar, scales as if they were discrete items in a questionnaire. Errors like this are common, even amongst more experienced researchers.

Interviewing

The advantages of the use of **interviews** to a large extent mirror the limitations of questionnaires discussed above. Interviews enable the researcher to explore complex issues in detail, they facilitate the personal engagement of the researcher in the collection of data, they allow the researcher to provide clarification, to probe and to prompt. Similarly the limitations mirror the advantages of questionnaires. Interviews are time consuming and thus place practical restrictions on sample size. Free form responses to open ended questions can be difficult to analyse and the direct interaction of the interviewer and the interviewee can give rise to forms of interviewer bias less evident in the setting of a self-completed questionnaire. As in our treatment of other ways of collecting information we will not attempt to argue the superiority of one method over any other. The selection of one particular method or combination of methods has to be related to the problem being addressed, and thus to the general theoretical framework within which the researcher is working, and to the particularities of the empirical setting.

In its most operationally **structured** form, an interview can resemble a personally administered questionnaire, with the interviewer following a standard format and reading a list of predetermined questions in an attempt to make the realization of the interview as consistent as possible across the sample. Each interviewee is offered a series of stimuli (the questions) in a standard form. That is, the same wording is used for the questions and the questions are always asked in the same order for each interview. The responses of the interviewee are recorded, usually in terms of pre-coded categories. The main advantage over the use of, say, a postal questionnaire is that the interviewer can provide clarification if the interviewee experiences difficulties or appears to misinterpret questions. It also enables the interviewer to collect contextual information not accessible using a respondent-administered questionnaire.

At the other extreme, the interview might be described as relatively **unstructured**. The term **semi-structured** interview is commonly employed. We have avoided this term, here, as it seems to leave open a space for an interview without any structure at all. We shall use the term 'unstructured interview' together with a caveat that it should not be taken too literally. There can be no such thing as an interview without any structure. The interviewer will always bring some agenda or general purpose to bear on the activity and will generally impose some theoretical and/or methodological selection in terms of the location and conditions in which it takes place and so forth.

With these qualifications, the 'unstructured interview' might be described as more closely resembling a conversation, with the interviewer working from a relatively loose set of guidelines. Here the questions are open and the format flexible. The prime concern of the interviewer might be to explore the world from the perspective of the interviewee and to construct an understanding of how the interviewee makes sense of their experiences. In this case the use of standard questions and a fixed format would be unduly constraining. The intensity of the interaction between interviewer and interviewee will necessitate that the interview is recorded in some way, for example, using an audiocassette recorder. The analysis will focus on making sense of what the interviewee says and how they say it.

These two forms of interview are often presented as the products of contrasting views of social knowledge. On the one hand, a positivist approach to social research is construed as a search for social facts which, therefore, gives rise to a closed, survey style interview. On the other hand, an interpretivist approach is understood as a search for meanings which generates a more open, ethnographic form of interview. More pragmatically the contrast is commonly drawn, firstly, between structured interviews and unstructured interviews. Between these two extremes a more or less complex typology of interviews is often constructed which variously combine structured components with opportunities for more open interaction.

Making sense of these forms of interview in terms of opposing **epistemological** positions (positivism *versus* interpretivism) is, in our opinion, not tenable and, in any event, is unlikely to advance your research in respect of your addressing of your specific problem. As with our earlier consideration of observational methods, we wish to look at this diversity neither in epistemological terms nor in terms of whether interviews are themselves structured, semi-structured or unstructured, but rather as a range of approaches that differ with respect to the point at which the researcher imposes structure on information to produce data. Rather than engage in an exposition of interview typology and the relative merits of each type, we will concentrate on those features of the design and conduct common to all forms of interview.

All interviews involve interaction. We shall consider both the form of the relation between interviewer and interviewee and the nature of the interview as an interactional context. The interviewer clearly has an agenda and has constructed what we might refer to as the **interview-as-event** as a setting for data collection. Each step in the construction of the interview-as-event warrants close attention. For instance, the **location** of the interview is important. In interviewing parents about their views on their child's school, for example, a strong identification of the interviewer with the school may have an inhibiting effect on the interviewee. The researcher thus has to consider whether the interviews should be held in the school, at the interviewee's home or elsewhere. If, in order to make the interviewee feel at ease, they are offered a choice of location, the researcher has to consider whether or not the data from interviews held in school and interviews held at home are comparable.

There is no 'correct' answer to this kind of question. There are no neutral locations, nor are there hard and fast rules for determining the effects of location, just as there is no way of determining what effect the presence of an observer has upon activity in a setting. It is incumbent upon the researcher to ensure that any obvious and unintended effects of the setting are minimized and taken into account when formulating the findings of the research. In particular, if comparisons are to be made, the researcher should ensure that, as far as possible, like is being compared with like.

Similar consideration has to be given to the manner in which **interviewers** present themselves to interviewees. Few interviews occur spontaneously. In most cases interviewers make a deliberate effort to introduce themselves to their interviewees, either by letter, telephone or in person. Exactly who the interviewee thinks they are talking to, and why, will affect what they say. The researcher thus has to consider what they tell the interviewee prior to the interview, both with respect to their own position and the nature of the research being carried out. Should letters asking parents if they are willing to be interviewed be written on university letterheaded paper? Should interviewers present themselves to teachers as colleagues, or outsiders? Often the interviewer is already known to the interviewee, and no introduction is necessary. Even more care has to be taken in considering the effects that this may have on the interview. The authority **relations** which characterize the relationship between a headteacher and a member of their staff, for instance, might not be conducive to a frank discussion of teacher attitudes to appraisal. A trainee teacher will talk in a particular way to a lecturer associated with their training programme. The nature of the interaction will change further once the trainee becomes a qualified teacher.

Consideration needs to be given to other features of the relationship between interviewer and interviewee and the positioning strategies brought into play in the interview setting. In some cases there are fundamental interviewer characteristics which have an unavoidable effect on the interview. For instance, children become accustomed to certain forms of questioning in school. Often questioning is used by teachers to test children's understanding or knowledge. The relationship between the child and the teacher is such that the child might make every effort to say what they think the teacher wants to hear. Any adults asking children questions can thus find themselves engaged in this kind of interaction.

Gender and social class relations will also affect the form an interview takes. An interview with a middle class man about childrearing practices might be viewed somewhat differently by working class as compared with middle class young mothers. Sometimes social distance can be useful in a research setting (for instance, talking to an obvious outsider might encourage interviewees to be more explicitly about their practices), in other cases it might prove inhibiting. In some circumstances, through deliberate control of the form of introduction, dress and manner, these effects can be manipulated or moderated; in others this is not possible and may not be desirable.

The brief discussion above illustrates the importance of thinking the interview through from the point of initial contact with the interviewee. The **management** of the interview itself requires equally close attention. Thought needs to be given to how the interview begins. What form of preamble do you need to place the interview in context? Do you need to provide reassurance that what is said will be treated as confidential and reported anonymously? Do you need to gain consent for the interview to be audio tape recorded? The initial stages of an interview are particularly important in helping the interviewee to feel at ease, so the preamble should cover the necessary ground but not be too formal; a short 'warm-up' period is generally advisable. Similarly at the end of an interview there is a need for a 'cool-down' period and closing section in which the end of the interview is clearly marked. Here the interviewee can be thanked and clarification given regarding what will be done with the information gathered.

At the beginning of the main body of the interview it is essential to provide the interviewee with initial stimuli — questions or activities — with which they can easily engage. As a rule it helps to move from the **particular** to the **general** as interviewees often find abstract questions difficult to address, particularly if they concern issues to which they have given little or no prior thought. Brown (forthcoming) showed parents examples of mathematical activities that they had previously carried out with their children. The initial questions asked for an account of what the interviewee had done with the activities. Later questions moved on to consider, in a more analytic fashion, what they thought the activities achieved and what they thought each activity was designed to teach. Following on from this the interviewee's criteria for the evaluation of school mathematics tasks were explored. To move directly from the preamble to abstract questions concerning criteria would not have been fruitful. Questions drawing on the direct experience of the interviewees and calling for a narrative response acted as a way in to detailed discussion of more general concerns.

Questions of a personal or sensitive nature, which the interviewee might feel awkward about answering, are also best left until later in the interview. Just what constitutes a potentially sensitive question is itself not always easy to judge and will vary between interviewees. As a general rule, it is better to be safe rather than sorry and leave all questions soliciting personal information (other than identification details) until the latter part of the interview. At this point there will be greater rapport between interviewer and interviewee. Furthermore, if the interviewee is reluctant to address a particular question, all is not lost as the main part of the interview will have been completed.

The form that questions take will vary according the type of interview. The interviewer needs to be clear about the extent to which it is important to ask the same questions in the same order, that is, to standardize the interview process. They also need to consider what **prompts** they will give if interviewees have difficulty in answering questions and decide how far they are willing to probe and what form their **probes** will take. As with the design of questionnaires, interviews should avoid double-barrelled, long and complex questions, questions involving technical or esoteric language, leading questions and loaded questions. In the interview itself the interviewer needs to show that they are engaged and interested, deliver questions in a clear and straightforward fashion and avoid providing cues. No matter how many interviews you have carried out or how much the interview process has become routinized, it is important to be seen to enjoy and value the interview and to listen attentively to what the interviewee says.

The points raised above provide very basic advice on the design and conduct of interviews. The researcher should have a high degree of control over the interview and it is important that sufficient thought goes into the design and realization. As with other means of data collection it is vital to carry out a number of pilot interviews and to refine the interview on the basis of this work. It is also important to practice interviewing as there are distinct interviewing skills which do not come naturally to everyone. Recording yourself and listening back through the tapes will help you to develop your interviewing technique. At the end of practice and **pilot** interviews you can ask the interviewee to reflect on the experience of being interviewed. This provides invaluable feedback and will help develop both the interview schedule you are working on and your own expertise as an interviewer.

The conduct of the interviews is, of course, just a start. Unless the responses are recorded using pre-coded categories, it will be necessary to **transcribe** the interviews. We suggest that, unless the number of interviews is prohibitive or you are working in a language in which you are not fully fluent, you should transcribe the interviews yourself. This fosters greater familiarity with the interview text and enables you to note the subtler nuances of the interaction. You will need to adopt a set of transcription conventions (see, for instance, those used by Silverman, 1993, p. 118). It is important to ensure that the level of detail of the transcription matches the use to be made of the transcripts. In some forms of analysis, such as **conversational analysis**, it is important to have a record of the duration of hesitations between utterances (usually measured in tenths of a second), but for most forms of analysis such detailed transcription is not necessary.

The production of accurate transcripts from **audio recordings** is, in any case, a lengthy process. It certainly helps if the source tapes are of a good quality. We recommend that you use good quality microphones, preferably lapel microphones for one-to-one interviews. Avoid the use of integral micro-phones which pick up a lot of noise from the motor of the tape machine. The use of a stereo rather than a mono recorder can also greatly enhance the clarity of your recording. With high quality source tapes and good typing skills, each hour of tape will take at least three hours to transcribe. With poor quality recordings and/or complex settings, such as a group interview, tran-scription can take a good deal longer.

Gathering Information and Asking Questions: Conclusion

In this chapter we have discussed a range of approaches to the use of accounts as a source of data. These accounts might be the product of a dir-ect encounter between the researcher and the subject in a setting specific-ally designed for the purpose (e.g. the clinical interview). In contrast the accounts might be the incidental products of everyday activity (e.g. policy documents produced within a school). As with the approaches to observa-tion discussed in the previous chapter, there might also be variation in the extent to which the method of data collection structures the data at a very early stage. The most marked contrast here is between the use of a self-completed postal questionnaire on one hand and the open-ended, appar-ently unstructured interview on the other.

In considering these contrasting forms of data collection we have attempted to evaluate the strengths and weaknesses of each and to make some practical suggestions regarding their use. We have taken care to avoid the promotion of one form of data collection over and above any other. This does not mean that we see the selection of methods of data collection in purely pragmatic terms. Whilst we have refrained from engaging in the form of epistemological positioning that would ultimately lead us to argue the essential superiority of a particular method, we have conducted our discus-sion within an overall approach that stresses the need to articulate the design of the empirical component of the research with the theoretical framework within which the research is conducted. To do this the researcher must be clear about the form of data they require and the logic of the various forms of data collection available to them.

The possibility of in-depth discussion and extensive probing that is offered by the clinical interview makes this approach particularly apposite for the exploration of types of human reasoning. The precise form of the interview and the manner in which the utterances and actions of the inter-viewee are interpreted are related to the theoretical perspective adopted by the researcher. There are, for instance, distinct differences in the form of clinical interviews carried out by Piaget and colleagues and those conducted by Luria (from a broadly Vygotskian perspective). There are even more marked differences in the manner in which the utterances and actions of the interviewees are interpreted.

A highly structured questionnaire would not be appropriate in these circumstances. A questionnaire simplifies the gathering of information from a large sample. Once the empirical data requirements pass beyond the informational, however, the limitations of questionnaires become clear. The questions by necessity have to be viewed as stimuli, held constant across the sample. The recipient of the questionnaire becomes a respondent, reading the question and marking their response. On collecting together the responses, the researcher can ascertain that when asked a given question a specific proportion of certain kinds of people responded in a particular way. For example, the statement might be made 'in our survey, 75 per cent of cat owners said that their cat preferred Tiddles cat food to any other brand'. Exactly what this might mean is, again, dependent upon the researcher's theoretical framework: what is it that enables cat owners to stand as key informants in respect of their pets' preferences, or is it, in fact, these preferences that are actually being measured? If not, just what are the concept variables that are being addressed via the survey? Ultimately, the selection of a particular technique and its realization in the empirical setting are the result of an interaction between the possibilities offered (and denied) by a particular form of data collection and the theoretical framework within which the research is conceived.

When dealing with accounts, the researcher has to be particularly clear about the **status** accorded to the accounts they are analysing. The survey of cat owners, for instance, does not tell us that Tiddles is the best tasting cat food nor that cats particularly like it. The human respondents are not in a position to judge this. They are only able to respond to questions that lie within the scope of their knowledge and experience. In a clinical interview, the responses of the interviewee are probed and tested by the interviewer and their utterances are interpreted as indicators of the operation of underlying cognitive processes. In an unstructured interview conducted from an interpretivist view point it is not the response of the interviewee to a given stimulus (e.g. a question) that is of interest but the manner in which this is interpreted by the interviewee. The interview is an investigation of the way in which the interviewee constructs meanings. In all these cases different status is accorded to what people say (and how they say it).

Whatever the status given to what is said and done by an interviewee or respondent there must be a clear distinction between the interviewee/respondent as the source of data and the researcher as the analyst of the data. In conducting a study you are not asking your interviewees to provide explanations, unless, of course, you are studying their explanations — in which case it is these that you have to analyse. Nor are you asking them to validate your analysis. The analysis is the responsibility of the researcher and in many cases may be at odds with the way in which the interviewee/respondent views their own behaviour. It is to the process of analysis that we now turn in Chapters 6 and 7.

References

BROWN, A.J. (1993) 'Participation, dialogue and the reproduction of social inequalities', in MERTTENS, R. and VASS, J. (eds) *Partnerships in Maths: Parents and Schools*, London: Falmer Press.

BROWN, A.J. (1994) 'Exploring dialogue between teachers and parents: A sociological analysis of IMPACT diaries', presented at Research into Social Perspectives on Mathematics Education, Kings' College, University of London.

BROWN, A.J. (forthcoming) *Parental Participation, Positioning and Pedagogy: A Sociological Study of the IMPACT Primary School Mathematics Project.*

BROWN, A.J. and DOWLING, P.C. (1993) 'The bearing of school mathematics on domestic space', in MERTTENS, R., MAYERS, D., BROWN, A.J. and VASS, J. (eds) *Ruling the Margins: Problematising Parental Involvement*, London: University of North London Press, pp. 39–52.

DONALDSON, M. (1978) *Children's Minds*, Glasgow: Fontana/Collins.

KELLY, G.A. (1969) *Clinical Psychology and Personality: The Selected Papers of George Kelly*, edited by B.A. Maher, New York: John Wiley.

LIKERT, R. (1932) 'A technique for the measurement of attitudes', *Archives of Psychology*, no. 140.

LURIA, A.R. (1976) *Cognitive Development: Its Cultural and Social Foundations*, Cambridge: Harvard University Press.

MERTTENS, R. and VASS, J. (1990) *Sharing Maths Cultures*, London: Falmer Press.

MERTTENS, R. and VASS, J. (eds) (1993) *Partnerships in Maths: Parents and Schools*, London: Falmer Press.

OPPENHEIM, A.N. (1992) *Questionnaire Design, Interviewing and Attitude Measurement*, (new edition), London: Pinter.

PIAGET, J. (1953) *The Child's Conception of Number*, New York: Humanities Press.

ROBSON, C. (1993) *Real World Research: A Resource for Social Scientists and Practitioner-Researchers*, Oxford: Blackwell.

SILVERMAN, D. (1993) *Interpreting Qualitative Data: Methods for Analysing Talk, Text and Interaction*, London: Sage.

6   Quality in Analysis

Introduction: From Information to Data

In this chapter and the one which follows we are going to deal with the stage of the research process which is very often attended by the greatest anxiety on the part of the beginning and the more experienced researcher. Unfortunately, it is also one of the two stages which are least likely to be made explicit either in research reports or in the research methods literature.[1] This is the stage at which the information which has been gathered is transformed into data via the process of analysis. The distinction that we are making, here, between **information** and **data** is crucial.

Essentially, data is information which has been read in terms of a theoretical framework or in terms of an analytic structure of some other kind. The use of a computer database provides a good illustration. Many of us will be in possession of diverse items of information about our family, friends, colleagues, various services which we use more or less frequently, etc. These will be in various forms, including, perhaps, entries in an address book, visiting cards, letters and postcards, scraps of paper and post-it notes, telephone directories, fading scribbles on the backs of our hands, and so on. Each of these items will have an individual form that is to a greater or lesser extent unique and specific to the particular context in which it was generated. However, suppose that we now decide to incorporate all of these items of information into a contacts list on a computer. The contacts list is a form of database that is designed to enable us to perform a number of tasks. For example, it may enable us to search our list under various headings, it may print address labels, allow us to make phone calls directly from the computer, enable the automatic importing and exporting of entries etc. In order for these functions to work in respect of each entry in the list, the entries must comply to a common format. The names, addresses and phone numbers must be entered in specific forms, we will be required to specify categories and, perhaps, keywords for each entry, and so forth.

When we have completed the contacts list, each item of localized information will have been transformed into a datum within a general structure. We will have lost something of the context specificity of the entries, but we will have gained a powerful tool. Powerful because of the generalizability of the database in retrieving and organizing its contents. This is, minimally, what theory does.

The power of our database will depend upon a number of things. Firstly, it should be as internally explicit and coherent as possible, so that its various categories are clear in terms of the ways in which they relate to each other. What, for example, is the distinction between the first and second lines of the home address in terms of the ways in which the database will make use of them? Secondly, it should be as relationally complete as possible. The various functions of the database cannot make full use of its contents unless they cover all of the various fields. Thirdly — and this is the central issue for the purposes of these two chapters — the information must have been entered in a way which is consistent with the operational intentions of the database. Clearly, there is a considerable amount of flexibility in terms of the entering of data. The database may not allow us to enter 'text' in a 'date' field, but it will not prevent us from entering a telephone number as the 'city' or in categorizing our grandmother as a plumber.

Similar criteria can be established for the evaluation of the analytic stage of the research process. Some form of theory is absolutely essential. There must be some structure that generalizes our local observations. The power of our analysis will then depend upon three criteria:

- the internal explicitness and coherence of the theory;
- the relational completeness of the theory;
- the integrity of the concept-indicator links.

The last criterion refers to the extent to which information is being read accurately and consistently, that is, to the validity and the reliability of the data, respectively.

Qualitative and Quantitative Data

Information can be transformed into data in many different ways. A distinction is often made in terms of whether or not the information is counted, that is, whether the analysis is made in **quantitative** or **qualitative** terms. For example, we could precode the addresses of our contact list database as London postal districts. The address for each record for a London address would be entered simply as a mark (say a '1') against the relevant district. This would enable us to plot out the distribution of our contacts in the London area as a chart and to investigate possible patterns in terms of the other precoded categories of our database (do the plumbers that we know tend to live in South London?). It would not, of course, enable us to print out the envelopes for our Christmas cards.

Unfortunately, in our view, a great deal of educational research has tended to be polarized as either quantitative or qualitative in approach. Indeed, many of the available books on research methods announce themselves, usually in their titles, as being concerned exclusively with one or the other. As with so many of the distinctions which are made in this area, the basis for the qualitative/quantitative polarization is frequently argued in terms of traditional **epistemological** divisions. Qualitative approaches are often associated with research which is carried out in an interpretative frame in which the concern is with the production of meaning. Quantitative methods are, correspondingly, associated with positivist forms of enquiry which are concerned with the search for facts. In turn, these forms have become polarized in politically motivated debate which has associated interpretivism with the so-called 'softer' social sciences and positivism with the 'hard' and more fundable natural sciences. This latter distinction was brought to the foreground by the insistence by the Conservative Secretary of State for Education and Science, Sir Keith Joseph, on the Social Science Research Council (SSRC) changing its name so as to eliminate the word 'science'; it became the Economic and Social Research Council (ESRC).

There are, in other words traditional and political motives for maintaining the qualitative/quantitative distinction. There are also reasons which relate to the training of educational and social science researchers. Specifically, a high degree of mathematical competence is not universally required or provided by university courses. This being the case, we are unlikely to be able to subvert the division by our argument in this book. In any case, we do see some value in sustaining the distinction for analytic and for pedagogic purposes, provided that we can resist any temptation to allow it to harden into a binary choice: either qualitative or quantitative, but not both.

As we shall argue in Chapter 8, empirical research is fundamentally concerned with the **generalizing** of local findings to wider ranges of empirical settings. The distinction between qualitative and quantitative approaches is, in our opinion, best described in terms of the different sets of resources that are deployed in establishing such generalizations. Quantitative approaches rely on **probability** theory. We cannot give an elaboration of this highly technical field in this book. Essentially, though, it construes the world as ultimately describable in terms of equally likely events. To take a simple example, the numbers 1 to 6 may be taken to represent, exhaustively, the six equally likely outcomes when you throw an ordinary die. Of course, the notion that these six outcomes are equally likely is built into the way in which we use dice in games or for gambling. The existence of such a close association between the elements of probability theory, on the one hand, and the structures of social practices more generally, or even those of natural phenomena, on the other, is far less obvious. In their recruitment of probability theory, then, quantitative research methods impose a particular theoretical framework, a particular **bias**, upon the world.

The considerable advantage of quantitative analysis, however, lies in the very high degree of coherence of this theoretical framework. This coherence enables issues of **reliability** and of generalization to be addressed with a high degree of consistency and, for those who are prepared to become familiar with statistical language, with a high degree of transparency. Paradoxically, the disadvantages of quantitative methods lie in precisely the same place. The coherence and **self-referentiality** of statistical knowledge also entails that it is relatively immutable with respect to local empirical settings and educationally specialized theoretical problems. In this respect, it might be argued with some justification that what quantitative methods gain in **reliability**, they lose in respect of **validity**. Statisticians, of course, will reply that they can measure validity. But, again, they can achieve this only by imposing the same probabilistic framework.

Qualitative approaches do not impose probability theory nor even, necessarily, the natural number system on their settings. They thereby lose both the power and the rigidity of quantitative methods. The researcher employing qualitative techniques is relieved of the requirement to specify their coding principles sufficiently uniformly to enable their data to be counted. But if it cannot be counted, then it must be represented in some other way. In general, accounts must include extracts from texts or transcripts, summaries of fieldnotes and so on. The researcher is then able to present an argument which establishes the validity of their interpretations, that is, they present an **elaborated description**. This process both develops and makes visible the operationalization of the theoretical problem, elaborating its validity. In our own experience, it is also an invaluable stage in the development of the theory itself. It is, however, immensely expensive in terms of both time and, in an account, space. A new description must be produced for each element of the data that is to be represented. Alternatively, an argument must be made — again in terms of elaborated description — as to the representative value of each data element that is presented as an example.

Unfortunately, there is a tendency for some researchers employing each of these approaches to hide behind the method and ignore the crucial area of theoretical development. The naive use of quantitative methods imagines that statistical techniques themselves will guarantee the value of the work. Correspondingly naive qualitative research tends to substitute narrative for analysis. On the other hand, the adoption of a dual approach involving both qualitative and quantitative techniques can help in overcoming such tendencies to what we might refer to as naive empiricism. The qualitative imagination will tend to demand that quantitative analysis explains itself in terms of the non-statistical concepts that it is claiming to measure. The quantitative imagination will demand a degree of precision in definition that qualitative work may slide away from. It is our position, then, that the best option will always be for a **dialogical** use of a combination of qualitative and quantitative methods.

For pedagogic reasons, however, we will continue to maintain a general distinction between the approaches. In the remainder of this chapter we will focus on qualitative methods of analysis. We will move on to quantitative techniques in Chapter 7.

We will add one caveat. There are, in our opinion, two very good reasons why research writing and, in particular, writing about research methods is comparatively silent on the process of data analysis. Firstly, the process is always intimately bound up with the very specific nature of the research problem and the local characteristics of the empirical setting and the information which has been gathered. This means that an adequate description of the analytic process must involve a considerable amount of contextual information. Secondly, in describing analysis, one is, in a sense, attempting to get at one's own thought processes. This is a project which is itself worthy of research. Writing about analysis is, in other words, difficult. You should be warned, then, that this may not be an easy chapter to read. Our intention is that your coming to grips with some of the analyses that we present will itself contribute to your apprenticeship as a researcher.

Reading the Signs: Semiotic Analysis and the Location of the Problem

We shall begin with an example of a **qualitative** analysis of a text — in this case an image. There has been an expanding interest in the analysis of texts in educational research over the past ten or fifteen years (see Dowling, 1998). In fact, however, we are using this example as an introduction to and illustration of approaches to qualitative analysis more generally. In particular, the analysis and the subsequent discussion illustrate the importance of defining adequately both the empirical setting to which the data relates and the theoretical problem which enables the researcher to think about the setting. Specifically, we shall indicate the importance of aligning the theoretical problem with the motivation for the research. The general methodological basis of the analysis in this section lies within the field of **semiotics** which, itself, is associated with structural linguistics and with the very broad theoretical fields of structuralism (which includes Piaget and is more loosely associated with Vygotsky and Luria), poststructuralism and postmodernist writing. These fields have been immensely influential in educational research and are becoming more so. Our example, then, also provides something of an overture to this substantial body of work.

The analysis which follows was originally conducted by Dowling as a part of a conference workshop which he ran on the analysis of **texts** (Dowling, 1995). Its object text is the photograph in *Figure 6.1*. This is the information that the analysis is to transform into data. The form of analysis that is being conducted, here, is, in general terms, referred to as semiotic analysis. We shall say a little more about this below.

Figure 6.1: 'Gun Law' (Photograph by John Gaps)

The text shows an American soldier suppressing a Haitian. The soldier is a very powerful man, rendered almost monumental by the camera angle. He is armed with a fearsome weapon which he is prepared to fire — his finger clearly rests on the trigger. The soldier is vigilant, on the watch for further trouble. Yet this is a benevolent soldier. Although he holds a deadly weapon, it is pointed downwards and not at anyone. He holds the Haitian down with his knee — a minimum amount of force.

The Haitian contrasts starkly with the soldier. He appears physically small — a feature exaggerated by the foreshortening effect of the camera angle. He is weak and easily suppressed by the soldier who does not need to use his gun. A stick lies on the ground. This might have been a weapon dropped by the Haitian as the soldier pinned him down; a primitive weapon for primitive people. There are two groups of Haitians in the background. One group, on the left, seems to be engaging in a brawl. The members of the other group, in the top right, appear indifferent to the action. Behind the soldier, lies a pile of rubble. Behind him and to his left, a media sound recordist is recording the action for the news.

Clearly, some interpretation has already taken place in this description of the text. The stick might not, after all, be a weapon, for example. This interpretation has been guided by an orientation to another level of description that we want to make, that is, of what we shall term the 'mythical' figures constituted by the image. The USA — represented by the soldier — is constituted as a powerful, but benevolent state. This state takes on an altruistic responsibility for other, less developed nations, protecting primitive societies from self-destruction. Haiti is represented as precisely such a society, characterized by criminality, apathy, and low-level technology; and already lying in ruins. The press, represented by the sound-recordist and by the photographer (in the place of the observer), is shown as a neutral organ, telling it like it is.

Now the question that must be asked is, does it matter where the photograph appears? If it appears on the cover of *Time* magazine, then we may well feel that the above reading is appropriate. Suppose, however, that it appears on the cover of *Living Marxism*. In this case we would probably reject the celebration of America and the disparaging of the Third World state. Rather, we would probably interpret the text as ironic: this is how America thinks of itself and of its neighbours and this is precisely the problem in contemporary global politics. After all, the gaze of the soldier resembles nothing so much as the optimistic gazes of the blond youths in so many Nazi images. In fact, the text is taken from the front page of *The Guardian*, a UK newspaper with a broadly centre-left editorial orientation. Here, perhaps, the text signifies the journal's own neutrality in the play between the literal and ironic readings of the photograph.

So now we have three readings of the text: a literal reading; an ironic reading; and a neutral reading. Which is the correct one, or is there another? Clearly, the choice depends upon the adequate definition of the empirical setting. In this case, this entails, minimally, naming the publication in which the image appears. However, the situation is more complex that that. In fact, each analysis violates the condition that the theoretical framework which enables it should be explicit. One or more of the analyses may appear plausible, but this is because they implicitly address interpretive frameworks that the reader already possesses. They make assumptions about the reader or, in other words, they construct an **ideal** or **model reader**. This being the case, they cannot tell us very much that we didn't already know, either about this particular image, about global politics, or about the news media.

Another example may help. Roland Barthes' *Mythologies* (1972) has been very influential in semiotic forms of analysis. Semiotics is an expression introduced by the linguist, Ferdinand de Saussure to refer to the study of signs. A **sign**, Saussure suggested, is constituted by a **signifier** and a **signified**. The former term refers to an acoustic or visual memory of a word, spoken or written; the latter refers to the concept to which the signifier attaches. Thus, the image of the word 'cat' attaches to a concept of a furry, domestic quadruped that catches mice. In *Mythologies* Barthes famously introduced another soldier. In this case, the text appeared as the front cover of an issue of the French popular journal, *Paris Match*. The illustration on the cover showed a young black soldier in the uniform of the French army. The soldier was saluting, his eyes raised, as if gazing on the tricolour. Barthes argued that this sign becomes the signifier in a higher order of signification, thus:

> France is a great Empire, that all her sons without any colour discrimination, faithfully serve under her flag, and [...] there is no better answer to the detractors of an alleged colonialism than the zeal shown by this negro in serving his so-called oppressors. (Barthes, 1972; p. 116)

The new, higher order sign, Barthes referred to as **myth**. The cover illustration appeared around 1954, at the height of the Algerian uprising. Barthes approached the text from a politically left of centre position. His reading of the myth was clearly constituted within the context of his understanding of the political positioning of *Paris Match*, which is to say, of its construction of its ideal reader. In the absence of such knowledge, it is clearly possible to constitute alternative myths, for example:

> France is a major colonial power. This soldier, serving in the uniform of his oppressors illustrates the extent of the domination of Algerian culture by the French hegemony.

Or, again:

> France has not been content with educating the savages of Africa, it has risked the contamination of its own culture by allowing them to participate in it. This soldier represents the extent of this contamination of a white race by black primitives.

The particular interpretation which is made depends upon the ideological position that is occupied by the interpreter. Because this is always

Figure 6.2: *Barthes' analytic schema*

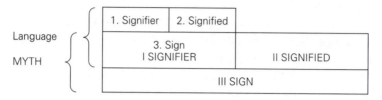

Source: Barthes, 1972, p. 115

implicit, it is no substitute for an explicit theoretical framework. Barthes' contribution, however, was less in the political specificity of his analyses — which, nevertheless, have considerable literary value — than in the general method that he was applying and which he summarized in a diagram which is reproduced in *Figure 6.2*.

Essentially, Barthes is extending the schema of the linguistic sign, as proposed by Saussure, to enable analysis to refer to broader cultural schemes. Language constitutes signs, but myth attaches higher order significations to these signs. The cover of *Paris Match* incorporates a number of signs which we can recognize because we participate in a common visual language. Thus, the image of the black soldier is understood to signify, precisely, a black soldier. Once the text is read within language, it is available for the higher order interpretation which is constituted by the level of interpretive frameworks which facilitated the analyses of both of the soldiers referred to here. This higher, mythical level of interpretation is dependent upon the 'linguistic' interpretation of the sign; if we don't recognize the image, then we won't be able to constitute the myth.

Barthes' interest is in how the text works culturally as well as strictly linguistically. The theoretical scheme is comprised of semiotic concepts — signifiers, signifieds, signs, language and myth. It provides a common framework for the analysis of potentially any text. But each analysis that we conduct will serve only to confirm that the analysed text can, indeed, be understood to be working according to Barthes' semiotic scheme. Each text is thus constituted as data in respect of a semiotic claim. There is, however, no way of choosing between the different ideological or mythical systems to which we refer the text. Each of the above analyses is, in this respect, equivalent. This is because Barthes' theoretical problem lies within the field of semiotics and not sociology or, say, political science. You may be interested in producing a semiotic grammar of the text. This would certainly be of value to an educator wishing to develop an educational programme in reading such texts. However, if you want to produce a sociological or a political analysis of the text, then your theoretical problem must comprise concepts which relate to these fields. Your theory must be concerned with what you are interested in, otherwise it is, like statistical methods, not a **theory** so much as a **technique**.

Biasing the Description

The discussion in the section above enables us to write a fourth criterion for the evaluation of the analytic stage of educational research to add to those which we introduced on page 81:

- the problem must relate directly to the system about which claims are to be made.

If you intend to constitute your information as psychological data, then your theoretical framework must employ psychological concepts. This, of course, entails that any text is susceptible to any number of analyses, depending upon the nature and specificity of the theoretical framework which we are employing. This is not to say, of course, that any analysis will do. Our position is that they must, at least, measure up adequately in terms of the other three criteria. Nevertheless, the text very definitely does not tell its own story. Rather, its description must be **biased** according to an explicit and coherent theoretical framework. Here, we are using the term 'bias' in a positive sense provided that it refers to an intentional and explicit structuring of the description.

Luria's work, that we described in Chapter 2, clearly performs well according to this fourth criteria (and, indeed, to the other three). To reprise, briefly, Luria proposed that societies which were limited to individualized production did not develop language to the extent that it could constitute independent systems. Rather, language in such societies was always used in such a way as to refer to direct experience. Since — as he further proposed — language provides the structure for thought, the thinking of individuals in such societies would be context-dependent, they would be characterized by 'participation'. More advanced societies which engaged in collaborative production developed language to a far greater extent so as to facilitate the production of relational or self-referential systems. The thinking of individuals in such societies would be taxonomic, which is to say, it would be governed by such relational systems as conceptual structures rather than by practical experience. This theoretical structure enabled Luria to predict that individuals of the simpler society would, when presented with questions relating to familiar or novel situations, always try to relate the questions to their own lives. Failure to make such a relation will result in failure to comprehend the task. Individuals of the more developed society would recognize the systematic structure of the questions and would be able to respond without such experiential references. Thus:

The following syllogism was presented: *White bears exist only where it is very cold and there is snow. Silk cocoons exist only where it is very hot. Are there places that have both white bears and cocoons?*

Subject: Kul., age twenty-six, peasant, almost illiterate.

> 'There is a country where there are white bears and white snow. Can there be such a thing? Can white silk grow there?' . . .

> 'Where there is white snow, white bears live. Where it is hot, there are cocoons. Is this right?' . . .

> 'Where there is white snow, there are white bears. Where it is hot, there are white silkworms. Can there be such a thing on earth?' . . . (Luria, 1972; p. 105)

Luria's theoretical structure and its operationalization enables him, firstly, to analyse this text in terms of the nature of the society in which the subject participates. The subject is a peasant and 'almost illiterate', which indicates that he has very little if any contact with more developed (in Luria's terms) forms of society. Secondly, Luria is able to categorize the subject's responses to the question as indicative of participative thinking. Referring to the sequence of transcripts in which the above is included:

> These examples show that syllogisms are not perceived by these subjects as unified logical systems. The subjects repeat different parts of the syllogisms as isolated, logically unrelated phrases. With some, the subjects grasp the interrogative form of the last sentence, which they then transfer to the formulation of both premises, which they have registered as two isolated questions. In other instances the question formulated in the syllogism is repeated regardless of the preceding premises; thus, the question is perceived as unrelated to the two interconnected premises. In all instances, when a subject repeated the premises he did not give them the character of universal assertions. Rather he converted each into a specific assertion logically unrelated to the other and unusable for drawing the appropriate logical conclusions. (*ibid*; p. 106)

Because Luria's theoretical structure concerns the relationship between the social, linguistic, and cognitive domains, he is able to make or confirm his assertions in respect of these domains. To return to the earlier analogy, the database of contacts can place telephone calls to individuals on the condition that its structure facilitates a direct relation between these domains and, further, that it relates the telephone data to a function which acts upon the telephone system.

Elaborating the Description

In the above extract from Luria's book we can see that he is **elaborating** an argument; he is providing some justification for his classification of these examples as instances of the lower level of thinking. This is a characteristic of qualitative forms of analysis. This is because there are generally limitations to the level of generalizability with which the principles of the analysis can be given. Luria's definition of participative thinking is, of course, given in terms of the other elements of his theoretical structure. His theory is, in this sense, **self-referential**. In fact, to use his own terms, it facilitates a particular formalization of taxonomic thinking. The practical problem of analysis involves the constitution and application of recognition principles whereby the theoretical concepts can be applied to information so as to constitute it as data.

This is comparatively easy with some of Luria's concepts. Thus, he presumably felt that there would be general agreement amongst his readership on a set of suitable indicators for the age and literacy status of his respondents. That is why these attributes are simply given and not elaborated. Also, the subjects have been selected on the basis of their participation in what Luria describes as comparatively simple or comparatively advanced societies. Having pre-coded his subjects in this way, he needs simply to record that Kul is a peasant.

Assigning Kul to a mode of cognition is a more complicated matter. This is because the originality of Luria's message lies precisely within this area of his theoretical structure. It is, of necessity, unfamiliar territory and so must be elaborated with worked examples of analysis. This process constitutes an apprenticing of the reader into the researcher's principles of recognition of his indicators. Ideally, it should enable the reader to reproduce Luria's own analysis with a high degree of reliability, which is to say that the reader's analysis should substantially coincide with the researcher's.

As is often the case, Luria presents his work in a form which suggests that his theoretical framework was substantially in place prior to his embarking on his field study. Because this framework rests heavily on the prior work of Lev Vygotsky, we may suppose that this was, in fact, the case. As we have indicated in Chapter 2, however, it is rarely the case that the beginning researcher can expect to begin their empirical work having already fully formulated their theoretical position. Indeed, to do so would be to minimize the impact of the empirical work on the study. Conceptual structure and data are, more commonly, generated together in a dialogue between the developing theoretical and empirical domains. An important strategy in this dialogue is to engage in precisely the kind of elaborated description that Luria offers.

Generating the Description: Network Analysis

The semiotic analyses presented at the start of this chapter were substantially tacitly biased insofar as they made claims within an untheorized space. Luria's analysis is biased by his well-developed theoretical problem. The real problem

Figure 6.3:   *Network for coding forms of evaluation reasoning*

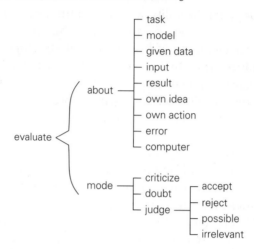

Source: Mellar *et al.*, 1994

of analysis, then, is how to move from the former to the latter situation. Decisions on the nature and specialization of the theoretical field, on the nature and localization of the empirical field and, crucially, on the articulation between them, are being made from the very start of the research process. These decisions begin to place a bias on the data long before you reach the stage of formal data analysis. In these and in subsequent analytic decisions your aim should be to make your principles as explicit as possible so that you can work towards the coherence that we are establishing as the fundamental criterion by which research is to be judged. We will try to illustrate this through a partial analysis of some diary data. The approach that we shall use in generating and refining analytic categories and structures is referred to as **network analysis** (see Bernstein, 1996).

Before looking at the diary data we shall describe what we mean by a network by reference to another study by Mellar and colleagues (Mellar *et al.*, 1994). This research sets out to explore school pupils' reasoning with computational modelling tools. The data analysed include interview transcripts and observation notes. Part of the analysis involves trying to identify the kind of reasoning used by pupils in particular contexts. To achieve this, five aspects of reasoning are identified: using knowledge; comprehension; planning or deciding; analysis; and evaluation. Networks are drawn up for each to enable a more delicate level of analysis to be carried out. The network for the evaluation component of reasoning is given in *Figure 6.3*.

The use of 'braces' (in this case, the connector defining the relationship between 'evaluate' to the left and 'about' and 'mode', to the right) in this kind of network signifies complementary subsystems of choices. Thus, the network in *Figure 6.3* entails that evaluative reasoning carried out by a pupil will be 'about' something *and* will be in a particular 'mode'. The other form of forked connective (e.g. connecting 'about', to the left and 'task', 'model', 'given data', and so on, to the right), signifies a mutually exclusive set of options. Thus, the evaluation may be about *either* a task, a model, given data and so on, but not more than one of these. The 'mode' of the evaluative reasoning will be *either* to criticize, doubt or judge. In 'judge' mode, the options are *either* to accept or reject or to judge something as being possible or as being irrelevant. Both forms of connective may be used at any level of the network, although in this case, the braces occur only at the first level.

The categories which are in braces constitute a logical set insofar as they can be taken to refer to what is evaluated and how it is evaluated. The categories at the second level of the network — 'task', 'model', 'given data', etc — seem to derive from the data, but it is not clear that they have been incorporated into the theoretical description of the problem. In other words, they represent untheorized aspects of the data. This is to be expected; your theory will never fully exhaust the description of your data. However, your intention should be to try to extend the theoretical description of the data in your development of the analysis. We shall try to illustrate what we mean by using some data from Brown's study.

Brown's data consists of written comments made by the parents of primary school children after they had worked at home with their children on some school mathematics tasks. These tasks, set by the school at either weekly or fortnightly intervals and carried out at home, were part of the IMPACT project, an initiative, now widespread, designed to foster greater involvement of parents in the mathematical education of their children. A key objective of IMPACT is to enable a dialogue to develop between parents and teachers by asking parents (and children) to comment on the tasks and to send these comments to the teacher. This is usually done in the form of an IMPACT **diary**, which provides, for each task, some boxes to be ticked and a space for a written comment. The IMPACT project provided Brown with 282 completed diaries (covering 1657 tasks) from four primary schools. These diaries were part of the on-going work of the schools and were not produced specifically for the purposes of research. Here is the entire text of two IMPACT diaries. They comprise the comments made by Charlene's and Jenny's parents to IMPACT tasks set by their teachers.

CHARLENE'S DIARY
1   Charlene finds it difficult to add with money.
2   Charlene found it difficult to understand but then she learn what was all about target.
3   Charlene had difficulty in counting over 100. Defining colours was easy.
4   It was just right.
5   Charlene found it interesting but easy.
6   Just right
7   Charlene found it a bit difficult and needed help.

JENNY'S DIARY

1 Jenny was aware of selecting items that were too expensive and replaced them without any guidance. PS please help her to write better than her Dad.

2 Jenny was not at all clear about what she had learnt. She thought it was about counting — how many smarties in a box etc. Presumably though this is part of Data Handling and probability?

3 We were not sure what to do — it was badly explained on the sheet. Once we sorted it out the game was good. We will spend more time on this later — Jenny is still not sure of 10s and units.

4 To follow the instructions and make 3 figure numbers we took the 10s out as well. This IMPACT must have been well explained in class as Jenny knew exactly what to do.

From initial inspection of these and the other diaries it was clear that some of the comments made by parents were lengthy and consisted of a range of observations about the child and the task, whereas others were very brief. Take the following example.

John enjoyed the activity. He coped well with the numbers under 20. The numbers over 20 we used Lego Bricks to help him work out the odds and the evens by making pairs. He needs a lot more practice at odds and evens.

Here information is relayed about the child's enjoyment of the task, how well the child was able to do part of the task, how the parent organized the task and about the parent's judgment of the child's competence in a particular area of school mathematics. This contrasts sharply with a comment that states bluntly that 'It was fun'. The task of analysis at this point is to be able to clearly identify and describe these differences in a principled manner. In the absence of a well defined theory, this involves working intensively through the diaries and developing descriptive categories. Producing a network is a useful way of organizing these categories.

In Brown's original analysis an initial distinction was made between comments that focus on the acquirer and those that focus on the task. These kinds of comments are then subdivided again to distinguish between acquirer focused comments that refer to the competence of the child (for instance, 'she was able to add the small numbers together') and those that refer to their dispositions (for example, 'John likes cutting and sticking activities'). The task-focused comments are divided into those which focus on the realization of the task (for example, 'we made a ruler from card') and those which focus on evaluation of the task (for instance, 'this was a good activity'). This gives four subsystems, differentiated in terms of the focus of the statement being described. This is illustrated in *Figure 6.4*.

In this case, subsequent levels of the network share the same structure. Firstly, a distinction is made between comments that are task-dependent, that

Figure 6.4: *Analytic network from Brown's data, 1*

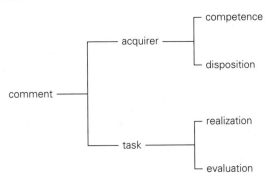

Figure 6.5: *Analytic network from Brown's data, 2*

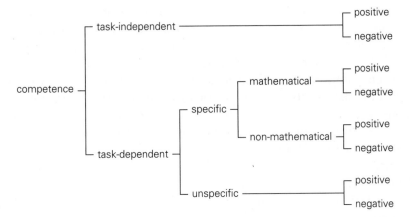

is comments that refer directly to the activity of doing the task (for example, 'she did some good colouring' or 'it was fun') and task-independent comments, that is those that pass beyond the context of the specific task and make more generalized statements (for instance, 'she knows her multiplication tables'). Task-dependent statements are then divided into those that are specific (i.e. make reference to a particular aspect of the task, its realization, the child's performance and so on) and those that are unspecific. Specific comments are further divided into those that make reference to school mathematics and those that do not. Finally, a distinction can be made between positive and negative comments. This generates the subordinate levels of the network which are shown in *Figure 6.5*. This diagram shows the continuation of the network from the upper track of *Figure 6.4*, that is, following the acquirer/competence route. The complete network is constructed by appending the additional levels shown in *Figure 6.5* to each of the terminal points of *Figure 6.4*.

At this point, you may notice that there is some resonance between some of the categories in the network and certain of the theoretical distinctions that we have been making in this book. In particular, the distinction between

Figure 6.6:   *Analytic network from Dowling's theory, 1*

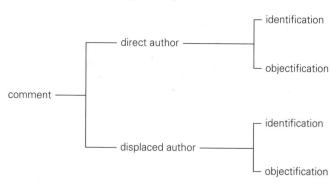

task-dependent and task-independent resonates with context-dependence/ independence. Clearly, Brown's organization of the empirical findings has been achieved with some sense of theoretical direction. However, it is quite apparent that the network is not fully theorized. It is not theoretically clear, for example, why a distinction should be made between acquirer and task or between competence and disposition. These categories are variables in respect of the data — they are indicator variables — but it is not clear, at this point, just what concept variables they are associated with. The development of this network is principally a process of **induction** from the information collected about the setting.

In order to develop the analysis further, we may move into the theoretical field. In this case, we can draw on a theoretical structure produced by Dowling (1995, 1998). We cannot present the theory fully here. Briefly (and with some necessary simplification and changes in terminology) Dowling proposes that all texts operate so as to establish or 'position' authorial and other 'voices'. In particular, the author of the text (e.g. the writer of the diary entry) may address the reader directly, or through another voice. In the diaries, the parent/author may describe the task that they and their child performed directly, or they may describe it in relation to, or through their child. These can be referred to as 'direct' and 'displaced' authors. In the latter case, the parent may make comments such as 'she is good at . . .' or 'she likes . . .'. In these examples, an attribute of the child is being 'identified' with the task.

Alternatively, the relationship between the child (or the parent) and the task may be described objectively, such as 'she/we put the numbers in rows . . .'. Note that 'we' is a first person pronoun and so serves as an indicator of a direct author. All of these categories have been or can be derived or **deduced** from Dowling's theoretical framework, although you will have to take this on trust, here (or refer to the source work). This analysis generates the network in *Figure 6.6.*

In our discussion of Luria's work, we have already made reference to the theoretical distinction between context-dependence and context-

Figure 6.7: Analytic network from Dowling's theory, 2

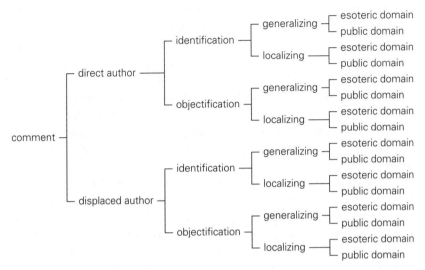

independence. Dowling makes a related distinction between localizing and generalizing. This distinction is given some elaboration in Chapter 7. Finally, Dowling establishes a distinction between specialized and non-specialized forms of text. These are referred to as 'esoteric domain' and 'public domain' respectively. This completes the theoretically generated network which is shown in *Figure 6.7.*

It is now possible to read the comments from Brown's data directly into locations on the theoretically generated network. Thus, 'she knows her multiplication tables' will be located on the branch signified by displaced author/identification/generalizing/esoteric domain. The new network, then, both describes the data and articulates it with a theoretically coherent problem. The data set as a whole can also be further analysed by mapping the distribution of comments of different categories of parents on the network.

There are two crucial points to be made. Firstly, the theoretically derived network has not, nor could it have been derived from the theory without any reference to the empirical data which it is to analyse. Thus the empirically induced network in *Figures 6.4* and *6.5* were necessary precursors to the further theoretical work.

Secondly, you may notice that the new network does not describe the data as completely as the empirically generated version. Specifically, it makes no distinction between comments relating to competence or disposition of the acquirer or between comments focusing on the task realization or evaluation. Further, it does not distinguish between positive and negative comments. There is, in other words, what Bernstein (1996) refers to as a **discursive gap** between the theoretical and empirical fields. Further analysis would seek to reduce this gap.

One approach might be to map the distribution of these different responses in terms of the different categories of parent (e.g. in terms of social class). In fact, Brown found that working class parents tended to make about the same number of dispositional comments about their children as they did competence comments, whereas middle class parents tended to make twice as many competence comments as dispositional comments. Further movement between these empirical findings and the theoretical problem might enable social class to be more fully incorporated into the theory so as to enable the network to describe the data more completely. Once the theory describes the data adequately, then you will have generated an **explanation**.

Data analysis, then, is properly conceived as a **dialogic** process which involves moving between the empirical and theoretical fields. The intention is, firstly, to produce as tight and coherent a definition of the problem and as extensive a description of the findings as is possible. Secondly, the articulation between problem and findings — that is, between concept variables and indicator variables — should be made as explicit as possible. It is only through this bringing together of the theoretical and empirical fields that the research is able to make more statements that extend in generality beyond its particular empirical setting. We shall return to the issue of generalizability in Chapter 8.

Managing the Analysis: Using Information Technology

Any form of detailed and systematic analysis of qualitative data will take a substantial amount of time. A significant proportion of this time can be spent organizing, annotating, coding, relating and recalling data. This requires a high level of organization and the development of effective systems for managing data and keeping track of one's analysis as it evolves. For the form of analysis described above, it is possible to mark codes for each segment of text on copies of the transcripts. Summary sheets of the results of the coding can be kept and a cross-referencing system developed. This enables one segment of data to be related to another. However, with a large amount of data this becomes cumbersome. Whilst there are no shortcuts in the process of data analysis, developments in **information technology** have produced a number of computer programs that can be of help. These range from familiar computer applications, such as word processors, databases and spreadsheets, through to programs specifically designed for the analysis of qualitative data. The following list, from Miles and Huberman (1994, p. 44), gives an indication of the wide range of ways in which computers can be of assistance in the process of conducting research and analysing qualitative data.

- Making notes in the field.
- Writing up or transcribing fieldnotes.
- Editing: correcting, extending or revising fieldnotes.
- Coding: attaching key words or tags to segments of text and making them available for inspection.
- Storage: keeping text in an organized database.
- Search and retrieval: locating relevant segments of text and making them available for inspection.
- Data 'linking': connecting relevant data segments and forming categories, clusters, or networks of information.
- Memoing: writing reflective commentaries on some aspect of the data as a basis for deeper analysis.
- Content analysis: counting frequencies, sequences, or locations of words and phrases.
- Data display: placing selected or reduced data in a condensed, organized format, such as a matrix or network, for inspection.
- Conclusion drawing and verification: aiding the analyst to interpret displayed data and to test or confirm findings.
- Theory building: developing systematic, conceptually coherent explanations of findings; testing hypotheses.
- Graphic mapping: creating diagrams that depict findings or theories.

It is clearly important for beginning researchers to consider carefully the ways in which a computer can be of help in their work. Certainly, the possibilities listed above will not all be relevant to every research project. Many of these tasks listed can be accomplished using readily available, non-specialist applications. A word processor, for example, can be used to make and edit notes, for transcription, to store and search data, to produce tables, and so on. A database can be used to set up a structure for the recording and storage of data, to enable links to be made between data segments and to facilitate the quick retrieval of data. A spreadsheet can be used in the numerical analysis of data and the production of graphical representations. A graphics or presentations program can be used to produce diagrams, networks and data displays. We have used all of these types of program in the production of this book. As a beginning researcher, you should explore what these programs offer and make use of them as and when appropriate.

Specialized qualitative analysis programs (such as the Ethnogaph, NUD.IST, HyperResearch and HyperSoft) are usually modelled on a particular view of the process of qualitative analysis. They all offer means by which text can be segmented and coded, and tools for the manipulation of codes and the recall of text. Used to manage information in this way, programs like these can speed up the process of coding and analysis. The range of facilities offered by the programs vary and it is important, if you are considering the use of a computer in your work, to be aware of the particular characteristics of each program (see the bibliography for sources of information). In many cases the researcher will not use all of the facilities which are offered. This will often be because the form of qualitative analysis they are employing differs from the model of qualitative analysis on which the program is modelled.

Brown, for example, used HyperResearch in his inductive analysis of IMPACT **diaries**. Each diary was transcribed and a word-processed text file created. Using HyperResearch, he coded segments from each diary. The program was then used to count how many times a particular code is used, to list all the diaries in which a specific code, or combination of codes, appears, to display all the segments of text that are given a particular code, and to produce summaries of the analysis at various points in the process. It was also used to add, change or delete codes as the analysis progressed. These facilities helped in the management of the process of analysis. The program also offers other facilities, such as hypothesis testing, that were not used because they had no part in the form of analysis being conducted.

Problems can arise where assumptions that have been built into the design of the software come into conflict with the research problem. For example, a doctoral student asked for assistance in using a text analysis program in her comparative study of linguistic structure in conventional (conversational and written) and computer mediated interactive texts. She had made use of a computer tagging service which 'tagged' her data texts so as to identify in linguistic terms each word in the text. So, she received back a text in which each word was labelled according to, for example, whether it was a noun, a verb, an adverb, and so on. She intended to use the text analysis program to identify instances of certain linguistic categories. Clearly, many words may be interpreted, contextually, as more than one part of speech. 'Play', for example, may be a verb or a noun. The tagging program made decisions on the basis of probability distributions which, themselves, had been derived from previous analyses of a large number of various kinds of text. It transpired, however, that no computer mediated texts had been included in this earlier work. The student was, therefore, proposing to compare computer mediated texts with other forms of texts using a device that had been constructed on the assumption that there was no such thing as a computer mediated text.

It is vital, then, that computers are seen purely as tools that can help researchers in their work. It is, after all, the researcher who carries out the analysis, not the computer. Sometimes beginning researchers select a particular analysis program believing that if they follow all the procedures listed in the manual, then the analysis will be done for them. It will not. The process of analysis cannot be codified, far less mechanized. As the case above suggests, much time and/or expense can be wasted putting data in the required form and working through it using a program only to discover that the form of analysis towards which you are being led is not appropriate.

In short, just because these programs are available, and offer certain facilities, it does not mean that you have to use them.

Qualitative Data Analysis: Conclusion

Quite clearly, there is a very limited extent to which it is possible to demonstrate the process of data analysis in a book like this one. Very often, the information that is to be processed as data constitutes a very substantial quantity of texts in a variety of forms. Ideally, perhaps, we might have incorporated such an extensive data set into the chapter and presented a narrative of our analytic activity. When we teach research methods courses, we try to proceed in this way by performing and getting our students to perform live analysis on visual and symbolic texts, video material, even the seminar room itself often ends up as data. We have tried to approximate to this by incorporating the deliberately incomplete network analysis of Brown's data. In the end, however, you will have to learn through your own engagement with your own empirical setting. Be warned, it will be a drawn-out and frustrating task. Unfortunately, if you are conscientious and produce a well-developed qualitative analysis, your presentation of it will, in all likelihood, completely conceal all of the angst that has gone into its production. Good analysis has the irritating tendency to look as if it was obvious all along. It wasn't, of course, and the fact that your reader is delighted with the simplicity of your conclusions certainly does not mean that they could have generated them with any lesser effort.

In the sections Introduction: From Information to Data and Biasing the Description, above, we introduced four criteria by which your development of your theoretical problem and its relationship to your findings should be judged. Here they are again, collected together:

- the internal explicitness and coherence of the theory;
- the relational completeness of the theory;
- the integrity of the concept-indicator links;
- the problem must relate directly to the system about which claims are to be made.

What we hope to have achieved in this chapter is to emphasize that qualitative data analysis of necessity entails a janusian attitude. Janus was the two-faced Roman god who looks both ways at a portal. You must be prepared to look both to the theoretical and empirical fields in your research. Assuming, however, that you have only a single face, your approach must be **dialogical**. You must have a good sense of your theoretical problem before you begin your data collection, let alone its analysis. But you are unlikely to have developed it fully (even if you think you have).

With your problem in mind, you will engage with your information set inductively, generating categories and organizing them, perhaps as a network of indicator variables, as we have illustrated. You will then cast your gaze into the theoretical field and do some developing of your concept variables perhaps, again, generating a network. The analysis then proceeds as a dialogical movement between the problem and findings, tightening up their respective structures and closing the discursive gap between them to generate the highest level of explicitness and coherence that is possible given the conditions under which you are working.

At some point you will have to stop and present your report. We will consider this stage of the process in Chapter 9. In the next chapter, however, we will move to a consideration of how quantifying your data may be of value to your research.

Note

1   The other stage being the writing-up, which is dealt with in Chapter 9.

References

BARTHES, R. (1972) *Mythologies*, London: Jonathan Cape.

BERNSTEIN, B.B. (1996) *Pedagogy, Symbolic Control and Identity: Theory, Research Critique*, London: Taylor & Francis.

DOWLING, P.C. (1995) 'A language for the sociological description of pedagogic texts with particular reference to the secondary school mathematics scheme *SMP 11–16*', *Collected Original Resources in Education*, **19**.

DOWLING, P.C. (1998) *The Sociology of Mathematics Education: Mathematical Myths/ Pedagogic Texts*, London: Falmer Press.

MELLAR, H., BLISS, J., BOOHAN, R., OGBORN, J. and TOMPSETT, C. (eds) (1994) *Learning with Artificial Worlds: Computer Based Modelling in the Curriculum*, London: Falmer Press.

MILES, M.B. and HUBERMAN, A.M. (1994) *Qualitative Data Analysis: An Expanded Sourcebook*, (2nd edition), London: Sage.

WOODS, P. and MERTTENS, R. (1994) 'Parents' and children's assessments of maths in the home' in MERTTENS, R. and WOODS, P. (eds) *IMPACT: Papers Presented at the Annual Meeting of the American Educational Research Association*, London: The IMPACT Project, University of North London.

7   Dealing with Quantity

This chapter is concerned with the production and presentation and analysis of data in **quantitative** form. It will include a discussion of the more common forms of data presentation as tables and charts. We will also be introducing the use of statistics in the analysis of quantitative data. We have included instructions for calculating several statistical measures. These may be helpful if your use of statistics is to be very limited and if your data is in a suitable form. In general, you would be better advised to make use of computer facilities, such as SPSS or a spreadsheet, for your statistical work. We have not introduced these facilities for two reasons. Firstly, it would have involved us in introducing the use of at least one computer software package, which would have extended the length of the chapter considerably. Secondly, as former teachers of mathematics, we believe that there is considerable value in running through the simpler computations to get some sense of how the mathematics is working, of what is going on inside the computer's head.

However, of more importance than these computational instructions are the descriptions of what these techniques do and of, when and how they can be used. These descriptions are also more easily understood when placed alongside the computations themselves. Often, in our experience, beginning researchers delegate their analysis to a sophisticated computer package or (perhaps even less appropriately) to a statistically competent colleague. The output is then presented without any discussion of the relevance or limitations of the tests which have been performed. The quantification and statistical analysis of data is potentially of immense value to all researchers. As with all methodological tools, however, they must be used with deliberation and reflection. Our intention is that this chapter will enable you to begin to make use of quantitative methods in this way in your own research and to ask appropriate questions of research produced by others. We also hope to provide you with an adequate basis to enable you to approach a statistical methods handbook with some confidence.

We have tried to present the instructions and descriptions so as to make them accessible to the non-mathematician. This has not, we have felt, ruled out the use of mathematical formulae where appropriate. However, we have given very little mathematical explanation of the formulae that appear in the text. If you wish to interrogate the mathematical rationales of the techniques, you will find suitable references in the bibliography.

Table 7.1: *Luria's summary for groups and method of classification*

Group	Number of subjects	Graphic method of grouping	Graphic and categorical methods of grouping	Categorical classification
Illiterate peasants from remote villages	26	21 (80%)	4 (16%)	1 (4%)
Collective-farm activists (barely literate)	10	0	3 (30%)	7 (70%)
Young people with one to two years' schooling	12	0	0	12 (100%)

Source: Luria, 1976; p. 78.

Quantifying Qualities

The presentation of results where a qualitative mode of analysis has been adopted generally employs elaborated description of one or more exemplary texts. Such **elaborated description** is an important strategy both in the development of theory and in the apprenticing of the reader of the research into the application of the theory in the construction of data out of information. However, it is often helpful to present an overview of the sample as a whole, particularly where the sample size exceeds that which can reasonably be presented in the form of elaborated description. *Table 7.1*, for example, is Luria's summary of the distribution of his subjects in respect of the classification tasks (described in Chapter 3).

The **table** is a **cross-tabulation** of the **frequencies** of the occurrence of the two variables, group and method of classifications. These indicators are both **ordinal scales**, which means that their values are ordered. Thus, the three values for 'group' shown in the first column of the table are given in an order which represents social and cultural development in terms of relations of production (individualized/collective) and level of literacy. The three values of 'method of classification' shown in the first row of the table are ordered according to the cognitive level which they indicate. 'Graphic method of grouping' is the lowest level and employs participation. 'Categorical classification' is the most advanced level and is taxonomic. 'Graphic and categorical methods of grouping' is an intermediate level. The relationship between the two variables is clearly represented by the structure of the table. That is, the non-zero entries in the main data columns (columns 3, 4 and 5) form an echelon. The inclusion of percentages in the table is important because the sample sizes within each group are different. Representing the figures as percentages as well as frequencies allows direct comparison.

In order to generate the table, Luria has had to quantify his data. However, although we now have numerical data — the figures in the table — there has really been no explicit change in the nature of the analysis. All that has happened is that the researcher has counted the number of subjects that he has already categorized in each way. The analysis itself remains qualitative in nature. The result of the counting, however, is a clearer picture of the overall distribution of the data. On the other hand, we have lost the specificities of individual responses. Furthermore, had the data been presented only in this way, we would have been unable to assess the **validity** or the **reliability** of Luria's coding of his subjects. There would have been no possibility of our apprenticing to the principles of his analysis. Clearly, Luria gets the best of both worlds by doing precisely as he has done, which is to provide both elaborated description and quantitative summaries of his data.

The elaborated description of qualitative analysis has advantages in respect of both the formulation of theory and the representation of the research. However, it tends to be very expensive in terms of time and space. Where the **problem** is sufficiently well defined, it is often possible to generate indicators for the concepts that can be described in simple terms and which are operationalizable to a high degree of reliability. Such a simplification of the analytic process can enable the coding and representation of a far greater amount of information than would be possible using elaborated description. We shall use, as an example, the analysis of a school mathematics textbook scheme by Dowling (1996, 1998). In discussing this example, we shall include some description of the process whereby an indicator variable is constituted in respect of a specific concept variable. You will recall that a **concept variable** is a theoretical object. An **indicator variable** is the empirical object which enables the recognition of the concept.

Dowling's research had involved a semiotic analysis of the scheme[1] which had employed elaborated description in the development of a theoretical framework. The theory included the definition of various categories of 'textual strategy' whereby a pedagogic **text** constructs its **ideal reader**. **Generalizing** and **localizing** constituted an opposing pair of strategies. The distinction between them is redolent of and was, to a certain extent, influenced by the distinction that Luria makes between taxonomic and participative thinking. For the present purposes, we can describe them in a way which more closely resembles Luria's distinction. Thus, generalizing strategies tend to constitute the text as relatively **self-referential** and so context-independent. Localizing strategies, on the other hand, tend to constitute the text as referring to something specific and concrete. It is this referent context that gives the text meaning, so that the text becomes context-dependent.

Dowling proposed that texts directed at 'high ability' students would be dominated by generalizing strategies, whilst those directed at 'low ability' students would be dominated by localizing strategies.[2] The **semiotic** analysis of the texts seemed to bear this out. However, the elaborated description did not allow coverage of a very substantial quantity of information. It was therefore decided to operationalize the strategies to enable a quantitative analysis of the texts. This kind of quantitative analysis of texts is often referred to as a **content analysis**.

Indicators were needed for the concepts, 'generalizing strategy' and 'localizing strategy'. These had to be described with sufficient precision to allow their occurrence in the books to be quantified. This was achieved by developing the additional concept variable, 'signifying mode'. Essentially, this refers to the way in which the text signifies. A visual image or 'icon', such as a realistic photograph or drawing, for example, signifies by physically identifying a viewpoint for the 'reader'. It constructs the page as a physical mapping of a specific physical location. Other forms of text, including symbolic, graphical and tabulated text, do not signify in this way. Written text may describe a concrete physical location. However, it does not achieve this by the physical reconstruction of the scene and by physically identifying the location of the viewpoint in relation to this reconstruction. It would seem, then, that icons more readily lend themselves to the purposes of localizing strategies by facilitating the more direct signification of specific contexts. Other modes of text are, by virtue of the way in which they signify, more readily incorporated into generalizing strategies.

This argument — which has been simplified for the present purpose — establishes a theoretical association between the two pairs of concept variables, that is, localizing and generalizing strategies, on the one hand, and iconic and non-iconic modes of signification, on the other. Iconic and non-iconic modes of signification, however, are comparatively easy to operationalize for the purposes of conducting a content analysis. We have to ask: 'does the text constitute the reader's physical position in relation to the page as a representation of the viewpoint in respect of the scene which it represents?' If the answer is 'yes', then the text, or section of text, is an icon, otherwise, it is not. 'Icon', defined in these terms, is an indicator for the concept 'iconic mode' and, by association, for 'localizing strategy'.

There remains a further decision to be made. Whilst it may be a comparatively simple matter to distinguish between icons and other textual elements[3], we have yet to determine how to quantify them. We may well be able to count the number of icons in a textbook. However, this would take no account of size. Furthermore, the study from which this example is taken required a comparative measure of a rather more complex structure of signifying modes than we shall be able to describe here. Clearly, alphanumeric text is rather more difficult to count in such a way as to enable a comparative measure to be made; is a picture worth a thousand words, or only one? It was decided, therefore, to quantify textual mode in terms of area. Operationally, a one-centimetre grid was laid over each sampled page. Each square was then coded according to the type of text that it contained and a distribution was constructed for each whole page. The **average** or **mean** page coverage by each type of text was calculated by dividing the total amount of each type by the number of pages sampled. These results, in terms of icons and other text are shown in *Table 7.2* for each of four books in the scheme.

Table 7.2: SMP 11–16: *mean signifying mode page coverage*
(total area of each page = 408 cm^2)

	Book G1 *n* = 40	Book G8 *n* = 40	Book Y1 *n* = 100	Book Y5 *n* = 100
Icon	116	77	39	13
Other	136	169	200	230

All figures given in cm^2.

Of the four books represented in *Table 7.2*, G1 is the first and G8 is the final book in the series targeted at 'lower ability' students. Correspondingly, Y1 and Y5 are, respectively, the first and final books in the series targeted at the 'higher ability' students. G1 and Y1 are intended for students of the same age cohort. From the table, you can see that the incidence of iconic mode of signification, indicated by the mean page coverage by icons, decreases substantially in the sequence, G1, G8, Y1, Y5. By virtue of the association which has been theoretically established between iconic mode and localizing strategies, it can be deduced that localizing strategies are employed in the G series to a greater extent than in the Y series. Further, the use of localizing strategies decreases between the first and final books in each series. Nevertheless, the incidence of icons in G8 is still approximately twice the level of that in Y1. The incidence of other types of text — indicating the level of use of generalizing strategies — also increases within each series. Again, however, the level in G8 remains substantially below that in Y1. The content analysis thus provides some support for Dowling's proposition that generalizing and localizing strategies are targeted at 'high ability' and 'low ability' students, respectively.

This study, like Luria's, started with a qualitative form of analysis, but also made use of quantification. Luria's use of counting did not alter the fundamentally qualitative nature of the analysis; it merely summarized it. Dowling, on the other hand, has moved from a qualitative to a quantitative mode by the use of an indicator which can be described in terms which enable it to be recognized with a high degree of reliability. Thus, a very substantial amount of information was made available to be transformed into the very small quantity of data represented by *Table 7.2*. Clearly, this kind of quantification entails a necessary loss of detail. However, as we suggested in Chapter 6, it is also quite likely to result in a certain loss in terms of the **validity** of the analysis. Another example from Dowling's study will illustrate this.

In the course of the content analysis an additional measure that was employed involved the counting of photographic icons. *Table 7.3* shows the number of photographs in each of the median, B series of books (targeted at 'average' students). 'Photograph' is a category of icon, which is, as we have said, an indicator for localizing strategies. The data in *Table 7.3* suggests that B4 employs localizing strategies to a far greater extent than the

Table 7.3: SMP 11–16: *number of photographs in the B series*

Book	Number of photographs
B1	0
B2	5
B3	4
B4	21
B5	6

other books in this series. Now it could be that the other B books incorporate more of the other categories of icon, 'drawing' and 'cartoon'. In fact, this is not the case. So why does B4 stand out in this way?

On studying the photographs in B4 it seems that eighteen of the twenty-one are incorporated into material which uses photographic enlargement as a metaphor for mathematical enlargement. Here, it is the photograph as photograph which is foregrounded, rather than the content of the photograph as the physical reconstruction of a scene. In other words, these photographs do not signify in quite the same way as is intended in the definition of 'iconic mode of signification'. This explanation quite clearly weakens the validity of 'icon' as an indicator for localizing strategies (although it does not invalidate it). However, because the specificity of the information text is lost in the quantification, this potential challenge is rendered invisible.

As we have represented it so far, quantification can enable the coverage of a larger amount of data than is generally possible using the elaborated description of qualitative analysis. It can also enable us to gain a clear overview of the data, whether or not qualitative analysis has also been employed. The quantification of data also constitutes it in a form which is accessible to mathematical manipulation. There are at least two reasons why you might want to manipulate the data mathematically.

- you may want to present your data in a mathematical table or chart;
- you may want to explore or interrogate your data statistically.

We will consider each of these forms of mathematical manipulation in turn.

Charting the Data

We will start this section with a warning against extravagance in the use of charts in your research. Modern computer software in the form of spreadsheets and presentation packages makes it a simple matter to generate an impressive range of charts and diagrams. A number of the beginning researchers with whom we have worked have been eager to take advantage of these **information technology** resources and have presented, in their draft reports, pages of colourful histograms and pie charts and line graphs. The fact that

Figure 7.1: SMP 11–16: *mean signifying mode page coverage*

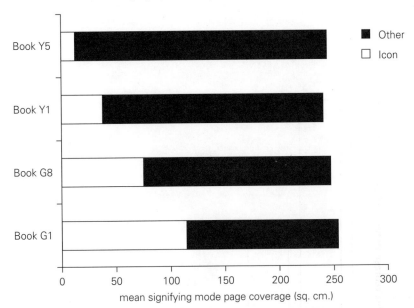

mean signifying mode page coverage (sq. cm.)

these presentational forms are possible, however, does not mean that they are always a good idea. The question that must be addressed is, how does the presentational form assist in making sense of the data. This question is relevant in the course of data analysis as well as in decisions relating to the final writing-up.

In our experience, a simple table is often the most expressive form for the written presentation of data. This is certainly the case with Luria's data in *Table 7.1*. This table provides access to the information in both absolute and percentage form and allows easy comparison between the cells. The structure of the results is clear because the two dimensions of the table show the scaling of the indicator variables. We could, of course, represent this data in a visually more imposing chart. However, it is likely that this would obfuscate rather than illuminate the results of the research. In our opinion, there need to be good reasons for representing data other than as a simple table. Where there are good reasons, then presenting information in diagrammatic form can be very useful. We will look at just two forms of **bar chart**.

When considering the data in *Table 7.2*, you will probably be making a number of comparisons. You will want to compare the two rows of data, also the G books and the Y books, and the first and last book in each series. It may be that a graphical representation of this data will make these comparisons easier. In this case, the iconic and other categories are exhaustive. If we discount the blank space, the page is made up of icons and other kinds of text. It may, then, be appropriate to use the kind of bar chart shown in *Figure 7.1*. The chart makes it very easy to obtain a fast visual comparison within each book and between books. Some of the precision

Figure 7.2: *Relative representation of each social class in home applicants accepted by universities through UCCA in 1991*

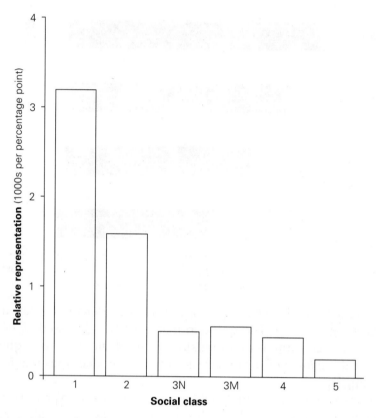

Source: Dowling (1998)

of the numerical data is lost, although this could be retrieved by labelling the chart more fully.

An alternative to the bar chart in *Figure 7.1* would have been to draw four **pie charts**, one for each book. However, we feel that a bar chart of the type that we have used always provides easier access to the data in comparison with pie charts. Our preference, then, is to avoid the use of pie charts.

Where the variable is of **ordinal** level of measurement, a different kind of bar chart may be often more appropriate, because this kind of diagram gives a sense of the shape of a distribution. *Figure 7.2* shows the social class representation of home applicants accepted by UK universities through the Universities Central Council on Admissions (UCCA) in 1991.

The categories for social class are those used by the Office of Population Censuses and Surveys (OPCS) in the analysis of census data up to and including the 1981 census. They are:

1   Professional, etc. occupations;
2   Intermediate occupations;

Figure 7.3: Social class profile of home candidates accepted by universities through UCCA in 1991

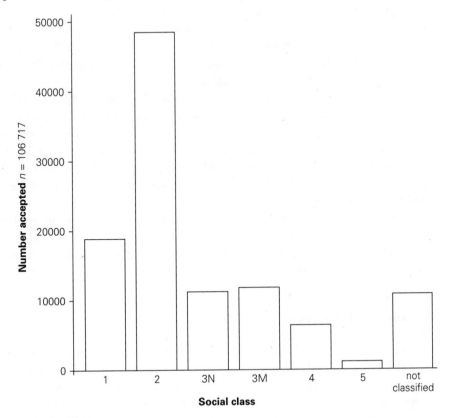

Source: Dowling (1998)

3   Skilled occupations
    (N) non-manual
    (M) manual
4   Partly skilled occupations;
5   Unskilled occupations
Source: OPCS, 1980

'Intermediate occupations' includes the 'junior' professions, teaching being an example. Of course, the assumption of ordinality in the variable 'social class' is open to challenge. After 1981, the OPCS abandoned the use of these categories in the analysis of census data.

The bar chart *Figure 7.2* shows the distribution of university acceptances in terms of social class in a very dramatic way. The particular choice of variable for the vertical axis is also important in this respect. It was obtained by dividing the number of acceptances in each social class by the percentage of the working population in that particular class. The picture is rather different if absolute numbers are used instead, as is the case in *Figure 7.3*.

The radical difference in visual impact of the two bar charts illustrates the crucial importance of labelling the axes as clearly as possible.

The charts in *Figures 7.1* and *7.2* are of clear value in representing the data in a report or as a part of a presentation. Whether or not they are of equal value in the analysis stage of the research process depends upon whether you find it easier to read a table or a diagram.

These charts were drawn using a presentation software package[4]. They could just as easily have been drawn using a spreadsheet or a modern wordprocessor. These programs offer a wide range of chart styles. In making a selection, you should not simply go for the one that you think looks the most impressive, but the one that most effectively displays the aspects of the data that you wish to highlight. In general, it is a good idea to try to keep your diagrams as simple as possible.

The second form of mathematical manipulation which may be applied to quantitative data is statistical analysis. In the next section, we shall give an introduction to some simple and commonly used statistical techniques and to the principles of their use.

Statistical Analysis

This is not a statistics textbook and we are not able to cover the range of **statistical** techniques which might be applied to quantitative data. We can, however, give an introduction to some simple, but widely used statistical measures and engage in some discussion of the circumstances under which they and related measures are appropriately used. We shall illustrate four statistics: the mean; the Mann-Whitney test; the chi square test; and Spearman's rho.

Try not to be put off by the terminology and symbols in these sections. We are not going to set you a test at the end of it. If you are not (yet) mathematically inclined, just try to follow the general lines of the arguments and, perhaps, gain some familiarity with some of the terms. This will help you when reading research which involves a statistical element. You can always come back to the chapter later or, indeed, move on to one of the more complete statistical manuals which we have referred to in our annotated bibliography.

The Mean and Frequency Distribution

Table 7.4 shows the number of alphanumeric symbols on each page of a random sample of twenty pages from each of two of the mathematics textbooks that were analysed by Dowling in the work cited earlier. Book G1 is the first book in the series targeted at 'lower ability' students; Book Y5 is the last book in the series targeted at the 'most able' students.

Table 7.4: *Number of alphanumeric symbols on each of a random sample of twenty pages of* SMP 11–16 Book G1 and Book Y5

Book G1	Book Y5
194	1121
306	941
744	562
531	1114
420	1129
377	1921
161	1037
424	958
503	1162
286	0
901	974
487	1336
557	850
498	586
486	513
574	985
586	701
658	792
285	585
718	390

Source: Dowling (1998)

From an inspection of the table it looks very much as if the pages in the G1 sample generally contain fewer symbols than those in the Y5 sample. Nevertheless, there is a certain amount of overlap. A measure for the **average** number of symobols per page in each sample can be obtained by finding the total number of symbols in each sample of twenty pages and sharing them out equally, that is, by dividing each total by twenty. This kind of average is called the **mean** (or **arithmetic mean** or **common average**). The mean of a set of measurements is calculated by dividing the total or sum of the measurements by the number of measurements. For the twenty pages in Book G1, the sum of the numbers of symbols is 9696, so the mean is calculated as follows:

$$\text{mean} = \frac{\text{sum of measurements}}{\text{number of measurements}} = \frac{9696}{20} = 484.8$$

Statisticians generally use the symbol $\bar{x}$ to represent the mean of the measurements (each called x), n to represent the number of measurements, and Σx to represent the sum of the measurements (Σ is the Greek character, sigma and represents 'sum of'). Symbolically, then, the mean of a set of measurements is represented by the following formula:

$$\bar{x} = \frac{\Sigma x}{n}$$

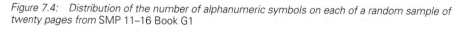

Figure 7.4: Distribution of the number of alphanumeric symbols on each of a random sample of twenty pages from SMP 11–16 Book G1

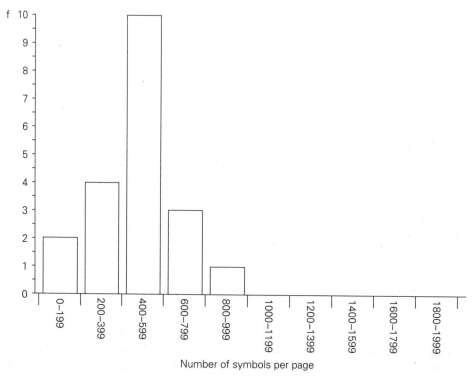

Number of symbols per page

If you perform this calculation on the data in *Table 7.4*, you will obtain 484.8 for the mean number of symbols per page in the G1 sample (as indicated above) and 882.85 for the Y5 sample. These figures seem to confirm the conclusion drawn from inspection that the G1 sample pages contain fewer symbols than those in the Y5 sample.

Although these means look very different, it is not absolutely certain that they indicate substantive differences between the two books. You would, in fact, be surprised if the means of two samples were identical, even if samples were drawn from very similar books or, indeed, even if the samples were drawn from the same book. You would expect the two sample means to be different purely on the basis of chance. The degree of difference will depend upon the mean number of symbols per page for each **population** from which a sample is drawn — in this case, for each book as a whole. It also depends upon the variation in the number of symbols per page within each population. Do most of the pages tend to have values close to the mean, or is there a wide spread of values?

It is clearer to see this in a diagram. We have grouped the data in *Table 7.4*, counting, for each sample, the number of pages having between 0 and 199 symbols, the number having between 200 and 399 symbols, and so on. The results are illustrated in *Figures 7.4* and *7.5*. The height of the first bar

Figure 7.5:   Distribution of the number of alphanumeric symbols on each of a random sample of twenty pages from SMP 11–16 Book Y5

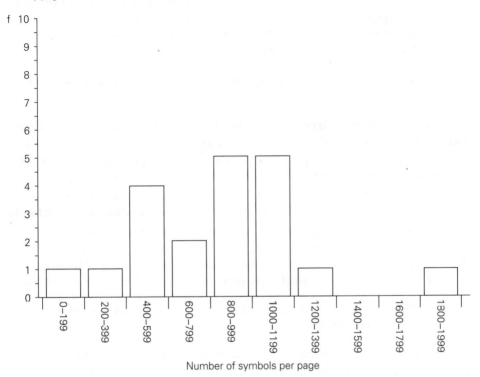

Number of symbols per page

in each chart shows the number of pages in the sample having between 0 and 199 symbols, the second bar shows the number having between 200 and 399 symbols, and so on. The number of occurrences in each group is called the **frequency**. *Figures 7.4* and *7.5* show the **frequency distribution** of symbols per page for each of the two samples. This kind of bar chart which represents a frequency distribution is commonly called a **histogram**.

Looking at the two histograms, it is clear that almost the whole of the distribution of the G1 sample is below the mean value for the Y5 sample. However, the G1 sample mean lies within the spread of values of the Y5 sample. How certain can you be, then, that the two samples come from populations which are substantively different? In order to measure this certainty, you may wish to conduct a statistical test of significance.

The Mann-Whitney Test

The argument which justifies the proposition about the two books runs as follows. For each book, a **random sample** was taken from the population which comprised all of the pages in the book. This means that every page in each book had an equal chance of being included in the sample for that book. The samples, then, are unbiased, and so can be claimed to represent the books. A difference was found in the mean number of symbols per page for each sample. Since the samples represent their respective populations, an **inference** is drawn to the effect that the difference in sample means is the result of a difference in population means. That is:

(i) Book Y5, as a whole, contains more symbols per page than Book G1 as a whole.

This is the **research hypothesis**. In this case, the hypothesis is **directional**. That is, it specifies which book has the greater number of symbols per page. This kind of hypothesis is called a **one-tailed hypothesis**. Had the hypothesis merely predicted that the number of symbols per page was greater in one book than in the other, but without specifying which was which, it would have been a **non-directional** or **two-tailed hypothesis**.

We indicated, above, that we are interested in using statistics to measure the degree of confidence with which we can propose this hypothesis. This is equivalent to a measure of the degree of confidence with which we can reject the opposite or **null hypothesis**. The null hypothesis states that:

(ii) There is no difference between Book Y5 and Book G1 in terms of the number of symbols per page.

Suppose, for the moment, that the null hypothesis is, in fact, true and that there is no difference between the books in terms of the number of symbols per page. The question that you now need to ask is, just how likely is it that you would draw two samples which are as different as the ones that you have. Or, to use the technical term, what is the **probability** of drawing the samples that you have if the null hypothesis is true? If it turns out that the probability is very low — say 0.05 (or 1 in 20) or less — then you could feel justified in rejecting the null hypothesis in favour of the research hypothesis. Fortunately, a measure of this probability can be obtained using a **test of significance**. We will conduct the **Mann-Whitney U test** for the figures in *Table 7.4* and then discuss its interpretation. Firstly, all forty measures from *Table 7.4* must be written down in order, smallest first and assigned **ranks**. The smallest measure is assigned rank 1, the second smallest rank 2, and so on. This has been done in *Table 7.5*. Notice that the twenty-first and twenty-second figures are the same, 586. They are each assigned the mean of these two ranks, that is:

$$\frac{21 + 22}{2} = 21.5$$

The ranks are then entered next to their respective measures in the original table (*Table 7.4*) and the two columns of ranks summed. This has been done in *Table 7.6*.

Table 7.5: *Mann-Whitney I: Assigning ranks*

Symbols	Rank(R)
0	1
161	2
194	3
285	4
286	5
306	6
377	7
390	8
420	9
424	10
486	11
487	12
498	13
503	14
513	15
531	16
557	17
562	18
574	19
585	20
586	21.5
586	21.5
658	23
701	24
718	25
744	26
792	27
850	28
901	29
941	30
958	31
974	32
985	33
1037	34
1114	35
1121	36
1129	37
1162	38
1336	39
1921	40

The Mann-Whitney statistic is called U. Two values are computed for U using each sum of ranks, respectively. The following formulae are used:

$$U_1 = N_{G1}N_{Y5} + \frac{N_{G1}(N_{G1} + 1)}{2} - \Sigma R_{G1}$$

$$U_2 = N_{G1}N_{Y5} + \frac{N_{Y5}(N_{Y5} + 1)}{2} - \Sigma R_{Y5}$$

N_{G1} and N_{Y5} are the sizes of the G1 and Y5 samples, respectively. In this case, they are both twenty, although the Mann-Whitney test works even where the two samples are of different sizes. ΣR_{G1} and ΣR_{Y5} are the sums of

Table 7.6: *Mann-Whitney II: ranks assigned to each sample*

G1	R_{G1}	Y5	R_{Y5}
194	3	1121	36
306	6	941	30
744	26	562	18
531	16	1114	35
420	9	1129	37
377	7	1921	40
161	2	1037	34
424	10	958	31
503	14	1162	38
286	5	0	1
901	29	974	32
487	12	1336	39
557	17	850	28
498	13	586	21.5
486	11	513	15
574	19	985	33
586	21.5	701	24
658	23	792	27
285	4	585	20
718	25	390	8
$\Sigma R_{G1} =$	272.5	$\Sigma R_{Y5} =$	547.5

the ranks assigned to the G1 and Y5 lists and are shown in *Table 7.6;* they are 272.5 and 547.5, respectively. Substituting these values into the formulae you will obtain:

$$U_1 = 20 \times 20 + \frac{20 \times (20 + 1)}{2} - 272.5 = 337.5$$

$$U_2 = 20 \times 20 + \frac{20 \times (20 + 1)}{2} - 547.5 = 62.5$$

The value that is used for U is always the lesser of the two values which are calculated; in this case, the value is 62.5. You will now need to consult a table of critical values for U. To do this, you will need the values of U and of N_A and N_B (in this case, both twenty) and whether your research hypothesis is one-tailed or two-tailed test. We used the tables provided in Clegg's (1990) introductory statistics book. Using these tables, we found that there is no more than a 1 in 200 (or 0.5 per cent or 0.005) probability of drawing these samples if the null hypothesis is true. This is a very small probability, so we can be confident in rejecting the null hypothesis, in this case.

Conventionally, you can reject the null hypothesis for probability values of 0.05 (or one in twenty or 5 per cent). A smaller probability increases the confidence with which you can reject the null hypothesis. If the probability value produced by the test allows you to reject the null hypothesis, then you can claim that your results are *significant*. In the above case, we can conclude that the results are *significant at the 0.005 level.*

'Significance', here, refers to **statistical significance**. A statistically significant difference between two samples is unlikely to have arisen purely by chance. Statistical significance does not reflect on the importance or absolute magnitude of the differences between the samples. Where sample sizes are very large, statistical tests will often show statistical significance even where the absolute differences between samples are really quite insignificant. Walden and Walkerdine (1985), for example, warn against placing undue emphasis on tests of significance in the comparison of girls' and boys' performances in school mathematics. The very large sample sizes of some of these comparisons result in quite trivial differences being declared 'significant'.

The Mann-Whitney test is appropriate where the two lists of data are **independent** of each other. In the textbook case, the two samples were drawn separately; the number of symbols on any G page is independent of the number of symbols on any Y page. The test can be applied where the size of each sample is different (if, say, Dowling had taken twenty pages from Book G1 and thirty pages from Book Y1).

Where the data is in the form of **matched pairs**, we need to apply a different test. For example, suppose that ten inspectors rate two teachers' performances. There will be ten pairs of ratings. However, these sets of ratings will not be independent, because the ratings in each pair will have arisen from the same inspector. One appropriate statistical test for such a set of data is the **Wilcoxon matched pairs signed ranks test**, which yields a statistic referred to as *T*. The Wilcoxon test also involves ranking the measures. You should refer to the bibliography which includes a number of statistical textbooks which provide further details and calculation schedules for this and other statistical tests.

Normal and Skewed Distributions

You may have noticed that the calculation for the Mann-Whitney statistic did not involve the actual measurements themselves, only their ranks. This is also true of the Wilcoxon test. This means that the only requirement that the test has of the data is that it must be in **ordinal** form, so that it can be ordered and ranks can be assigned. No assumptions are made about the shape of the distribution of the scores. These tests are referred to as **nonparametric tests**. There are other tests which, whilst more powerful, in the sense that they provide better estimates for the probabilities, are rather more picky in terms of the kind of data that is required. Commonly used examples are the matched and independent *t* tests, which correspond to the Wilcoxon and Mann-Whitney tests, respectively.

The *t* tests are **parametric tests**. They make assumptions about the population distribution, which must be in the form illustrated in *Figure 7.6*. *Figure 7.6* includes a curve drawn through the tops of the bars of the

Figure 7.6:   *The normal distribution*

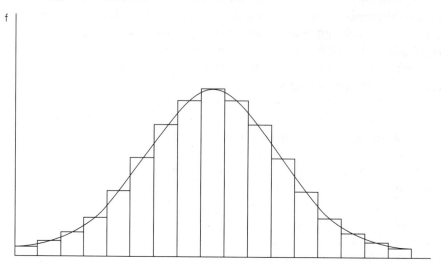

Figure 7.7:   *The normal frequency distribution curve*

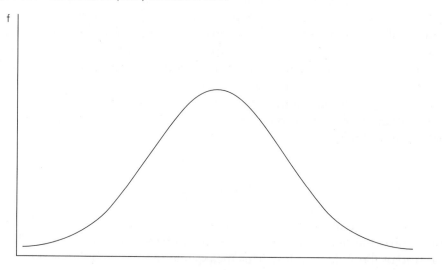

histogram. *Figure 7.7* shows the same curve, but without the bars. This bell-shaped curve is symmetrical about the group having the highest frequency. This group is called the **modal** group. A distribution which conforms to this shape is called a **normal frequency distribution**.

Commonly, the data does not conform to this specification and its distribution is a different shape. *Figures 7.8* and *7.9* illustrate distributions which are **skewed**, so that the shape is not symmetrical. The shape of the distribution illustrated in *Figure 7.8* is referred to as *positively skewed*, because the long tail of the graph is on the positive side (right) of the mode. *Figure 7.9* illustrates a *negatively skewed distribution*.

Figure 7.8: *Positively skewed distribution*

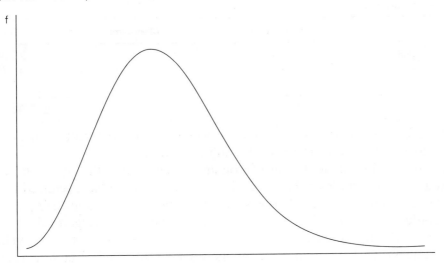

Figure 7.9: *Negatively skewed distribution*

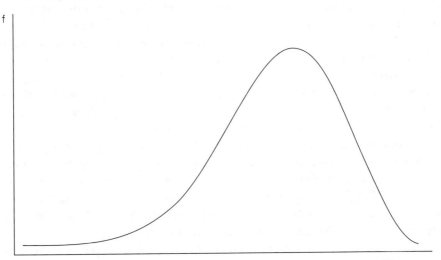

The Chi Square Test

The next test that we shall consider operates by a comparison of the shapes of the distributions of two samples. It is called the **chi square measure of association**, often written χ^2 (χ is the Greek letter which is pronounced chi). The chi square test measures the probability that two (or more) samples could have been drawn from the same population. Again, if this probability is found to be sufficiently small (less than 0.05) then you can have a degree

Table 7.7: *Distribution of generalizers and localizers amongst parents at East Wood and Chambers Schools*

	East Wood	**Chambers**	**Totals**
generalizers	28	6	34
localizers	28	48	76
Totals	56	54	110

of confidence that the samples were, in fact, drawn from different populations. In other words, you can reject the null hypothesis.

We shall illustrate the calculation and application of the chi square test on a set of results from the research by Brown that we have referred to in Chapters 5 and 6. *Table 7.7* shows the distribution of two samples of parents according to whether they are classified in Brown's work as 'generalizers' or 'localizers'. The samples are drawn, respectively, from parents whose children attend East Wood and Chambers schools. This kind of table is called a **contingency table**. It is important for the chi square test that the figures in the cells are frequencies and not percentages or scores of some other kind. The chi square test also imposes two other requirements on the data. Firstly, the items in each cell of the table must be independent of each other. In the case of Brown's data this condition holds, because the unit of analysis is the individual parent and each parent is classified as either a generalizer or a localizer and as either an East Wood or a Chambers parent. Each parent, then, is classified in only one cell of the table. The final condition is that the expected frequency should not be less than five for any cell; we will explain what is meant by the *expected frequency* below.

Inspecting the table, you will notice that the East Wood sample is divided equally between generalizers and localizers, whilst the Chambers sample is heavily dominated by localizers who outnumber the generalizers by a ratio of eight to one. It is hardly necessary to draw the histograms of the two sample distributions to see that they are very different in shape. Nevertheless, the histograms are drawn in *Figure 7.10*.

Now, it looks very much as if the two samples of parents are drawn from populations which differ in terms of the distribution of generalizers and localizers. Nevertheless, there is, as with the textbook data, a finite probability that even such obviously different samples could have been drawn from the same population or from two populations with the same characteristics. Chi square will enable you to estimate this probability.

The null hypothesis states that there is no difference between the populations from which the two samples are drawn. If this were to be the case, then the best estimate for the ratio of generalizers to localizers would be the same for each sample of parents. Altogether, thirty-four of the 110 parents are generalizers and seventy-six of them are localizers. If the fifty-six East Wood parents were divided between generalizers and localizers in this proportion, then:

Figure 7.10:   *The distributions of East Wood and Chambers parents*

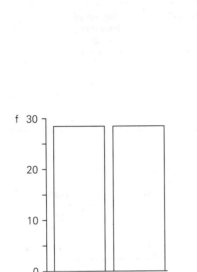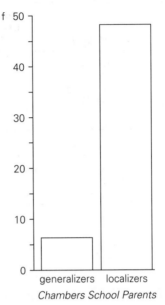

East Wood School Parents   Chambers School Parents

$$\text{the number of East Wood generalizers} = \frac{34}{110} \times 56 = 17.309$$

$$\text{the number of East Wood localizers} = \frac{76}{110} \times 56 = 38.691$$

Similarly:

$$\text{the number of Chambers generalizers} = \frac{34}{110} \times 54 = 16.691$$

$$\text{the number of Chambers localizers} = \frac{76}{110} \times 54 = 37.309$$

Obviously, the East Wood sample could not actually have been divided between 17.309 generalizers and 38.691 localizers, since the categories are mutually exclusive. Each parent has been classified as either generalizer or localizer and not a bit of each. Nevertheless, these figures are those which a proportional distribution of generalizers and localizers would give. They are called the **expected frequencies**. As we have mentioned, the use of the chi square test requires that these values should not be less than five for any cell. As you can see, this condition is met by Brown's data. The original, observed frequencies and the expected frequencies are shown in *Table 7.8*. The final column in *Table 7.8* includes the calculation of chi square.

Table 7.8: *Calculation of chi square*

School	Category	Observed frequency O	Expected frequency E	$\dfrac{(|O - E| - 0.5)^2}{E}$
East Wood	generalizers	28	17.309	6.000
	localizers	28	38.691	2.684
Chambers	generalizers	6	16.691	6.222
	localizers	48	37.309	2.784
			χ^2 = total =	17.690

Table 7.9: *An incomplete 2x2 contingency table*

	α	β	Totals
A	?	25	60
B	?	?	50
Totals	40	70	110

The formula[5] for chi square is:

$$\chi^2 = \Sigma \frac{(|O - E| - 0.5)^2}{E}$$

This needs a little explanation. $|O - E|$ means the positive difference between O and E. That is, you should subtract the lesser value from the greater so that the result is always a positive number.

Before referring to tabulated values of chi square, there is one more consideration. In a 2x2 contingency table, such as the one used here (that is, it is 2x2 without the totals), then provided that the totals are known, only one other figure needs to be known in order to enable you to fill in all the rest. Try it on *Table 7.9*.

The table is described as having one **degree of freedom**. The chi square test can also be used (calculated in exactly the same way) where the contingency table has more cells. More cells means more degrees of freedom. A 3x4 table, for example, has six degrees of freedom, because you need to know the values of at least six cells, in addition to the totals, in order to fill in the rest. The number of degrees of freedom of a table is calculated by multiplying one less than the number of rows by one less than the number of columns. So, an 8x5 table has $7 \times 4 = 28$ degrees of freedom.

You need to calculate the number of degrees of freedom, because the critical value of chi square depends upon it. In the case under consideration, here and in all 2x2 tables, the number of degrees of freedom, or *df*, is 1. Referring to the tabulated values for chi square in Wright (1997), we found

Figure 7.11: *Positive correlation*

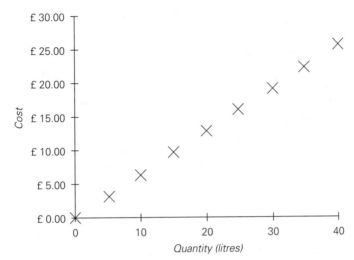

that Brown's results are significant at at least the 0.01 level for a one-tailed test. The null hypothesis can comfortably be rejected. We can infer that the populations of East Wood and Chambers parents are significantly differently distributed in terms of generalizers and localizers.

Correlation

The last kind of statistical technique that we shall consider provides an estimate of the strength of association between two variables, or the extent to which one variable is *correlated* with another. Such a statistic is called a **coefficient of correlation**. Two variables are said to be correlated when an increase in one variable is regularly accompanied by an increase or by a decrease in the other. For example, the cost of filling up your car with petrol is correlated with the quantity of petrol that you have to put in, because the more petrol you buy the more it will cost.

There is a range of ways in which two variables can be correlated. The petrol example is an instance of **positive correlation**. If you draw a **scatter graph** of the cost of petrol against the quantity, you will get something like *Figure 7.11* (at 1997 prices).

The term 'scatter graph' or **scattergram**, which denotes this kind of diagram, is rather a misnomer, in this instance. You will notice that the points in the graph lie in a straight line. The correlation is *positive* because both of the variables are increasing together, so that the graph goes upwards from left to right. Negative correlation is also possible. *Figure 7.12* graphs the distance remaining of a (fictitious) 300 mile journey against the time that a motorist has been driving at a steady fifty miles per hour. The correlation is

Figure 7.12: *Negative correlation*

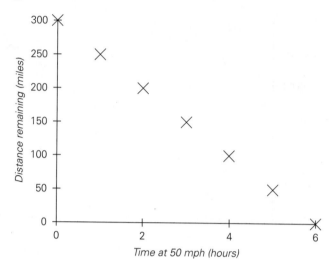

negative, because an increase in one variable is accompanied by a decrease in the other, so that the graph goes downwards from left to right.

Both of these examples are artificial. They have been produced using mathematical relationships rather than empirical observations. Empirical observations, even of physical phenomena observed under laboratory conditions, rarely produce such simple relationships. You could, of course, reproduce the first graph empirically by purchasing the various quantities of petrol and recording the cost. But you had better make sure that you use the same filling station and that the price doesn't change during your 'research'. Producing the second graph empirically might prove an interesting, if dangerous challenge.

Empirical observations, then, are likely to produce rather more messy arrays of points. For example, *Figure 7.13* shows examination performances and authorized absences for the secondary schools in a local education authority. This time, the data are 'real'. From an inspection of the scattergram, it looks as if there is some degree of negative correlation between these variables. It is clearly not a perfect negative correlation. Indeed it would be astonishing if it were to be so. Moving from one point to another from left to right sometimes involves a downward movement, sometimes an upward movement, and sometimes a horizontal movement. In other words, an increase in authorized absence between two particular schools might be associated with either an increase or a decrease in examination performance, or their examination performances might be the same. Nevertheless, there are clearly more downward moves than upward moves.

Unlike the previous examples, there is no straight line that will pass through all of the points in *Figure 7.13*. However, there are statistical techniques which enable the calculation of the position of the line which is

Figure 7.13: *Negative correlation: GCSE passes and authorized absences at schools in one LEA in 1994–5*

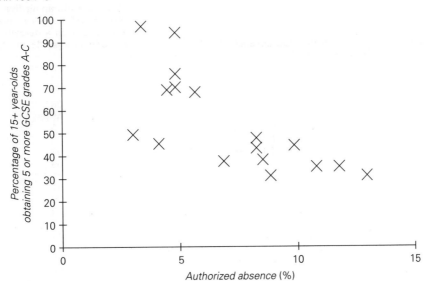

Figure 7.14: *An example of zero correlation*

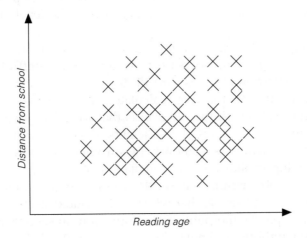

closest to most of the points. This line is called a **line of best fit**, or a **regression line**.

If you were to take a sample of secondary school students and graph the distances of their homes from the school against their reading ages, you would probably be surprised to find any pattern of association at all. In fact, you might expect, the variables reading age and distance from school, both to be **normally distributed.** That is, clustering around the central values with few extreme points, as in *Figure 7.7.* When two normally distributed variables are graphed against each other, the result is a roughly elliptical cluster of points as shown in the artificially produced *Figure 7.14.* For this

Table 7.10: GCSE passes and authorized absences at schools in one LEA in 1994–5

School	Authorized absence (%)	Students obtaining five or more GCSE passes at grade C or above as a percentage of students aged 15 or above
A	3.1	95
B	8.3	47
C	6.9	37
D	8.6	38
E	4.1	45
F	4.8	70
G	11.8	35
H	3.4	97
I	4.5	69
J	8.9	31
K	13.0	31
L	4.8	76
M	3.0	49
N	5.7	68
O	9.9	44
P	8.3	43
Q	10.9	35
R	4.8	94

scattergram there is no single line of best fit. A rectangular pattern of points would also have no line of best fit. In these cases, the level of **correlation** is **zero**.

The strength of correlation between two variables ranges between perfect positive, through zero, to perfect negative. The **coefficients of correlation** that correspond to these are +1, 0 and −1, respectively. In virtually all cases, the coefficient that you calculate will lie between 0 and +1 or between 0 and −1. As with the other tests that we have discussed, you can use tables giving critical values of coefficients of correlation to determine the significance level of the association between your variables.

We are going to illustrate the calculation of a particular coefficient of correlation called **Spearman's rho**. Rho is another Greek letter, written ρ. The data that we shall use is that which is illustrated in the scattergram in *Figure 7.13*. It is part of the published information on schools in a particular local education authority in England for the year 1994–5. The data is shown in *Table 7.10* and shows the rate of authorized absence and the percentage of students obtaining five or more General Certificate of Secondary Education (GCSE) subject passes at grade C or above.

As we indicated above, the shape of the scattergram suggests a negative correlation between absences and examination performance. This is interpreted to mean that schools having lower absence rates tend to have higher rates of examination passes and vice versa. The coefficient of correlation is therefore expected to lie somewhere between 0 and −1. In order to calculate the coefficient, we have completed the values in *Table 7.11*.

Table 7.11:   *Calculation of Spearman's rho*

School	Absence (%) A	GCSE passes P	R_A	R_P	$D^2 = (R_A - R_P)^2$
A	3.1	95	2	17	225
B	8.3	47	11.5	10	2.25
C	6.9	37	10	5	25
D	8.6	38	13	6	49
E	4.1	45	4	9	25
F	4.8	70	7	14	49
G	11.8	35	17	3.5	182.25
H	3.4	97	3	18	225
I	4.5	69	5	13	64
J	8.9	31	14	1.5	156.25
K	13.0	31	18	1.5	272.25
L	4.8	76	7	15	64
M	3.0	49	1	11	100
N	5.7	68	9	12	9
O	9.9	44	15	8	49
P	8.3	43	11.5	7	20.25
Q	10.9	35	16	3.5	156.25
R	4.8	94	7	16	81
				$\Sigma D^2 =$	1754.5

The values in the fourth and fifth columns of *Table 7.11* are the ranks, R_A and R_P, assigned to absences *A*, and percentage of students obtaining five or more GCSEs at grade C or above, labelled *P*. The ranks were assigned in the same way as for the Mann-Whitney test, described earlier in this chapter, except that each column (*A* and *P*) was ranked separately. The values in the final column of *Table 7.11* are obtained by squaring the difference between the ranks for each school. For example, the ranks for School A are 2 and 17; the difference between the ranks is 15; the square of 15 is $15 \times 15 = 225$. This final column is totalled to give the sum, 1754.5. Rho is calculated according to the following formula:

$$\rho = 1 - \frac{6\Sigma D^2}{(N^3 - N)}$$

where ΣD^2 is the sum of the squares of the differences between the ranks, 1754.5, and *N* is the number of schools. Thus, in this case:

$$\rho = 1 - \frac{6 \times 1754.5}{(18^3 - 18)} = 1 - \frac{10527}{5832 - 18} = 1 - 1.811 = -0.811$$

You will immediately notice that the prediction that the coefficient would be negative is confirmed. It remains to determine the level of significance of the negative association. Referring to Clegg's (1982) table of critical values for Spearman's rho, we found that the results are significant at at least the

Figure 7.15:   Histogram: authorized absences in schools in one LEA

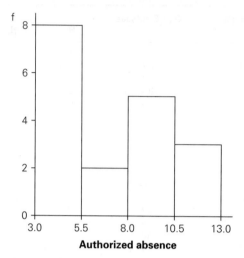

0.005 level for a one-tailed test. Therefore, the null hypothesis, which states that there is no association between authorized absences and GCSE passes, can be rejected. You can conclude that there is a negative association between authorized absences and GCSE passes which is significant at the 0.005 level.

There are other coefficients of correlation which can be used. **Pearson's product-moment coefficient**, *r*, is one that is commonly used. However, as is the case with the *t* tests, Pearson's test is parametric. This places additional demands on the data including that the two lists of scores should be normally distributed. In the case of the schools data, both lists are heavily weighted towards the lower values — they are positively skewed. The data is represented in the histograms in *Figures 7.15* and *7.16*. On visual inspection, they are clearly not normal distributions.

Another requirement of the Pearson product moment technique is that the association between the two variables must be **linear**. That is, the scattergram must approximate to a straight line. This is, in fact, the case with the schools data, as can be seen from *Figure 7.13*. However, it is possible that two variables may be related in a way that is **non-linear** and that the scattergram may cluster around different shaped curves, such as the one illustrated in *Figure 7.17*. Pearson's statistic is not appropriate here. The Spearman technique, on the other hand can be applied in a wider range of cases, including the one illustrated in *Figure 7.17*.

In general terms, the parametric techniques, some of which we have mentioned, but have not described in detail, provide better estimates for the significance level or for the coefficient of correlation. However, they will do this only if the data conforms to much more stringent requirements. If you are considering using these tests, or if you are assessing other work which uses them, you should consult a statistics textbook, such as those which we have included in the bibliography.

Figure 7.16: Histogram: GCSE performances in schools in one LEA

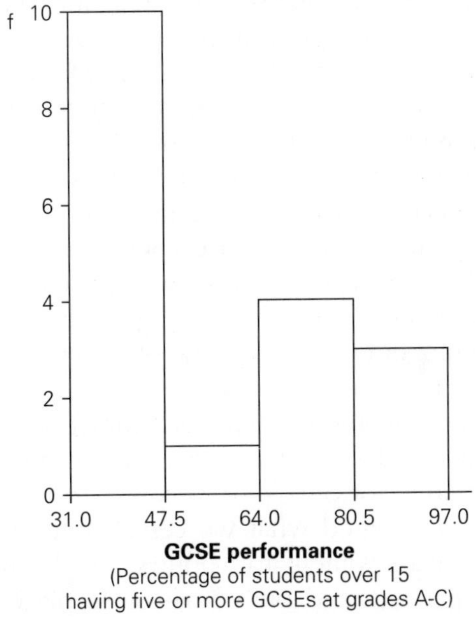

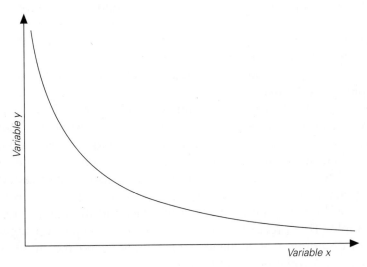

f
10
8
6
4
2
0
31.0
47.5
64.0
80.5
97.0
GCSE performance
(Percentage of students over 15
having five or more GCSEs at grades A-C)

Figure 7.17: A non-linear association

Variable y
Variable x

Some Caveats

Our own research has tended to be dominated by qualitative methods. Unlike some authors of books on research methods, however, we do not perceive a rigid divide between qualitative and quantitative approaches. Few would regard the Luria research as quantitative, yet he has counted and tabulated

his findings in support of his conclusions. We have both, in our own work, made use of the kind of quantitative representation and statistical analysis of data that we have introduced in this chapter. Our feeling is that this has significantly added to the quality of our work. Furthermore, few researchers in education can avoid engaging with research that is more extensively statistical in nature. In part, the intention behind this chapter is that it should enable you to engage with such work with at least some degree of understanding of how the claims that are being made are justified. We also hope that you will be encouraged to make use yourself of some of the quantitative strategies that have been introduced, where their use will extend and develop your work, either in conception or in presentation. We should, however, emphasize a number of caveats, some of which we have already made in the course of this chapter.

Firstly, and rather counter to the general thrust of this chapter, presenting essentially qualitative data in quantitative form can have negative results. For example, a colleague of ours — a very experienced and widely published researcher — submitted what we certainly felt to be an interesting paper on educational assessment to a journal in the field of educational assessment. The paper reported on a small-scale piece of research which had involved clinical interviews with a couple of dozen school children using National Assessment Standard Assessment Tasks as the focus of the interviews. The paper made a number of important points about the students' interpretation of these tasks and about the validity of the tasks for the purposes of assessing the UK National Curriculum. Our colleague had collated some of the results in much the same kind of tables as Luria's in *Table 7.1*. The editor of the journal rejected the paper on the grounds that the sample was too small.

Now this certainly suggests a fundamental lack of understanding of the relevance of sample size on the part of the editor. Presumably, they would also have rejected Luria's work on the same grounds. Whilst the tabulation of the data had been intended to provide a clear overview of the sample, it had allowed the research, in the editor's mind, to be interrogated as if it were of a quantitative nature. Where resources are finite, there is bound to be a trade-off between the richness of the data and the number of subjects in the sample. This precisely corresponds to the comparison between the elaborated description of qualitative presentation and the more extensive but summary potential of quantification.

Secondly, there is commonly a certain tendency amongst those offering advice on research to a doctrinaire attitude to statistical testing. This attitude insists that where data is in quantitative form, it should always be subjected to statistical analysis. In our opinion, such a position is misguided. As we have indicated, statistical **significance** should not be confused with significance per se. Where sample sizes are sufficiently large, almost any difference is likely to prove statistically significant. Furthermore, the availability of

Table 7.12: *Pronoun use by primary school children*

	Masculine	Feminine	Neutral	Totals
girl	26	12	112	150
boy	59	0	91	150
Totals	85	12	203	300

statistical packages as computer software has enabled and even encouraged the unprincipled application of highly sophisticated statistical tools in lieu of serious analysis. As Tony Halil, a statistician and former colleague of ours, used to say, if you torture data sufficiently, it's bound to confess to something. The danger is that if you are not really clear on what the techniques do or how they work or what assumptions they are making about your data, it is difficult to see how you can have any confidence in the conclusions you build on these 'confessions'. This having been said, if your data is or can be organized into an appropriate form and if you have a specific question to put to it, then statistical techniques may be of considerable use and should be considered. All instruments of analysis, however, should be used deliberately, correctly and with an explicit purpose in mind.

We will give an example of an inappropriate use of a statistical technique from a case that we have already mentioned in an earlier chapter. A student on one of our courses wanted to see whether there was any difference between the use of gender-specific and gender-neutral pronouns by primary age girls and boys. The students presented a number of primary school students with a series of sentences which they were to complete. The sentences had been designed so as to encourage the use of a pronoun in their completion (although some of the students used alternative parts of speech). Each sentence ending was recorded as either masculine (he, him, his, etc), feminine (her, she, hers, etc), or neutral (it, its, etc). The results were tabulated according to whether the response was made by a girl or a boy, giving a table similar to *Table 7.12*[6].

The table is a 2 × 3 contingency table. It looks ripe for a **chi square test**. So the test was run, the value for χ^2 being calculated as 24.101. With two degrees of freedom, significance for a one-tailed test was claimed at at least the 0.005 level. Where's the problem?

The problem is that the items in the cells are not **independent**. The unit of analysis, here, is the individual sentence completion. But there were several different sentences and a classful of girls and boys. Endings provided for the same sentence are not independent of each other insofar as the form of the sentence influences the choice of ending. Endings provided by each individual girl or boy are not independent of each other insofar as each may be expected to respond with a degree of consistency.

In fact, given that the interest was in responses made by individuals, the research should more properly have been designed so as to make the individual the unit of analysis as is the case, for example, in Luria's table (*Table 7.1*). This could have been done by rating each individual in terms of, say, the following score:

$$\frac{\text{masculine endings} - \text{feminine endings}}{\text{all endings}}$$

This would have face validity as a measure of the tendency to masculine-dominated pronoun use. It is not an ideal measure. It would not, for example, distinguish between those making equal use of masculine and feminine endings, on the one hand, and those making exclusive use of neutral endings; in both cases, the rating would be zero. Nevertheless, it would enable the ranking of the two groups (girls and boys) and, if necessary, the application of the Mann-Whitney test.

This example emphasizes the need to be clear about the assumptions that you are implicitly making about your data by using a statistical test. Just because, as here, the numbers will fit into the formula or the computer package, doesn't mean that the test is appropriate.

The next point concerns the distinction that must be made between **association** and **cause**. Take, for example, the regression analysis that we conducted on the schools data. We found that there was a negative correlation between absences and GCSE performance which was significant at the 0.005 level. Now a politician may wish to infer that a high level of absence is directly responsible for poor examination performance. A politician of a different persuasion may want to argue that the students of a school which has a low examination performance rate might reasonably feel that there is not much point in going to school, so that the absences are, in a sense, caused by the examination performances. The prevalence of this kind of inappropriate inference is quite possibly exactly what Disraeli meant when he pronounced that there were lies, damned lies and statistics.

The fact of the matter is that the data that we have provided and the analysis that we have conducted does not entitle you to make either **inference**. It is not appropriate for us to speculate, here, on the causes of such differences between schools. However, they are, we feel, likely to be the outcome of a highly complex set of factors that will, in all likelihood, operate somewhat differently even between schools exhibiting similar statistical profiles. The finding that there is an association between two or more factors does not, then, provide an answer, so much as raise a question for further research.

In addition, the manner in which we have obtained the data — from the published lists available on the Internet — does not allow us access to the way in which they are produced. The list of schools, for example, contains both independent and state schools. These two sectors do not have the same requirements when it comes to the publishing of their results. 'Absences' are recorded as 'authorized' absences. It is unlikely that all schools have the same procedures for registering authorization. These and other questions can and should be asked about the validity and reliability of these figures as measures of school culture and performance.

Finally, unless your own use of quantitative techniques is very limited, we strongly suggest that you go on from this text to one of the more sophisticated handbooks that we have listed in our annotated bibliography. If you are registered on a course at an academic institution, you may well have access to specialist advice from professional statisticians. If this is the case, then it is generally a good idea to seek their advice very early on. A final word of warning is appropriate here, as well. Do not go to the statistical adviser or, indeed, the book, with the expectation that they will tell you what to do with your data; far less that they will do it for you. What they will want to know from you is precisely what you want to know of the data. Only then, will they be in a position to advise on the selection of the appropriate statistical techniques. Statistical tools are no different from any other methodological techniques in that they are resources to be recruited in a deliberate and reflective research endeavour, whether it be your own research or reading someone else's. It is the integrity and enthusiasm of such deliberation and reflection that measures the quality of your research, not the sophistication of your statistics.

Notes

1 School Mathematics Project (1983–5) *SMP 11–16*, Cambridge: CUP.
2 In Dowling's analysis, 'low ability' and 'high ability' refer to the constructions of the ideal reader of the texts. They do not, in other words, constitute necessary attributes of the students or teachers who actually make use of these books. It is for this reason that these expressions are enclosed in quotes.
3 Although there remain some operational problems which are discussed in Dowling, 1995.
4 The program used was Claris Impact on a Macintosh computer.
5 The formula presented here includes Yates' correction. This involves the subtraction of a value of 0.5 as shown. This is omitted in some expressions of the formula and there is some disagreement amongst statisticians as to its value. However, we suggest that you include it for 2x2 tables or where the sum of the frequencies (the figure in the bottom righthand cell of the contingency table) is less than 25. Its effect is to make the test more demanding.
6 In fact, the data has been modified slightly. Two categories have been combined in order to simplify the explanation offered here. This modification does not impact on the argument being made and is probably an improvement on the original organization.

References

CLEGG, F. (1982) *Simple Statistics: A Course Book for the Social Sciences*, Cambridge: Cambridge University Press.

DOWLING, P.C. (1995) 'A language for the sociological description of pedagogic texts with particular reference to the Secondary School Mathematics Scheme *SMP 11–16*', *Collected Original Resources in Education*, **19**.

DOWLING, P.C. (1996) 'A sociological analysis of school mathematics texts', *Educational Studies in Mathematics*, **31**, pp. 389–415.

DOWLING, P.C. (1998) *The Sociology of Mathematics Education: Mathematical Myths/Pedagogic Texts*, London: Falmer Press.

OFFICE OF POPULATION CENSUSES AND SURVEYS (1980) *Classification of Occupations*, London: HMSO.

WALDEN, R. and WALKERDINE, V. (1985) *Girls and Mathematics: From Primary to Secondary Schools*, Bedford Way Paper no. 24, London: Institute of Education, University of London.

WRIGHT, D.B. (1997) *Understanding Statistics: An Introduction for the Social Sciences*, London: Sage.

8 Specializing, Localizing and Generalizing: A Mode of Interrogation

In this book we are taking a particular stance on educational research. Essentially, we are presenting a description of educational research activity as the production of a coherent set of statements. These are established and located within explicitly stated theoretical and empirical contexts. The research process, conceived in this way, begins with vagueness and hesitance and plurality and moves towards precision and coherence. You can think of this as the imposition of order, which we refer to as a **constructive** view. Alternatively, you may consider yourself to be engaging in the discovery of order — a **realist** view.[1] For the record, we are inclined towards the former and, in this chapter, we have for the most part chosen our language accordingly. We feel that this is appropriate, especially as the language chosen throughout the earlier chapters is probably more consistent with a realist position. However, constructivism and realism are **epistemological** and not methodological positions. They are concerned with the origins of structure rather than its practical description or production. From our perspective, then, it is no more necessary to resolve your epistemology in your empirical research than it is to incorporate a declaration of your religious affiliation. Unfortunately, however, the tendency to make a pass at epistemological discussion is commonly presented in lieu of adequate theoretical development.

We have tried to give an introduction to a range of methodological resources which you may draw on in your research activity. In many instances, our exposition of these resources has been the explicit message of our text. At a more implicit level, we have also attempted to provide some guidance on how to move towards coherence. It is coherence which we are claiming to be the fundamental criterion by which educational research is to be judged. Research must be generalized and generalizable in relation to its local empirical contexts. In this respect, it must be more like theoretical knowledge than situational knowledge, to borrow Luria's terms. In this final chapter we want to be more explicit about the process whereby the coherence of such 'theoretical knowledge' is to be produced. This will involve bringing together and organizing elements of the discussions of the earlier chapters and particularly the contents of Chapters 2 and 3.

We must first re-emphasize another feature of the approach which we are taking. Essentially, if structural coherence is the intention of your research activity, then the search for structural coherence must inform your interpretation of research which has been carried out by others. The process that we are proposing for doing research is, to this extent, precisely the same as that to be adopted in the reading of research. You don't have to interview the author. But you do have to ask precisely the same kinds of questions of someone else's interviewing procedures as you do of your own.

The act of asking questions is crucial. We want to maintain that it is the process of asking questions that drives the development of structural coherence. The kind of questions to be asked and the way in which they are put comprises a **mode of interrogation**. Our intention, in this chapter, is to make as explicit as we can the nature of this mode of interrogation. We shall argue that there is a sense in which it is the mode of interrogation which defines the activity — in this case, research. The activities of educational practitioners other than researchers generate alternative modes of interrogation. In this conception, educational research and other educational practices must be regarded as separate spheres. This position has implications for the practitioner researcher and, in particular, for the approach to educational research that is often referred to as **action research**. We shall illustrate, briefly, an action research project in Chapter 9. We shall discuss the issue of the practitioner researcher more generally in Chapter 10. We shall also make some reference to it in the discussion in this chapter in which we concentrate on the presentation of the research mode of interrogation.

The Research Mode of Interrogation: Specializing the Theoretical Context

Since we are introducing a mode of interrogation, we felt that it would be appropriate to organize the discussion under headings which are the principal questions to be addressed in either conducting or reading research. We have collected these questions together into a schema for the mode of interrogation at the end of the chapter. The first set of questions concerns the development of the theoretical context of the research. We have referred to this process as **specialization**.

What is the General Theoretical Field Within Which the Work is Located?

In Chapter 3 we referred to the **theoretical field** as a nebula of debates, theories and empirical findings. But the theoretical field more appropriately refers to a notional community of researchers and/or practitioners as well as to their output. Your work, or the work that you are reading, is entering into discursive relations with this community. In other words, the theoretical field comprises, firstly, the authors of whom the researcher is a reader. These are

authorities within the theoretical field. Authors' names and journal titles in the bibliography should provide some sort of an indication of the relevant authorities. But it may also be important to consider the relevance of **disciplinary knowledge** to the research. An academic discipline, such as sociology, for example, incorporates a range of journals and practitioners, but it also entails a canon of knowledge and texts that are its foundations. This canon will constitute the content of undergraduate work in the discipline and therefore is generally assumed by more advanced writing in the discipline.

The theoretical fields within which educational research is developed is not confined to the academic disciplines and certainly not to the traditional, academic disciplines. There are also what might appropriately be referred to as **professional disciplines** related to the curriculum and to assessment and also to educational management and administration. These will also be associated with journals and practitioners and will also generate what might be referred to as canonical knowledge. The latter might include current and historical details of the development of a particular educational system. UK authors addressing UK audiences will probably assume some knowledge of (at least) the 1944 and 1988 Education Acts and the structure of the public examination system and of school inspection, for example. Writing within professional disciplines will include academic educational research, but it will also include non-academic writing directed at practitioner and lay audiences. The professional journals of school subject associations and governmental publications, for example, fall into this latter category.

The second component of the theoretical field includes the readers or potential readers of the researcher's own writing. The researcher cannot anticipate all possible members of the second category. They can and should, however, have a clear sense of their ideal reader and make this explicit. This is the **readership** of the theoretical field. The relationship between authorities and readership is an important one in defining the nature of the work. Where the work is research, its readership may be understood as a subset of the authorities of the field. Research adopts a position and presents findings for peer evaluation. If you are constituting yourself as a reader of research in these terms, then your responsibility to the field is to participate in its evaluation or, as we are presenting it here, its interrogation.

On the other hand, a work which is primarily pedagogic stands as an authority in relation to its ideal readership; naturally, this does not preclude the possibility that the actual reader might reject this authority. The extent to which the authorities and readership of research coincide determines the extent to which the researcher can assume knowledge of the former. We can read this the other way. An important indicator of the coincidence of the authority and readership components of the theoretical field is the amount of field knowledge assumed by the text. Field knowledge is assumed by a text which indexes but which does not elaborate upon its authorities.

What is the Problematic?

The notional community which constitutes the theoretical field is inevitably very broad. In conducting and reading research, you must specialize. This entails the denoting of key work, positions and debates which define what we might call the **problematic** within which the research is situated. The problematic may be one that is already established. For example, the research may be concerned with factors effecting school effectiveness. In this case, there is an established body of work which is concerned with this area. This body of work may be conceived as a specialization within a more general field comprising educational researchers, administrators and practitioners as well as, perhaps, politicians and public commentators. This field clearly incorporates a diverse range of motives and **genres**. In defining the school effectiveness problematic, it would be important to mark out the research as distinct from, for example, journalism and inspectors' reports. This is not because research is being constituted as superior, in any absolute sense, to these other genres. Rather, the mode of interrogation that is applied to any genre of work should be specific to that genre. In a sense, it is the mode of interrogation that defines the specificity of a genre.

On the other hand, the problematic may not be one that is established as an area of interest. Under these circumstances, the researcher must organize a space for themself. A range of work is to be cited in such a way as to make clear how each item relates to the specialized area which is the problematic under construction. Again, however, the problematic is to be constructed with reference to work in the research genre.

What is the Specific Problem?

At this point, the level of theoretical development is at its sharpest and most specialized. The researcher is making one or more specific propositions or hypotheses and/or asking one or more specific questions. We shall refer to this highly specialized region as the **problem** of the research. At the end of a research write-up, the **propositions, hypotheses** or **questions** may be recast as **conclusions**. The problem is given in theoretical terms. It stands as an **abstraction** in relation to any local **empirical setting**. That it is an abstraction, however, does not entail that it may be vague. On the contrary, the interrogation of the propositions, hypotheses, questions or conclusions should aim to establish them to a high degree of precision whereby their terms are defined by the problematic.

For example, the articulation of a problem concerned with school effectiveness entails the shaping and/or selection of a definition (which may be multidimensional) of 'school effectiveness' in relation to or drawn from the school effectiveness problematic. When the problem is fully stated, its concepts will also be defined in relation to each other. That is, the problem recruits as much of the problematic as is necessary in order to establish itself as internally complete and consistent. Essentially, the **concepts** involved in the problem should be developed to a degree which enables their empirical measurement or operationalization.

Operationalization involves the movement between the theoretical and empirical contexts of the research. We shall now move on to the empirical sphere, starting at the level of the empirical field.

The Research Mode of Interrogation: Localizing the Empirical

What is the General Empirical Field Within Which the Work is Located?

The **empirical field** may be glossed as the broad range of practices and experiences to which the research relates. Examples might be the management of schools or children learning mathematics or attitudes to alcohol. Like the theoretical field, the empirical field also constitutes a community or communities. Again, these may be more notional than substantive. The field is being constituted by the research as an object of study which is to be described in terms of the theoretical problematic. It is this relationship of **objectification** which distinguishes between the theoretical and empirical fields. The **theoretical field** objectifies the empirical field and not the other way around. The community or communities comprising the theoretical field engage in the production and interrogation of research and of other modes of commentary on the empirical field.

This does not mean that there is a necessary division between those who are observers and those who are observed. Indeed, all educational practice entails both activity and reflection upon that activity. Our position, however, is that the theoretical field consists of **genres of reflection** which are distinguished from the practices and experiences upon which they reflect. Preparing or evaluating a lesson both involve reflection upon teaching, but they are genres of reflection which are incorporated within the practice of teaching. It would be inappropriate to apply the mode of interrogation which defines the research genre to a lesson plan. On the other hand, it would be an interesting and possibly useful task to construct a mode of interrogation for lesson planning and to mark out the sources of its distinction from the research mode. Teachers as educational researchers are participating in a theoretical field; teachers as teachers are participating in what might be an empirical field for an educational researcher. The researcher may quite appropriately be the teacher themself. The division, then, is between the practices in which the human subjects are involved rather than between human subjects themselves.

What is the Local Empirical Setting?

We have referred to the development of the theoretical context from theoretical field through problematic to problem as a process of specialization. This follows Dowling's (1998) use of the term in his own language of description, referred to as **social activity theory**. The corresponding process relating to empirical development is referred to as **localizing**. The distinction is important. Specialized propositions or questions remain at a level of **abstraction** with respect to any particular empirical context. You can think of them as being measurable in a whole range of possible **empirical settings**. The task of empirical development in research is to localize this empirical space. This is essentially a process of selection in terms of research design, sampling strategies and data collection techniques. These categories are to be understood as reservoirs of methodological resources. They have been illustrated and discussed in Chapters 3, 4 and 5. Localizing the empirical setting entails a selection from these reservoirs of resources and the deployment of the selected resources within the empirical field.

There will inevitably be contingent opportunities and difficulties in conducting empirical research. For example, the researcher may decide to enlarge the sample when offered unanticipated access to contexts or subjects. On the other hand, sample sizes may be reduced by circumstances beyond the control of the researcher. Any project which is carried out over an extended period of time is likely to be faced with a degree of **mortality** of its subjects. That is, subjects who are selected in the sample and participate in the early stages of the research become unavailable subsequently. The use of questionnaires rarely achieves anything like a 100 per cent **response rate**; the researcher may anticipate this and inflate the planned sample size. This does not, of course, account for any possible **bias** which is introduced because of disparities between the characteristics of those responding and those not responding.

So you can expect inconsistencies within the empirical domain between what might be referred to as the planned setting and the achieved setting. We have emphasized consistency as the fundamental criterion for the evaluation of research. It is, therefore, important that attempts be made to reconcile these inconsistencies at least to the point of exploring their possible implications for the research.

What are the Empirical Findings?

The terminal point of empirical localization is the production of the **empirical findings**. These are descriptions or summaries of the relations between **indicator variables**. They constitute the empirical correlates of the theoretical propositions and/or questions which comprise the problem. These propositions and/or questions are in the form of relations between concept variables. Findings may be presented in the form of tables, charts, protocols, transcripts, narratives, and so forth.

A central question in relation to the findings concerns the issue of **reliability**. In Chapter 3, reliability was defined as the repeatability of the process. For example, to what extent will the data be coded in the same way by different researchers employing the same coding instructions. The most direct way to address this issue is to incorporate a test of reliability which involves the comparison of the coding results of two or more coders. This is most easily achieved where the data is in quantitative form.

Where data is presented in qualitative form, there will commonly be a need for selection. It is rarely possible to present all of the data that has been gathered. Neither is it necessarily desirable to do so. Nevertheless, it is important that the research justify its particular selection. The term reliability can be expanded to include the measure of the extent to which the data presented is representative of the data generally. This may be addressed by presenting data in different forms, possibly employing a degree of quanti-fication. This was the strategy employed by Luria which was discussed in Chapter 7.

The Research Mode of Interrogation: From Specializing and Localizing to Validity and Generalization

The mode of interrogation describes the problem and findings as having been generated via the specialization of the theoretical domain and the localization of the empirical domain, respectively. This does not mean that either the chronological 'story' of the research process or its 'plot' as realized in its write-up necessarily take this path. Applying the mode of interrogation, as it has thus far been introduced, in reading or in doing research affects or, at least, moves towards a coherent organizing of the research in terms of theoretical specialization and empirical localization. This has been described as a dual movement which focuses in on the central concerns of the research from the theoretical and empirical directions separately, as is illustrated in *Figure 8.1*. The dual process has brought the theoretical domains and empir-ical domains into contact in a very specialized and highly localized region which relates the problem to the findings. At this point, we now have to consider the validity and reliability of this articulation and the nature of the implications of the research beyond this specialized and localized region.

How is the Link Between the Problem and the Findings Established?

The link between the theoretical problem and the empirical findings is concerned with the question of **validity**. In Chapter 3, we glossed validity

Figure 8.1:   *Theoretical and empirical domains*

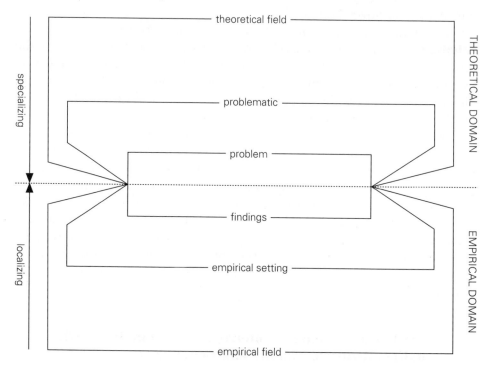

as a measure of the extent to which you are measuring what you think you are measuring. It is concerned with the plausibility of the relationship between, on the one hand, the indicator variables that constitute the findings and, on the other, the concept variables that constitute the problem. All research should incorporate an argument which attempts to establish this relationship. This argument may or may not include statistical measures of validity. In any case, the question that is to be put here is precisely how does the research justify its empirical measurement of its theoretical propositions? Alternatively, put the other way round, how does the research justify its theoretical interpretation of its empirical findings?

How is the Research Generalized?

We have stated that that which distinguishes the theoretical from the empirical domains is that statements within the former are abstractions with respect to situations within the latter. In particular, the problem stands in a relation of abstraction or context independence with respect to the findings. This entails that it can be construed as **preconceptualizing** the **findings** of research conducted in alternative empirical settings. Thought of in this way, the problem imposes a **bias** upon future research; this is consistent with what we described earlier as a **constructive epistemology**. Alternatively, a **realist** epistemology might interpret the problem as **predicting** the findings of future research. Again, we do not believe that the choice of epistemological position itself imposes any particular bias upon the research. Nevertheless, whether you think in terms of preconceptualization or prediction, the relationship between the problem and future research is an important one. It defines the **theoretical generalizability** of the research. Essentially, no piece of research is of any value at all unless it does impose upon the way in which you interpret the world on subsequent occasions.

Central to the issue of generalizability is the concept of **implication**. We shall elaborate this concept by reference to an example. In Chapter 7 we conducted a chi square test of Brown's data on the incidence of generalizers and localizers at two primary schools. Generalizer and localizer are the two values of the **variable** 'semantic selection'. The other variable is social class, Woods and Merttens (1994) having characterized East Wood as mixed middle class and working class and Chambers as predominantly working class. We should note that these two variables are operating on different **units of analysis**. Semantic selection refers to individual parents; social class refers to the school. Brown is transferring the school variable ascription to the parents. He is claiming that if the school is, for example, predominantly working class, then there is a relatively high probability that any given parent sending their child to that school will be working class.

The group of parents who are represented by this data constituted a **sample**. The **population** from which this sample was drawn might be described at a range of levels. Minimally, the sample could have been a 100 per cent sample of this particular group of parents. On the other hand, it could have been a very small sample of the population of all parents having children currently attending primary schools in the UK. Or, the population might be defined to lie anywhere between these extreme values. However the population is defined, the assumption is being made that it varies in terms of the two variables, semantic selection and social class.

The **null hypothesis**, in this case, states that there is no **association** between these variables in the population from which the sample was drawn. From the results of the chi square test, we know that the probability of drawing this particular sample from a population having no association between these variables is very small — less than 0.01. We can, therefore, be confident in rejecting the null hypothesis. In doing so, we are making an **inference** that there is an association between social class and semantic selection for the population as a whole. In other words, we are making a generalization of the findings as they relate to the particular sample analysed by Brown to a larger population and therefore to a greater or smaller range of potential empirical settings. The theoretical structure that has enabled this generalization is statistical knowledge. Generalizations of this form are referred to as **statistical inference**.

Statistical tests can tell you that you are justified in inferring an association between two variables. They cannot provide an explanation for this association. In order to address this issue, you will need to move into the theoretical domain. Nevertheless, the research may be designed in such a way as to enable certain explanations to be ruled out — again, in probabilistic terms — in the same way that the null hypothesis is ruled out.

For example, you may suspect that the gender of Brown's subjects has implications for their mode of semantic selection, that is, that gender is a **confounding variable**. If this were the case, then the findings might be explainable simply in terms of the different gender composition of each group of parents. The researcher might have attempted to **control** the variable, gender, by testing for an association between gender and semantic selection. In fact, information on the gender of the parents was not consistently available to Brown. Thus, gender is an **uncontrolled variable** in this part of his work.

Control techniques are important strategies in eliminating confounding variables and in moving towards the explanation and so generalization of one's findings. Of particular importance is the control of the **Hawthorne effect**, which may be glossed as the proposition that knowledge of their involvement as subjects of research may itself change people's behaviour. The Hawthorne effect is discussed in Chapter 4. Control strategies cannot, ultimately, provide **explanations**. Explanations are available only within the theoretical domain. Indeed, a degree of theoretical development is needed in order to establish which variables might need to be controlled. The move has to be made from indicator variables to concept variables.

In Brown's research, semantic selection and social class are both **indicator variables**. They refer directly to the organization of the data. Semantic selection indicates the state of the **concept variable**, 'cultural orientation'. The indicator variable, social class indicates the state of its theoretical equivalent, which is a concept variable, also referred to as social class. The inferred association between social class and semantic selection may be attributed to one of three theoretical possibilities for the relationship between the concepts, social class and cultural orientation. Firstly, you may argue that the value of social class has an implication for the value of cultural orientation. Alternatively, you may try to establish that the value of cultural orientation has some implication for the value of social class. Thirdly, it may be that there is a third variable which has some implication for both of them.

The identification of implication is explored in terms of the ways in which the concept variables are defined. We shall not consider Brown's work further in this respect as this would entail considerable additional theoretical discussion. We can, however, refer again, briefly, to Luria's study. Essentially, the association that Luria established between the concept variables social relations and cultural practices was interpreted as the product of social evolution. Taking the society as the unit of analysis, Luria proposed that the development of collective relations of production demanded corresponding linguistic developments. The latter were not, on the other hand, a feature of societies exhibiting individualized relations of production. Luria further proposed that the terminal level of individual human cognition would correspond to the level of linguistic development exhibited by the society. Thus, individuals participating in the more advanced society should display higher forms of cognition than those participating only in the more primitive society. This constitutes, in simplified form, Luria's problem. Its concepts are defined in relation to each other. The definitions of social relations and linguistic development are implicated in the argument that establishes their association as are the definitions of societal linguistic development and individual cognitive development.

The **problem**, in other words, is constituted as a coherent and **self-referential system**. The ways in which the concepts, social relations, linguistic development, and cognitive development are defined entails that the value of one has implications for the value of the others. Thus, if a society exhibits collective social relations, then it will have developed literacy. If an individual participates in a literate society, then they will have developed taxonomic thinking. Thus the theoretically developed problem imposes a bias on findings relating to other potential empirical settings. Alternatively, you may say that the problem predicts the outcomes of research which may be carried out in additional empirical settings. That is, it comprises one or more testable propositions. If you were to adopt this alternative formulation, you may also be inclined to speak in terms of causality rather than implication.

The Mode of Interrogation

The **research mode of interrogation** consists of three moves which are, respectively, **specializing**, **localizing** and **generalizing**. The first move establishes the theoretical specificity of the research **problem** in relation to a wider **problematic** and general **theoretical field**. The second move makes explicit the local **findings** of the research in the context of the particular **empirical setting**, the latter being a selection from a general **empirical field**. The third move challenges the research to move beyond its local findings via processes of empirical and theoretical generalization.

The mode of interrogation may be thought of as a frame or a jig, perhaps. The kind of tool that holds in place the components of an object while it is under construction. This metaphor highlights two crucial features of the mode. Firstly, it is equally appropriate for use in reading and doing research. In either case, the finished product emerges from an extended process of organization and clarification. Secondly, there is no necessarily optimum sequence of application of the mode of interrogation. In effect, you can start anywhere and move along any of the three dimensions of the mode of interrogation.

Figure 8.2: The research mode of interrogation

DIMENSION 1: Specializing

1 *What is the general theoretical field within which the work is located?*

  authorities
    academic disciplines
    professional disciplines

  readership

2 *What is the problematic?*

  key antecedent work
    research
    other commentaries

3 *What is the specific problem?*

  system of concept variables
    propositions
    hypotheses
    questions
    conclusions

DIMENSION 2: Localizing

4 *What is the general empirical field within which the work is located?*

    practices
    experiences

5 *What is the local empirical setting?*

    research design issues
    data collection techniques
    sampling techniques
    practical issues

6 *What are the empirical findings?*

    indicator variables
    reliability

DIMENSION 3: Generalizing

7 *How is the link between the problem and the findings established?*

    concept variables and indicator variables
    validity

8 *How is the research generalized?*

    relationships between indicator variables
    units of analysis
    statistical inference
    control of variables

    relationships between concept variables
    implication/causality

The notion of a jig is a useful metaphor, but it should not be taken too literally. A jig is a rigid tool and, as such, it is prescriptive. The mode of interrogation is, by definition, interrogative. It asks particular kinds of questions of the research, it does not provide the answers. Furthermore, a response to one question may have an impact on a response to another that has already been made. Thus the mode of interrogation is an inherently dynamic kind of jig. There is, ultimately, no necessary termination point to its application. The situation is similar to that of sculpture, where the decision as to when a piece is finished must rest with the artist. Having made the decision, the sculptor may care to ponder on the nature of the object of their labour. Is it that their skill and imagination has enabled them to engage with the marble in constructing a statue, or have they simply revealed to the world a figure that was there in the stone all the time?

We shall terminate our presentation of the mode of interrogation with the schematic summary of its three dimensions in *Figure 8.2*.

Note

1   Constructivism and realism are themselves contested terms and certainly not everyone would oppose them in quite the way that we are doing here.

References

DOWLING, P.C. (1998) *The Sociology of Mathematics Education: Mathematical Myths/ Pedagogic Texts*, London: Falmer Press.

WOODS, P. and MERTTENS, R. (1994) 'Parents' and children's assessments of maths in the home', in MERTTENS, R. and WOODS, P. (eds) *IMPACT: Papers Presented at the Annual Meeting of the American Educational Research Association*, London: The IMPACT Project, University of North London.

9 Opening and Closing the Account

In this, penultimate chapter we want to focus on the end points of the research process. We have already given some consideration to the early stages of doing research in Chapter 2. Here, we shall revisit this phase by looking at the first steps in developing some initial ideas for small-scale research projects. We also want to give some attention to the terminal point in the research process, which is the construction of an account of your work. These two phases are of necessity separated in time. But they logically go together as the portals into and out from your research activity.

Entering the Mode of Interrogation

Here, are four of the initial ideas for research questions proposed by a group of education lecturers at a workshop which we held in Fortaleza, Brazil recently:

- What is the influence of computer use on children's intellectual development?
- Can nutrition education improve health?
- Can the use of educational television improve schooling?
- How are gender relations formed and maintained in schooling and how do they influence career choice?

The questions reflect, perhaps, anxieties about the effectiveness and/or equity of the professional practices with which the lecturers were associated. They may also be tied to political motives concerning the transformation of these practices. As they stand, the questions are very open. It is not immediately clear how you might move forward with them in either the empirical or theoretical fields. In order to initialize the operation of the research mode of interrogation, it is necessary to give them sharper focus and begin to think about possibilities for data collection. In the following discussion, we shall outline and explain our preliminary reformulations of the questions. We should emphasize that our reformulations reflect a combination of our own interests and our interpretation of the interests of the original proposers. To this extent, they are arbitrary. Our purpose is to illustrate some possible moves from an initial expression of interest to something which will enable the research process to begin.

The first question signals, perhaps, a professional interest in the use of information technology in schools, but seems to want to treat computer use as a unitary activity. Children use computers for video arcade games as well as standard tool packages (wordprocessing and so on) and a whole variety of educational uses, ranging from computer assisted learning programs to aid spelling and basic arithmetic to simulations of historical events and scientific processes to programming languages, such as Logo. It is unlikely that the effects of such a diversity of computer use will be undifferentiated.

The question is also pretty vague on the nature of the effects which might be expected, nor does it specify an age range. Does 'intellectual development' refer to cognitive level or to the acquisition of specific skills or knowledge? Are we talking about pre-school, or primary- or secondary-age children. We decided to interpret the question as expressing an interest in cognitive development focusing on the early years of elementary schooling, that is, at ages 5–6 years. This drew us to think of cognitive development in terms of Piagetian conservation (see, for example, Piaget, 1952; Donaldson, 1978). This is a long-standing and contentious area in educational research, and one with which most teachers will have some familiarity through their initial training. Approaching it from the direction of *new* technology looks interesting (although we are not claiming that it is completely original).

We are aware of work that has been done looking at the potential of interaction between children in the development of conservation (for example, Perret-Clermont, 1980). We therefore decided that the research should consider the possible effects of an interactive computer conservation training program. The research question thus became:

- Can an interactive computer conservation program contribute to children's cognitive development?

We decided upon an **experimental design** using the program as a **treatment**. There remained a decision to be made concerning which aspects of the treatment should be **controlled**. We decided to control the conservation training element, using an interactive drawing program for the treatment to be administered to the **control group**. We produced the following as a potential scheme of action:

(a) Design (or select) an interactive conservation of number training program (using number conservation tasks of various forms (rearrangement, addition, subtraction), voice-simulator instructions, three choices (more, same, less) and demonstration (of correct solutions).
(b) Select or design interactive drawing program.
(c) **Pre-test** opportunity sample of 5–6-year-olds, using **clinical interviews** to select samples of non-conservers and intermediates on conservation of number (experimental task) and other conservation tasks (e.g. conservation of volume).

(d) **Allocate** subjects to experimental and control groups by **strati-fied random sampling** (stratified by cognitive level) (or **quota sample** if sample size is small).

(e) Administer treatment: conservation program to experimental group, drawing program to control group.

(f) Administer **post-test** and delayed post-test (using clinical inter-views) to both groups.

The second and third of the four original questions exhibit similar problems. They are, again, inexplicit regarding the particular educational programme and do not suggest how improvement or effectiveness might be measured. The question on nutrition education introduces a particularly contested concept, that of 'health'. Because of this, we felt that the question lent itself particularly well to an **action research** project. Action research is a term which is applied to projects in which **practitioners** seek to effect transformations in their own practices. In general, the processes of determin-ing the objectives of such a project and of evaluating their effectiveness are themselves incorporated into the project. Some advocates of action research suggest an approach whereby objectives are redefined after each cycle of a rolling project. In this sense, there is no obvious natural termination to the programme. We decided to impose an arbitrary terminal point via the need to produce an account, in this case, after two cycles of the research.

In action research as we have interpreted it, it might be inappropriate to impose an academic or medical definition of 'health' on the community within which the project is to be located. We have, therefore, adopted this approach in our plan. Our revised research question is:

• Can we design and implement a nutrition education programme that transforms health-related nutritional practices?

The use of the 'can we' mode enabled us to interpret a project aiming at action as also embodying a question and, therefore, as legitimate empirical research, in our terms. Our initial proposals are, briefly, a follows:

(a) Identify a range of health problems that are believed to be miti-gated through changes in nutritional practices by reference to **key informants** in the community in which the project is to be located.

(b) Design nutrition education programme targeting forms of informa-tion relating to problems and related changes identified in (a).

(c) Implement programme.

(d) Immediate and delayed evaluation of changes in practices.

(e) Adaptation of programme and re-implementation.

(f) Immediate and delayed evaluation of changes in practices.

(g) Produce account.

This plan begs a large number of questions concerning, in particular, data collection under phases (a), (d) and (f). This is entirely appropriate. The ethos of action research, in particular, discourages the taking of important decisions other than by direct reference to the participating community (however that may be defined). The **mode of interrogation** which we have introduced in this book is, as we have indicated, to be applied continually throughout the research process. It thus takes the place of the individual whom Bridget Somekh (1995) — an exponent of action research — refers to as a 'critical friend'. It is, in other words, analogous to the academic supervisor or 'outsider' of practitioner research. We do, however, claim, that the difference between our position on action research and that of some of its major voices is that we advocate the full apprenticing of the practitioner researcher into the research mode of interrogation, rather than establishing a division of labour between participating individuals as practitioners, on the one hand, and academics, on the other. We shall return to this point in Chapter 10.

Clearly, the third question might also be interpreted as an action research project. However, the lecturer who proposed this question was particularly concerned with a scheme which is already in place in the State of Ceará, Brazil, where we were running the workshop. In effect, the scheme involved the use of video television programmes and non-specialist 'learning orientators' as substitutes for subject specialist teachers. The scheme was managed by the Secretary for Education at the State Ministry of Education. It incorporated subject curricula, which were represented by the content of the videos, and instructional procedures, which were overseen by a 'learning orientator supervisor', an official at the Ministry. We can refer to these as the official principles of the scheme. The lecturer's interest was in the extent to which the realization of the scheme accorded with the official programme; her own subject specialism was in science education. Her own expectations were that the exigencies of the classroom would effect a transformation of the official principles of the scheme and generate one or more sets of local principles. We reformulated the question as:

- What is the nature of the recontextualization of science discourse and pedagogic theory in the operationalization of an educational television programme? How is the recontextualization related to the structure of social relationships in the classroom (position of learning orientator with respect to official knowledge and students, relations between students, etc)?

Our preliminary ideas on a plan of action were as follows.

(a) Select **case study** classroom and one thirty minute biology TV programme.

(b) Access the official principles of the discourse and pedagogy via **interview** with learning orientator supervisor and analysis of programme.

(c) Interview learning orientator regarding local principles of discourse and pedagogy.

(d) **Observe** and video lesson having **habituated** the students and the learning orientator to the researcher and the video-camera over a period of two weeks.

(e) Re-interview learning orientator.

(f) Interviews with four students (two girls and two boys) at top and bottom of class performance (as indicated by learning orientator), plus group interview with some or all of the other students in groups of five or six.

The question on gender relations is immense in scope, covering, it would seem, the entire school age-range. It reflected a general concern, on the part of the proposer, with the issue of gender inequality in society. This is a concern which we share. However, a great deal of work has been done in this field and we felt that it was important to try to get a particular (which is not to say necessarily original) angle if the research was to generate something that would be likely to extend beyond the completely predictable. The question also needed to focus on a tighter age-range. We proposed the following question:

- How do school leavers negotiate counter gender-stereotypical career choices?

Our proposed scheme of action was as follows.

(a) Generate large **opportunity sample** of imminent school leavers. Administer four-question **questionnaire** (name, contact address, sex, intended career).

(b) Identify likely **critical case** studies.

(c) Administer sequences of loosely structured interviews over a period of two years: prior to leaving school; during job-seeking process, if applicable; on taking-up career; after one year; after two years.

These revised questions and associated plans of action took an average of twenty minutes discussion to generate. We are not claiming that any of them would remain unmodified either in the initial phases of literature review and planning or in the longer term of the research. Indeed, it would run counter to our description of research as a continuous application of the mode of interrogation if we were to make such a claim. We do claim that they enable the researcher to begin to identify some of the elements of their theoretical and empirical fields. In other words, they constitute entries into the research process. They are sufficiently precise to enable the application of the research mode of interrogation.

As we have suggested, the original questions may have been associated to a greater or lesser degree with professional and political motivations. Initial thoughts regarding research questions may also be coloured by methodological or locational interests: it may be that what you really want to do is some participant observation or spend some time in a rural school in Brazil. It may even be that you feel that your career or social position would be enhanced by being able to put 'Dr' before your name in your chequebook. Beginning researchers enter the research process with a variety of motivational baggage. In our experience, however, the more of this baggage that can be left at the door, the more effectively the research mode of interrogation can be applied. Even in our initial revisions of the research questions which we have introduced in this section, there has been a substantial cooling out of the anxieties and political interests that shaped the original versions. Motives are not, however, to be lost. The baggage can be collected at the other end of the research process. It is to this phase that we shall move in the next section.

Exiting the Mode of Interrogation

We have described the research mode of interrogation as a continuous complex process involving specializing, localizing and generalizing. In this interpretation, there is no unambiguous point of completion of the research although particular research activities — such as data collection and library searches — may have planned beginnings and endings. You can, however, establish a point of exit from the process by addressing a **readership**, that is, by producing an **account** of or **reporting** your research.

In Chapter 8 we defined the potential readership of your research as a component of the **theoretical field**. Therefore, the process of clarifying the nature of the audience of your account is itself a **specializing** of this field. There are, of course, many possibilities for the readership. In particular, we have distinguished between practitioner or professional readerships and academic readerships. Your choice of readership is important, because it defines the **genre** in which you will be writing. In this chapter, we shall concentrate on the genre of academic writing. We noted, in Chapter 8, that the readership of academic writing should be thought of as a subset of its **authorities**. In writing an account of their research, then, the beginning researcher is making a claim to academic authorship. There is a sense, then, in which the account is a submission for evaluation by the field. We are of course asserting that the nature of the evaluation is precisely the mode of interrogation that we have introduced in this book. This clearly has implications for the content, emphasis and style of your account. We shall describe a possible structure for the account.

For example, your account must enable the reader to situate your work within a region of the general theoretical field. That is, it must construct its **problematic**. This involves an organized discussion of your key authorities, which is generally referred to as a literature review. The principal purpose of a literature review, however, is less to inform your readership of what work has been done in your area of interest, than to position your own research in relation to this body. Of course, an annotated summary of related research can provide a useful resource, not least for other beginning researchers whose own literature searches may benefit from your groundwork. However, you should avoid adopting a pedagogic attitude in constructing your review; you are locating yourself within the field, not enlightening its members.

A useful approach is to organize the contents of your library search into categories that relate to your own work. You can then discuss the categories in terms of the ways and extent to which your work coincides with or deviates from them. Individual items may be used in the form of examples of the work in each category. Where your work is very close to research in a particular category, you will need to enter into more detailed discussion in order to clarify the particular specialization that you have adopted. Categories which are more obviously distinct from your approach may be dealt with more briefly. An initial, coarse classification may be made in terms of research that focuses on related empirical settings, on the one hand, and work that adopts related methodological or theoretical approaches, on the other. Work that falls into both of these categories is clearly that which is most closely related to your own.

In organizing your account, you may choose to present the full statement of your research problem and the details of your empirical setting as emerging from your literature review. In this case, the initial statement of the problem and description of the empirical site will be made in general terms. The literature review will then provide entry into a full theoretical elaboration of the conceptual space that constitutes your **problem** which, in turn, will provide an entry into the description of decisions relating to your **empirical setting**.

The problem having been established, you will be in a position to mark out the empirical setting in terms of research design issues, sampling, data collection techniques etc. Now, clearly, the empirical work will have been shaped by deliberate decisions, on the one hand, and by contingencies, on the other. The latter will relate to opportunities that were or were not available, response rates of less than 100%, mortality rates of more than 0%, your own errors in respect of interviewing technique and practicalities, and so forth. Deliberate decisions can, to a greater extent than contingencies, be justified in relation to your problem. However, this does not entail that you should present an apology for the unintended features of your empirical work.

Both the intentional and unintentional circumstances which have shaped your empirical setting and findings have implications for your conclusions, including the generalizability of your research. However, the conclusions are not constructed until the empirical work has been completed. They should, therefore, be formulated with reference to both the intended and the actual context of your empirical setting. This being the case, you should describe contingencies in terms of the qualifications and limitations that they impose upon your conclusions. You will also want to include some reflexive discussion on alternative decisions or approaches that might have been adopted with hindsight. This discussion would commonly (but not necessarily) be incorporated into a concluding chapter or section. It is appropriate for this section or chapter also to look beyond your particular project to implications and suggestions for further research and, indeed for professional practice. What you should not do is produce a list of excuses for not doing the job properly in the first place.

The termination of the localizing process is the construction of the **empirical findings**. Here, you will need to make decisions relating to the form in which these are to be presented. We have suggested that research can often benefit from a combination of qualitative and quantitative approaches. If your approach is predominantly qualitative, then you will be presenting your findings via **elaborated description**. This clearly raises questions regarding the representativeness of the examples that you select from your data set. As we have pointed out in Chapter 7, the use of quantitative summaries can be of value here. Again, the fact that you have quantified your work does not entail that you have to carry out statistical analysis. Nor does it require you to present the results as anything more than simple tables. More sophisticated quantitative analysis and charts should be used only where they add to the force or clarity of the argument which you are making.

So far, in our description of a possible account, we have made reference to the following contents:

(i)   general statement of the problem and outline of the empirical setting;
(ii) establishing of the problematic in terms of key antecedent work categorized by empirical setting and by theoretical and methodological approach;
(iii) detailed theoretical exposition of the problem;
(iv) description of decisions made and contingent circumstances relating to the empirical setting;
(v)   findings;
(vi) conclusion.

These items could quite clearly be interpreted as sections of a 6000 word article, or chapters of a 20 000 word masters dissertation or parts (some of which may contain more than one chapter) of an 80 000 word doctoral thesis or book. In our experience, a great many successful accounts do indeed adopt such a format. However, it is not intended as a prescription and another form of structural organization may be more appropriate in your particular case. Nevertheless, each of these elements should be included. They must be addressed with clarity and with a clear indication of their role in the general line of argument that you are seeking to establish.

You will notice that our original description of these items has not been given in precisely the same order in which they appear in the summary list. Furthermore, it is unlikely that either order will coincide with the sequence of events and decisions that actually constituted the research process itself. After all, we have defined this process as the continuous application of the mode of interrogation and not as a sequence of neatly delineated phases. Nor will the order of the above list necessarily coincide with the order in which the account is written.

In describing literature, the Russian formalist school of literary scholars made a distinction between the story, or *fabula*, and the plot, or *suzhet*. Shklovsky described the technique of art as:

> . . . to make objects unfamiliar, to make forms difficult, to increase the difficulty and length of perception because the process of perception is an esthetic end in itself and must be prolonged. Art is a way of experiencing the artfulness of an object; the object itself is not important. (Shklovsky, quoted by Kozulin, 1990; pp. 29–30)

This would certainly be an exaggeration were it to be applied to the relationship between the research story and its plot as realized in its account. Even so, the distinction provides a useful metaphor. As we have said, the account is always addressed to an audience. Its author will also wish to incorporate at least some of the motivational 'baggage' that they left at the door of the research process on the way in (of course, some of it may have been repacked somewhat in their absence). Furthermore, the structure of the argument which you are making will also impose itself upon your account. These considerations must have implications for decisions relating to the order, emphasis and style of the account. Nevertheless, if you are writing within the academic genre, you must not lose sight of the mode of interrogation which, we are claiming, will constitute the basis of the evaluation of your work.

There is a corollary. The fact that the structure and ordering of a written account is likely to deviate from the structure and ordering of the research process that it represents has an additional implication. Essentially, it means that you should not take research reports as simple guides to the doing (or even the reading) of research.

We shall conclude this section with some brief practical advice for beginning authors. We shall focus on four issues that have sometimes caused problems for students whose work we have been required to assess. Firstly, the question of language. The first issue that we must mention here concerns the need to avoid the use of sexist language or terms which are or which may be interpreted as derogatory with respect to ethnic or other cultural categories. We will not provide detailed guidelines here, but guidelines on avoiding **sexism** and **racism** in sociology, for example, are available from the British Sociological Association office, Unit 3G, Mountjoy Research Centre, Stockton Road, Durham DH1 3UR.

Secondly, in relation to language, it is not entirely inappropriate to include figurative and other literary devices in a research account. However, your principal concern should be to be understood as you intend to be understood. Essentially, this means writing clearly and explicitly. All educational researchers are dealing with ideas that are new, at least to themselves. Getting these ideas down into a wordprocessor file is often a tortuous business. It is, then, very likely that your first write through of a section or chapter or of the whole account will consist of excessively long and complex sentences comprising excessively long and complex paragraphs which are woven into a confusing and incoherent structure; confusing to others, if not to you. Go through it again. Lay out the central structure of what you want to say. Then rearrange your paragraphs. Remember that if you are starting a sentence with an expression such as 'although', or 'whilst', or 'in order to', and so on, you are going to need at least two clauses (see the beginning of the next paragraph). Better to make two sentences.

Because putting difficult ideas into coherent English is a challenging task, there is sometimes a temptation to make use of someone else's words. This is quite acceptable where it takes the form of a **quotation**. All quotations should be indexed as such. Where the quotation is no more than a few words, you may use quotation marks and run it into your own text. If you want to use a quotation of more than one or two lines, then you really should indent it as we have done with the Shklovsky quotation above. It is also a good idea to use a smaller font size for emphasis. All quotations should be followed by a reference, including the number of the page on which the original appears.

There are three caveats regarding the use of quotations. Firstly, they should not be too long. For most purposes, you should consider 200 words to be an absolute maximum and generally aim to use shorter quotations. Secondly, you should not overuse quotations. Use them where an author has put something in a particularly apposite or elegant way, or where you want to discuss a particular phrase or definition that they have used. Too many quotations makes the text hard to read and inhibits your imposition of your own authorship on your work. Thirdly, and most importantly, all quotations must be signalled as such, either by the use of quotation marks or indenting and with an adequate reference. Do not represent other people's words as if they are your own, even in slightly modified form. Minimally, this weakens the authority of your text. In serious cases, it constitutes **plagiarism**. Where your account is being submitted as part of the requirements for a higher degree, this could result in failure and the possibility of being banned from re-entering.

One method of uncluttering an account is to make use of **footnotes** (notes at the bottom of the page) or endnotes (notes at the end of the chapter). We have generally avoided them in this book, although both of us make extensive use of footnotes or **endnotes** (depending upon the publisher's house style) in our research writing. In our opinion, a footnote or endnote should be introduced for much the same reasons as an **appendix**. That is, it should contain details or information which is useful or relevant or interesting, but which is not central to the line of argument which is being developed. Essentially, it must be possible to read the work without references to footnotes, endnotes, or appendices.

If you have any choice, we would suggest that you do not use footnotes or endnotes simply to list **references**. We say this for two reasons. Firstly, we feel that references are vital to the interpretation of an academic account and should be run in with the main text; more about this in a moment. Secondly, if you want your readers to read even some of your footnotes or endnotes, then you should make all or most of them interesting. This is unlikely to be achieved if most of your footnotes or endnotes contain no more than publication details. On the other hand, you may want to make a statement about a particular reference, like this:

> see, for example, Brown and Dowling (1998), which includes a brief discussion of the use of footnotes and endnotes in academic writing.

An annotated reference of this form would be an appropriate candidate for a footnote or endnote.

In our opinion, the identification of references is a crucial feature of the academic **genre** of writing. This is because an academic account is participating in a field of discourse which is populated and constituted by its authors. Your declaring of references assists your reader to position your work within this field and may help them to interpret any technical terms which you are using. Although house styles vary, our preference is for the reference in the text to consist simply of the author's name and date of publication. This should enable the reader to locate unambiguously the relevant item in your bibliography. Thus, if there are two items by Brown and Dowling which are both published in 1997, then refer to them in the text and in the bibliography as Brown and Dowling, 1997a and 1997b.

We are firmly of the opinion that references should be used to assist the reader both to follow-up on the cited work and ideas and to interpret and position your work. They should not, in our opinion, be used to bolster support for an assertion or a decision which you are not otherwise going to defend. Thus:

> I decided upon a non-directive interview approach (Cohen and Manion, 1994).

Cohen and Manion provide a very useful summary of a wide range of research methods and their book has possibly been the most widely used research methods handbook in the field of education in recent years. The mere mention of their names, however, cannot provide authority for your research decisions. Minimally, you would need to include some discussion of the nature and advantages and disadvantages of the approach that you adopt. You will then need to defend its selection in your particular case by reference to the questions which constitute the research mode of interrogation. Unfortunately, you will find many instances of the use of references to lend spurious support to assertions and decisions, even amongst experienced authors of research accounts. Indeed, we are all guilty of it at times. Nevertheless, try to avoid it.

This concludes our brief discussion of the writing-up phase of the research process. It also concludes this practical chapter on entering and quitting the research process. In the final chapter we shall present our 'Manifesto' for educational research which, of course, derives from the position that we have been introducing throughout the book.

References

Brown, A.J. and Dowling, P.C. (1998) *Doing Research/Reading Research: A Mode of Interrogation for Education*, London: Falmer Press.

Cohen, L. and Manion, L. (1994) *Research Methods in Education*, fourth edition, London: Routledge.

Donaldson, M. (1978) *Children's Minds*, Glasgow: Fontana/Collins.

Kozulin, A. (1990) *Vygotsky's Psychology: A Biography of Ideas*, New York: Harvester/Wheatsheaf.

Perret-Clermont, A-N. (1980) *Social Interaction and Cognitive Development in Children*, New York: Academic Press.

Piaget, J. (1952) *The Child's Conception of Number*, London: Routledge and Kegan Paul.

Somekh, B. (1995) 'The contribution of action research to development in social endeavours: A position paper on action research methodology', *British Educational Research Journal*, **21**, 3, pp. 339–355.

10 The Practitioner and Educational Research: A Manifesto

We have claimed, in this book, that the fundamental criterion for the evaluation of empirical educational research is that it should aim at coherent closure. There are at least two directions from which we may be challenged on this claim. Firstly, a number of authors within what may (very) loosely be referred to as the postmodern school self-consciously seek to avoid closure in producing their own texts. These are intended to reveal the deconstruction of what are only apparently closed texts produced by others. Well, we see value in such writing, too, just as we see value in modernist epistemological debates between, say, constructivists and realists. We occasionally engage in it ourselves. Such work is important in the generation of critical dialogue on and within the research activity. Suffice it to say, perhaps, that if there were no texts that aspired to closure, the postmoderns would have very little to do.

The second line of challenge comes from the pragmatic professionals. Here, the criticism is that undue emphasis on internal consistency is onanistic. Whilst trumpeting the potential value of research as the basis of professional practice, this position claims that what is really important is that the research should help practitioners in their work (for example, see Barber, 1996). We also think that educational research should help practitioners in their work. However, our position, in a nutshell, is that educational **practitioners** need to move outside of their professional practice and into the distinct activity of educational **research**. This is essential if they are to generate the dialogue between research and practice that is a necessary condition for their mutual development. It is this position that we shall argue in this final chapter.

The mode of interrogation that we presented in Chapter 8 is intended and designed for application in the reading as well as in the doing of research. Research, then, is to be interrogated. This is not, however, the only way of utilizing research. Here, for example, is an extract from a policy document which is arguing for a particular approach to the choice of medium of instruction in schools:

> The gradual introduction of the language of wider communication as a language of learning is based on the *research evidence* which strongly suggests that the conceptual development of children is facilitated by initial learning in their home language. (ANC, 1994; p. 64; our emphasis)

The African National Congress — the authorial voice of this text — is laying claim to a reading of research. However, the form that the reading takes completely subordinates the research to the principles of the quite different activity in which the ANC is involved. This is a political activity. 'Language of wider communication' means English, but this cannot be stated as, to do so, would rule out Afrikaans. English, as the language of the struggle, is acceptable in the new South Africa, but must not be allowed to dominate the African languages which most of its population speak. A clear space must be established for each. The ANC document recruits 'research' in achieving precisely this. The 'research' itself is not identified or elaborated or criticized in any way. Nor should it be, because to do so might encourage a shift from the political activity of governance to the academic activity of enquiry. This is not an interrogation, but a consumption of research which entails its recruitment as a resource by political strategies (see Dowling, 1998).

Here is another extract, this time from the field of academic educational research:

> The results [of this study] support the thesis proposed by Luria (1976) and by Donaldson (1978) that thinking sustained by daily human sense can be at a higher level than thinking out of context in the same subject. (Nunes et al., 1993; pp. 23–5)

Surprisingly, perhaps, the research cited in this piece is also being recruited for what might metaphorically be described as political purposes. It is being used to lend additional support to the authors' claims in what Dowling (1995, 1998) describes as a 'positioning strategy'. Luria and Donaldson do no 'work' in this text. Their omission would not alter the sense of the claim that is being made. Furthermore, the citation elides the quite fundamental differences between the three pieces of research. Luria, as we have stated earlier in this book, was working with adult subjects in a remote area of the Soviet Union in the 1930s. Donaldson was drawing on work with the very young children of university staff in Edinburgh in the 1970s. Nunes and her colleagues were working in the early 1980s in Recife, Brazil, with 9 to 15-year-old children from 'very poor backgrounds'. Further, and more importantly, there are very substantial theoretical differences between the studies. It will be apparent from our description of Luria's work that his position was quite incompatible with that attributed to him in the extract.

In each of the two extracts the author attributes a degree of authority to the research, but denies it its own voice. The cited work is almost arbitrarily chosen in respect of its specific content. The ANC text would probably have worked as well by using an appeal to commonsense. The excision of Luria and Donaldson from the second extract would weaken its authority, but not significantly alter its sense. The specificity of the language research and of the work of Luria and Donaldson are not allowed to speak. In each case, then, the consumption of research entails the transformative recontextualizing of its principles in subordination to another project.

In his presentation of his **social activity theory**, Dowling has argued that a more or less radical transformation in the principles of a practice occurs whenever it is recontextualized between distinct activities. The practices of the recontextualizing activity include *strategies* which recruit those of the recontextualized activity as *resources*. Precisely what is recruited as a resource has a degree of arbitrariness. The manner in which resources are recruited, however, entails a subordination to the principles of the recontextualizing activity. For example, Dowling (1996, 1998) has illustrated this recontextualizing with respect to the recruitment and transformation of domestic and other practices by school mathematics. Elsewhere, we have illustrated the recruitment and transformation of domestic practices by a professionally motivated parental involvement scheme in the primary phase (Brown, forthcoming, Brown and Dowling, 1993) and we (Dowling and Brown, 1996) and Ensor (1995) have problematized the relationship between teacher education and classroom practice.

We want to maintain that the general field of professional educational practice and academic research constitutes a range of distinct activities. Dowling has defined *activity* as the contextualizing basis for all social practice. Any particular activity — say, teaching — establishes a range of positions which can be occupied by human individuals. The activity also constitutes a range of practices which are distributed to these positions. Thus, teachers are specialized according to their discipline and phase and also according to their post. Students are differentiated according to age, 'ability', 'needs', and other attributes such as gender, ethnicity and social class. Parents may be attributed differential levels of cooperativeness, and so on. What it means to be a teacher, a student, or a parent, is contingent upon the activity. For example, Brown (forthcoming) has found that teachers who are also parents maintain a high degree of differentiation between these positions. Teachers, when speaking as teachers, can describe what parents are like, without appearing to accept these descriptions as applying to themselves.

Academic educational research, as an activity, defines a different set of positions and practices. In particular, the output of academic research is subject to peer review through the procedures of publication in journals and books and through conference arrangements. Furthermore, the nature of this output is always an abstraction from the immediate empirical context of the research. Local contingencies are more or less effectively eliminated through definition and/or control, so that the empirical setting is constituted as a laboratory. Research output is, in other words, relatively context-independent, indeed, this is a condition of its generalizability. The empirical site of educational research is, in this sense, consumed by research and this consumption entails the transformative **recontextualization** of the site.

Professional educational practice and academic educational research, then, are distinct fields of activity. They are not, however, restricted to specific institutional sites. Teachers and other educational professionals can and do become involved in the production as well as the reading of research and universities are teaching as well as research institutions. In general terms, we might say that educational activities constitute the empirical basis of educational research which is constituted as an arena for the interrogation of educational activities. The two fields stand in dialogic relation to each other. We want to maintain that this is potentially a productive relationship, but only to the extent that the dialogic potential is maintained. In other words, failure to recognize the distinctive natures of the two fields will result in the one being unduly subordinated to the principles of the other.

Thus, psychological research which defines out the social and political structuring of the classroom may well be good psychology, but it is perhaps an abstraction too far in respect of educational research. Some approaches to **action research** (though not all and not, we would claim, ours) aim at the direct development of professional practices, but perhaps give too little scope to the research to organize its own theoretical space. In these cases, educational research and professional educational practice respectively recruit the other as a reservoir of resources for the elaboration of their own strategies.

One of the outcomes of the failure to regard research as a distinctive activity is the plundering of research for the techniques which will facilitate the genesis of the all-singing/all-dancing **practitioner-researcher**. This accords with the view that all the teacher needs is some interviewing skills and a methodological lexicon in order to turn them into a research-based professional. Thus you find the curricularizing within higher education of the practices of research in the construction of research methods courses and books on research methods for educational practitioners. A curriculum is an educational programme which of necessity constitutes a content as a sequence of topics (whether or not they are spirally revisited). So, there are research methods books and courses which comprise a chapter or seminar on surveys, one on case studies, another on interviews, another on participant observation, yet another on the use of secondary data, and so on. We do not in any way wish to deny the potential usefulness of such courses and books and have, indeed, appended to this volume an annotated bibliography which includes such items. Furthermore, we are clear that there is a degree of inevitability about this or some equivalent form of organization and have not avoided it in our own presentation. Nevertheless, there are a number of potential dangers to the extent that the specificities of the research activity are subordinated to the exigencies of the educational activity.

One of these dangers is that an unprincipled organization of the diversity of methodological approaches to research may lead to the fetishizing of methods. **Case study** — which we referred to in Chapter 3 — is, indeed, a case in point. One of us recently attended a professorial presentation (not in our own institution) on 'Case study research in education' given to a group of about fifty masters students. After the presentation, a number of the students asked the professor to rule on whether the approaches that they had adopted in their respective studies were or were not appropriately described as case studies. The professor appeared to find it very difficult to rule one way or the other in most of the cases which were introduced. Just what is and what is not a case? One of the quotations that the professor had cited on the first page of his handout was from Robert Stake. Unfortunately, the reference was not supplied by the professor, so we were unable to verify its authenticity. Whether or not Stake wrote it, however, it presents a widely held image of case study research;

> Case studies are special because they have a different focus. The case study focus is on a single actor, a single institution, a single enterprise, maybe a classroom, usually under natural conditions so as to understand it — that bounded system — in its natural habitat.

This is a mythologizing of research and a romanticizing of the world in general. The 'natural' world is presented as thinkable in terms of a collection of mutually independent (bounded) systems which are nevertheless transparently knowable to us. We, as the observers, are able to dispense with our preconceptions and motivations. It recalls, perhaps, an image of a whispering David Attenborough tiptoeing around a tropical forest followed by an equally silent production crew using night-sights on their cameras and telling it like it is — or, rather, like it would be, even if they weren't there. But of course Attenborough and his production and editorial teams are highly skilled producers within a hugely costly media enterprise. They can and must act selectively and productively, that is to say transformatively, on their object environment in constructing their programmes, irrespective of the relationship that they or their viewers believe might exist between the programme and the pristine environment (whatever that might be).

Stake's description is also mythologizing in its reference to the singularity of the object of the case study. The expression 'single actor' may seem clear enough. But what is to be the context in which the actor is involved. Will educational research consider the behaviour of the subject in their domestic and leisure activities as well as in the classroom? Will it address the entire lifecycle and, indeed, family history of the subject? Will it be concerned with physical aspects such as the subject's cardiovascular system? The fact of the matter is that even a single actor participates in a multiplicity of research sites upon which research acts selectively, which is to say, it samples. To assert that each of the potential research sites is independent of the others is to constitute a radically schizoid subject. The situation becomes even more complicated when the unit of analysis becomes institutional.

There is, in other words, no such thing as 'the case study approach' other than as constituted by the curricularizing of research methods. Within the context of a specific research study, the use of the term 'case' is probably best interpreted as simply a way of describing one's sampling procedures.

Our position, then, is that research must constitute its object just as educational practices have constituted 'the case study approach'. That is to say, research must impose selective and organizational principles upon its object site in establishing the empirical basis for its data. The rationality of these principles is precisely realized in the principles of the research activity which we have presented in Chapter 8 as the research mode of interrogation. The motivational source for research may, as in the action research tradition, be a question or a problem that arises within professional educational practice. However, if the dialogic relationship between professional and research practice is to be maintained, the nature of the imposition of research upon its site must be constituted as a gaze from another position and employing the practices of another activity. A dialogue, by definition, involves more than one voice. The professional practitioner intending to engage in educational research in the interrogation of their own practices will need to acquire the principles and not merely the trappings of these research practices. This entails a kind of apprenticeship into the practices of research. This book is intended to stand as a contribution to such an apprenticeship.

References

AFRICAN NATIONAL CONGRESS (1994) *A Policy for Education and Training*, Johannesburg: ANC.

BARBER, M. (1996) *The Learning Game: Arguments for an Education Revolution*, London: Gollancz.

BROWN, A.J. (forthcoming) *Parental Participation, Positioning and Pedagogy: A Sociological Study of the IMPACT Primary School Mathematics Project.*

BROWN, A.J. and DOWLING P.C. (1993) 'The bearing of school mathematics on domestic space', in MERTTENS, R., MAYERS, D., BROWN, A.J. and VASS, J. (eds) *Ruling the Margins: Problematizing Parental Involvement*, London: University of North London Press, pp. 39–52.

DOWLING, P.C. (1995) 'Discipline and Mathematise: The myth of relevance in education', *Perspectives in Education*, **16**, 2, pp. 209–226.

DOWLING, P.C. (1996) 'A sociological analysis of school mathematics texts', *Educational Studies in Mathematics*, **31**, pp. 389–415

DOWLING, P.C. (1998) *The Sociology of Mathematics Education: Mathematical Myths/ Pedagogic Texts*, London: Falmer Press.

Dowling, P.C. and Brown, A.J. (1996) *Pedagogy and Community in Three South African Schools: A Classroom Study* at http://www.ioe.ac.uk/ccs/ccsroot/ccs/dowling_brown/1996.html.

Ensor, P. (1995) 'From student to teacher: Continuity or rupture', presented at the Kenton Educational Association Conference, Grahamstown, October 1995 (available from the author at the School of Education, University of Cape Town).

Nunes, T., Schliemann, A.D. and Carraher, D.W. (1993) *Street Mathematics and School Mathematics*, Cambridge: Cambridge University Press.

Evaluation

Whenever we have presented the courses out of which this book has developed, we have included a session for participant evaluation. This is a little difficult when writing a book. We would, however, like to invite you to contact us with your response to the book. We are keen to receive critical comments (regarding both what works and what doesn't), suggestions and anecdotes about your research experiences. Most of all, we would like to see the opening up of the vast amount of authoritative writing on and practice in education to the rigorous scrutiny of the research mode of interrogation which we have introduced.

Andrew Brown & Paul Dowling
Culture Communication & Societies
Institute of Education
University of London
20 Bedford Way
London WC1H 0AL

email: a.brown@ioe.ac.uk & p.dowling@ioe.ac.uk

Annotated Bibliography

We have listed a number of books which we and/or our students have found to be useful. The short comments we have provided are intended to give some indication of why we feel a particular book to be interesting.

We have not included any journal articles. It is within journals that some of the most vigorous methodological debate takes place. There are some journals, such as the *International Journal of Qualitative Studies in Education* which are dedicated to the exploration of methodological issues. Journals which are principally concerned with the publication of research reports, such as the *British Education Research Journal*, also publish papers of methodological interest from time to time. We recommend that everyone carrying out research should become familiar with the journal collection in their library.

The annotated bibliography has been divided into two sections. The first gives a short selection of general research methods books. Each of these attempts to give a comprehensive introduction to educational or social research. The second part of the bibliography contains more specialized books.

General Research Methods Books

BELL, J. (1993) *Doing Your Research Project: A Guide for First-Time Researchers in Education and Social Science*, 2nd edition, Buckingham: Open University Press.

A clearly presented and straightforward guide to **designing**, conducting and producing **accounts** and **reports**. The process is laid out sequentially and practical advice is given at every stage. In attempting to cover so much in a short book, superficial treatment of techniques and issues is inevitable.

COHEN, L. and MANION, L. (1994) *Research Methods in Education*, 4th edition, London: Routledge.

A useful reference book. Covers a wide range of approaches to educational research. Good on **research design**. Provides a reliable source of information on approaches such as **personal construct theory** which are given little space in other introductory research methods texts. With so much to cover, the accounts given can only act as starting points.

GILBERT, N. (ed.) (1993) *Researching Social Life*, London: Sage.

This collection of papers provides an accessible introduction to the conduct of small scale qualitative and quantitative research. Includes the design of

questionnaires, the measurement of **attitudes**, **interviewing** and **ethnographic** work. Not specifically aimed at educational researchers but a useful introductory text nonetheless. Different approaches to research are exemplified by accounts of three contrasting research studies.

HITCHCOCK, G. and HUGHES, D. (1995) *Research and the Teacher: A Qualitative Introduction to School-Based Research*, 2nd edition, London: Routledge.

Comprehensive introduction to educational research aimed specifically at teachers. Includes consideration of research **ethics**. Covers issues in the **design**, conduct and in producing **accounts** and **reports** of **qualitative** research. Provides good coverage of data collection techniques (including **interviewing**, **observation**, **diaries**, **life histories** and **document analysis**).

ROBSON, C. (1993) *Real World Research: A Resource for Social Scientists and Practitioner-Researchers*, Oxford: Blackwell.

A very thorough and comprehensive introduction to conducting small-scale research. The author has a clear image of what he sees as constituting worthwhile research. Provides good, clear, practical advice on specific data collection techniques and approaches to the analysis of **qualitative** and quantitative data. Good sections on **interviewing**, on **observation** and on the analysis of **quantitative** data. Not aimed specifically at the educational researcher. Has a distinct bias towards psychological research.

Specialized Books

ADELMAN, C. (ed.) (1981) *Uttering, Muttering: Collecting, Using and Reporting Talk for Social and Educational Research*, London: Grant McIntyre.

The papers in this collection focus on talk in educational and other settings. The accounts of research given cover **interviewing** adults in the context of institutional **case studies** (Simon) through to the exploration of forms of speech in teacher child **interaction** (Wells). In the appendix to the latter paper there is an example of a set of **transcription** conventions.

ANTAKI, C. (ed.) (1988) *Analysing Everyday Explanation: A Casebook of Methods*, London: Sage.

A collection of papers illustrating a wide range of approaches to the analysis of explanations. Each paper contains an outline of the theoretical perspective from which the research is carried out, an example, in **qualitative** mode, of analysis of a fragment of data and an evaluation of the approach adopted. This format draws attention to the need to address both the **theoretical field** and the **empirical setting** when designing and evaluating research.

BANNISTER, D. and FRANSELLA, F. (1986) *Inquiring Man: The Psychology of Personal Constructs*, 3rd edition, London: Croom Helm.

Thorough and readable introduction to **personal construct theory** and the use of **repertory grids**.

BARTHES, R. (1973) *Mythologies*, London: Paladin.

First published in French in 1957, this short book provides examples of Barthes' form of **semiotic analysis**. Barthes takes as the objects of his analysis a range of popular cultural phenomena, from the world of wrestling to the brain of Einstein. The final chapter outlines Barthes' method, paying particular attention to the notion of **myth**.

BECKER, H.S. (1986) *Writing for Social Scientists: How to Start and Finish Your Thesis, Book or Article*, Chicago: University of Chicago Press.

A practical book about academic **writing** that is actually interesting to read. Becker takes a serious sociological interest in both the producers of academic texts and their **readership**.

BERNSTEIN, B.B. (1996) *Pedagogy, Symbolic Control and Identity: Theory, Research Critique*, London: Taylor & Francis.

Bernstein directly addresses the research potential of his thesis. Part One provides an exposition of his current work. Part Two clearly lays out the distinctive approach to research that has characterized the empirical work of Bernstein and his colleagues for over three decades. Chapters 5 and 6 deal specifically with the movement between the **theoretical field** and **empirical** data and the development of **network analysis**.

BLACK, T.R. (1993) *Evaluating Social Science Research: An Introduction*, London: Sage.

Provides a thorough guide to reading **quantitative** research in the social sciences and education.

BLISS, J., MONK, M. and OGBORN, J. (eds) (1983) *Qualitative Data Analysis for Educational Research*, London: Croom Helm.

An introduction to the use of **networks** in the analysis of **qualitative** data. Includes a number of short papers in which researchers give accounts of the process of analysis. In most cases the networks are not theoretically derived and tend to provide a means for the organization rather than analysis of data. The paper by Holland is a notable exception.

BRYMAN, A. (1988) *Quantity and Quality in Social Research*, London: Unwin Hyman.

A careful consideration of the relationship between qualitative and quantitative approaches to social research. The author argues that the practices of researchers should be taken into account in addressing the **qualitative/quantitative distinction** and that the **epistemological** polarization of approaches that often characterizes debate in this area is not fruitful.

BURAWOY, M., *et al.* (1991) *Ethnography Unbound: Power and Resistance in the Modern Metropolis*, Berkeley: University of California Press.

Collection of **ethnographic** research by graduate students attending Burawoy's participant observation course at Berkeley. The introduction and conclusion by Burawoy place the empirical studies in a distinctive theoretical and methodological context. **Participant observation** is viewed as exemplifying 'what is distinctive about the practice of all social science' (p. 3).

Burgess, R.G. (ed.) (1985) *Issues in Educational Research: Qualitative Methods*, London: Falmer Press.

Burgess, R.G. (ed.) (1985) *Strategies of Educational Research: Qualitative Methods*, London: Falmer Press.

Two complementary collections of papers by educational researchers using **qualitative** methods. Together they give an overview of issues and approaches.

Burgess, R.G. (ed.) (1986) *Key Variables in Social Investigation*, London: Routledge & Kegan Paul.

A valuable discussion of important conceptual issues in the **design** of research. Each paper takes a particular variable common in social research (gender, for instance) and explores the movement from **concept** to **indicators**. The contributors are all experienced empirical researchers. The bibliographies provide good starting points for further reading.

Carr, W. and Kemmis, S. (1986) *Becoming Critical: Education, Knowledge and Action Research*, London: Falmer Press.

A well-argued critique of naive approaches to **action research**. Drawing on critical theory, the authors advocate an alternative basis for the development of **practitioner research** in education.

Clegg, F. (1982) *Simple Statistics: A Course Book for the Social Sciences*, Cambridge: Cambridge University Press.

Straightforward introduction to **statistics** and **quantitative analysis**. Useful for beginning researchers looking for a non-threatening introduction to basic concepts. By necessity lacking in detail and limited in scope.

Coffey, A. and Atkinson, P. (1996) *Making Sense of Qualitative Data*, London: Sage.

An accessible account of the process of **qualitative analysis**. Focuses mainly on **ethnographic** work. Using examples from their own research, the authors illustrate the movement from data to an analytic account. They compare the coding of qualitative data with forms of narrative analysis. Useful sections on **writing** research **accounts** and **reports** and the use of **information technology**.

Croll, P. (1986) *Systematic Classroom Observation*, London: Falmer Press.

Provides a guide to systematic observation as a research technique in classroom settings. Includes advice on the use of **observation schedules** and examples from the **ORACLE study**.

Delamont, S. (1992) *Fieldwork in Educational Settings: Methods, Pitfalls and Perspectives*, London: Falmer Press.

The early chapters focus on the reading and **writing** of research **accounts** and **reports** and the judgment of quality in **qualitative** research (and specifically **ethnographic** work). The latter part of the book traces the progress of the research project from the choice of a topic to writing an account.

Denzin, N.K. and Lincoln, Y.S. (eds) (1994) *Handbook of Qualitative Research*, Thousand Oaks, Calif.: Sage.

A collection of thirty-six specially commissioned papers covering a wide range of issues and approaches to **qualitative** research. Includes papers on particular perspectives on inquiry (e.g. **feminist** approaches), specific ways of approaching research (including **grounded theory**, **ethnography** and the use of **case studies**), methods for the collection of data (including **observational** techniques and **interviewing**) and modes of analysis (including **semiotic analysis**, the interpretation of personal experience and the use of **information technology**). Each paper has an extensive bibliography.

DEY, I. (1993) *Qualitative Data Analysis: A User-Friendly Guide for Social Scientists*, London: Routledge.

Dey views the analysis of **qualitative** data as an iterative process of **coding**, classifying and connecting. Data is broken down into bits which are categorized, linked and combined to produce an analytic account. He illustrates the process, which includes a form of **network analysis**, using extracts from a Woody Allen comedy routine. The approach is specifically related to the use of **information technology** in the analysis of qualitative data, but the techniques described are also appropriate for researchers who are not using a computer.

DOWLING, P.C. (1998) *The Sociology of Mathematics Education: Mathematical Myths/ Pedagogic Texts*, London: Falmer Press.

This work provides the **general methodological** basis for the position that is being taken in *Doing Research/Reading Research*. In particular, it elaborates the approach of **constructive description** and **social activity theory**. It also represents an example of a combination of **qualitative** and **quantitative** approaches in the **semiotic** and **content** analysis of educational **texts**, in this case, in the area of mathematics.

ELLIOTT, J. (1991) *Action Research for Educational Change*, Milton Keynes: Open University Press.

Provides an introduction to Elliott's particular approach to **action research**. Elliott takes the view that action researchers set out to investigate activity within a specific setting with the express intention of improving practice within it. This places action research at the heart of the development of professional practice. This book includes practical advice for **practitioners** intending to carry out action research projects.

FEYERABEND, P. (1975) *Against Method: Outline of an Anarchistic Theory of Knowledge*, London: Verso.

This work has been influential in debates on the **epistemology** of the sciences. See also the item by Kuhn.

FOUCAULT, M. (1970) *The Order of Things: An Archaeology of the Human Sciences*, London: Tavistock.

This is a very important work in debates in the general area of the **epistemology** of the human sciences. It does, however, place heavy demands on the reader both in terms of knowledge and understanding of philosophical work and in respect of the sophistication of its own arguments.

GITLIN, A. (ed.) (1994) *Power and Method: Political Activism and Educational Research*, London: Routledge.

The contributors to this collection of papers directly engage with the relationship between **political** activism and educational research. The approach is multi-disciplinary and a variety of positions, including **feminist** and **gay** and **lesbian** perspectives, are explored. Conventional views of the relationship between the interests of the researcher and those of the researched are problematized and alternatives proposed.

HAMMERSLEY, M. (ed.) (1986) *Controversies in Classroom Research*, Milton Keynes: Open University Press.

HAMMERSLEY, M. (ed.) (1986) *Case Studies in Classroom Research*, Milton Keynes: Open University Press.

Two collections of papers. The first addresses issues in the **design** and conduct of classroom research. The second provides examples of the diversity of forms of classroom research. The controversies considered include debates around **action research** and the use of **case studies**, the comparison of systematic **observation** and **ethnographic** approaches and the relationship between macro and micro analysis. The studies illustrate different approaches to the exploration of teaching style, classroom tasks and teacher expectations.

HAMMERSLEY, M. (1992) *What's Wrong with Ethnography?*, London: Routledge.

Hammersley raises questions about the forms of **ethnographic** research for which he himself has been an active advocate. Very useful in the development of criteria for the judgment of one's own and other people's research (Chapter 4 is particularly helpful in this respect).

HAMMERSLEY, M. (ed.) (1993) *Educational Research: Current Issues*, London: Paul Chapman Publishing.

Useful collection of papers addressing contemporary issues in educational research. Consideration is given to issues of **causality** and the **generalizability** of educational research.

HAMMERSLEY, M. and ATKINSON, P. (1995) *Ethnography: Principles in Practice*, 2nd edition, London: Routledge.

Thorough consideration of **ethnographic** approaches to social research. Provides much in the way of practical advice (including the **management of field relations**, collecting accounts and recording, organizing and analysing data) as well as tackling **epistemological** questions (such as those raised by **naturalism** and other **realist** positions). Includes consideration of the **ethics** of **ethnographic** research.

HODGE, R. and KRESS, G. (1988) *Social Semiotics*, Cambridge: Polity.

This book provides a very readable introduction to **semiotic analysis** and includes a range of examples of semiotic analysis of very diverse **texts**. The particular approach taken shifts the focus of semiotic analysis towards an interest in social structure.

IRVINE, J., MILES, I. and EVANS, J. (eds) (1979) *Demystifying Social Statistics*, London: Pluto Press.

Introductory **statistics** books understandably focus on the strengths of **quantitative** approaches. The authors of the papers in this collection raise numerous questions about the history, foundations and applications of statistical analysis (for instance, in questioning the development of **tests** of **statistical significance**) and the use of statistics (for instance, the production, analysis and use of **opinion polling**).

KELLE, U. (ed.) (1995) *Computer-Aided Qualitative Data Analysis*, London: Sage.

A collection of papers exploring the possibilities and implications of the use of **information technology** in the **analysis of qualitative** data. These papers begin to move beyond the novelty of the use of computers in qualitative analysis and address broader issues. The final chapter provides a useful review of programs. Demonstration versions of many of these programs can be downloaded from the CAQDAS Networking Project world wide web site (http://www.soc.surrey.ac.uk/caqdas/).

KUHN, T.S. (1970) *The Structure of Scientific Revolutions*, 2nd edition, Chicago: University of Chicago Press.

This has been a very influential book in debates on the **epistemology** of science. Although its focus is clearly on the natural sciences, it has also been widely cited in discussion on the nature of social science. See, also, the item by Feyerabend.

LAREAU, A. (1989) *Home Advantage: Social Class and Parental Intervention in Elementary Education*, London: Falmer Press.

The appendix provides an interesting narrative account of the process of carrying out an **ethnographic** research study (in the manner of Whyte's appendix to *Street Corner Society*).

LEE, R.M. (ed.) (1995) *Information Technology for the Social Scientist*, London: UCL Press.

A useful introduction to the range of possible uses for **information technology** in the research process. The papers in this collection cover the use of generic computer tools (such as word processors, spreadsheets and databases) through to more specialized analysis programs and expert systems.

LINCOLN, Y.S. and GUBA, E.G. (1985) *Naturalistic Inquiry*, Beverley Hills, Calif.: Sage.

Thorough consideration of the possibilities of conducting **naturalistic** research. Includes practical advice on appropriate forms of data collection, analysis and reporting of results. Includes a critical discussion of **causality** and the social sciences.

LOFLAND, J. and LOFLAND, L. (1984) *Analysing Social Settings*, 2nd edition, Belmont, Calif.: Wadsworth.

Concise introduction to techniques for the in-depth exploration of specific social settings. Provides advice on the collection and analysis of data. Focuses particularly on the use of intensive **interviewing** and **participant observation**. Includes advice on making **fieldnotes**.

Marsh, C. (1982) *The Survey Method: The Contribution of Surveys to Social Explanation*, London: Allen & Unwin.

Classic text on the use of **surveys**. Gives a detailed and theoretically sophisticated account of both the strengths and weaknesses of surveys. Pays particular attention to **causality**.

Marsh, C. (1988) *Exploring Data: An Introduction to Data Analysis for Social Scientists*, Oxford: Polity.

Accessible introduction to the analysis of **quantitative** data. Provides numerous examples and exercises. Focuses on the development of an understanding of the logic of quantitative research and of the construction of **causal** explanations.

Maynard, M. and Purvis, J. (eds) (1994) *Researching Women's Lives from a Feminist Perspective*, London: Taylor & Francis.

An exploration of the conduct of social research from a **feminist** perspective. The contributors draw on examples from their own research in the exploration of a range of **epistemological**, **political** and operational issues.

Miles, M.B. and Huberman, A.M. (1994) *Qualitative Data Analysis: An Expanded Sourcebook*, 2nd edition, London: Sage.

The authors outline a number of ways of analysing **qualitative** data, with a strong emphasis on **diagrammatic** forms of representation. They also address means of drawing and verifying conclusions. A useful reference book.

Oppenheim, A.N. (1992) *Questionnaire Design, Interviewing and Attitude Measurement*, new edition, London: Pinter.

Comprehensive guide to the design and conduct of **survey** and **interview** based research studies. Consideration is given to analytic and descriptive surveys and to standardized and exploratory interviews. Includes specific advice on **pilot studies**, the wording of questions and the development of **attitude scales**. Also covers data processing and **statistical analysis**.

Outhwaite, W. and Bottomore, T. (eds) (1994) *The Blackwell Dictionary of Twentieth-Century Thought*, Oxford: Blackwell.

A concise and comprehensive introduction to a range of **epistemological** positions. More of an encyclopedia than a dictionary, many of the entries are by leading academics in the field (the entry for **realism**, for instance, is written by Roy Bhaskar).

Potter, J. and Wetherell, M. (1987) *Discourse and Social Psychology: Beyond Attitudes and Behaviour*, London: Sage.

Begins with a review of various approaches to the analysis of accounts (including **semiotic** approaches and **ethnomethodology**). Building on this the authors explore the possibilities offered by **discourse analysis** to social psychological research. They outline a ten step process for the analysis of discourse.

Powney, J. and Watts, M. (1987) *Interviewing in Educational Research*, London: Routledge.

Practical guide to **interviewing**. Includes guidelines for practice and advice on **transcription**.

Rose, G. (1982) *Deciphering Sociological Research*, Basingstoke: Macmillan.

Rose provides a structured approach to reading sociological research which will also be of interest to beginning educational researchers. The book contains useful chapters on **concepts** and **indicators**, **sampling**, and an introduction to **quantitative analysis**. The book also includes a number of sociological research reports which have been reprinted so that the reader can try out Rose's approach to 'deciphering'.

Scott, J. (1990) *A Matter of Record: Documentary Sources in Social Research*, Oxford: Polity.

Discusses the nature of social research and considers the place and status of documentary evidence. Provides guidance on the treatment of **official documents** (e.g. census material), the products of the mass media (e.g. newspapers) and personal documents (e.g. **diaries**).

Silverman, D. (1993) *Interpreting Qualitative Data: Methods for Analysing Talk, Text and Interaction*, London: Sage.

Offers an approach to the analysis of various forms of sociological data (including **observations**, **texts**, **interviews** and **transcripts**). Considers questions of **validity** and **reliability** and the practical relevance of sociological research.

Strauss, A.L. (1987) *Qualitative Analysis for Social Scientists*, Cambridge: Cambridge University Press.

Strauss, A. and Corbin, J. (1990) *Basics of Qualitative Research: Grounded Theory Procedures and Techniques*, London: Sage.

Both books give descriptions of the **grounded theory** approach to conducting social research and analysing **qualitative** data. The first book details the process with copious examples and gives a flavour of the training seminars run by Strauss. The later book gives a sequential account of the process of conducting research in this style. This includes explication of various forms of **coding** of data, **theoretical sampling**, the development of **theory** and **writing** a **report** or thesis.

Tesch, R. (1990) *Qualitative Research: Analysis Types and Software Tools*, London: Falmer Press.

Tesch reviews a wide range of approaches to **qualitative** analysis in the social sciences (including education). Approaches are grouped and the logic of each form of analysis explored. This provides the basis for examination of specific **information technology** data analysis programs. Many of these programs have now been superseded. Despite this, the book provides insight into the way in which computer analysis programs work and the circumstances in which they might be useful.

Vaus, D.A. de. (1991) *Surveys in Social Research*, London: UCL Press.

Gives detailed consideration of the design of **survey research** and the analysis of **quantitative** data. Addresses the need to clarify the relationship between

concept and **indicator variables**, describes various forms of **sampling** and details issues in the construction of **questionnaires**. Includes consideration of the use of **cross-tabulations** and alternative means of bivariate analysis.

WALFORD, G. (ed.) (1991) *Doing Educational Research*, London: Routledge.

Formal research reports rarely give a clear picture of the mechanics of conducting a research study. In order to give the beginning researcher some insight into this process, thirteen educational researchers give narrative accounts of their research. Provides necessary reassurance that there are always contingencies to be addressed and compromises to be made in the **operationalization** of a research **design** or strategy.

WEBB, R. (ed.) (1990) *Practitioner Research in the Primary School*, London: Falmer Press.

Opens with an historical account of the development of **practitioner research**. The other papers provide examples of small-scale research carried out by teachers.

WEITZMAN, E.A. and MILES, M.B. (1995) *Computer Programs for Qualitative Data Analysis*, London: Sage.

Gives detailed reviews of a wide range of **qualitative analysis** programs offered by **information technology**. The programs are categorized according to the forms of analysis they support (e.g. a number of programs are grouped under the heading 'code-based theory-building programs'). The reviews include examples of the use of the program. There is a chapter providing guidance on the selection of appropriate analysis programs. Current demonstration versions of many of the programs reviewed can be downloaded from the CAQDAS Networking Project web site (http://www.soc.surrey.ac.uk/caqdas/).

WHYTE, W.F. (1955) *Street Corner Society: The Social Structure of an Italian Slum*, 2nd edition, Chicago: University of Chicago Press.

The main part of the book is an account of an early urban **ethnography** which has been very influential. This edition also includes an appendix which reflects on some of the methodological issues involved in the study, including the **validity** of the use of **key informants**.

WILLIAMSON, J. (1978) *Decoding Advertisements*, London: Marion Boyers.

This book provides a large number of examples of the **semiotic analysis** of mainly visual **texts**. It also includes some discussion of anthropological, psychoanalytic, semiotic and sociological work which is involved in the **theoretical field** within which the analysis takes place.

WINTER, R. (1989) *Learning from Experience: Principles and Practice in Action Research*, London: Falmer Press.

Introduction to the practices of **action research**. Includes some examples of teacher action research projects.

WRIGHT, D.B. (1997) *Understanding Statistics: An Introduction for the Social Sciences*, London: Sage.

Considers the foundations of **statistical** theory (including discussion **of probability**, **levels of measurement** and forms of **sampling**) and introduces a range of forms of statistical analysis of **quantitative** data. These include methods of hypothesis testing, comparison of means, regression, **correlation** and the comparison of proportions. Provides numerous examples and exercises.

YOUNG, R. (ed.) (1981) *Untying the Text: A Post-Structuralist Reader*, London: Routledge & Kegan Paul.

Good introduction to post-structuralist approaches to the analysis of **texts** (including **semiotic** analysis). Papers by Foucault and Barthes are of particular interest.

Keyword Index

Page references in **bold** are main references, those in *italics* refer to items in the annotated bibliography.